RESEARCH HIGHLIGHTS IN SOCIAL WORK 24

Child Abuse and Child Abusers

Protection and Prevention

Edited by Lorraine Waterhouse
Foreword by Professor Olive Stevenson

Jessica Kingsley Publishers
London and Bristol, Pennsylvania

Research Highlights in Social Work 24
Editor: Lorraine Waterhouse
Secretary: Anne Forbes
Editorial Advisory Committee:

Professor G. Rochford	University of Aberdeen
Professor J. Cheetham	University of Stirling
Ms I. Freeman	Strathclyde Region Social Work Department
Mr D. Gough	Japan Women's University, Tokyo (formerly at University of Glasgow)
Dr J. Lishman	Robert Gordon University, Aberdeen
Dr A. Robertson	University of Edinburgh
Dr P. Seed	University of Dundee
Mr J. Tibbitt	Social Work Services Group, Scottish Office

University of Aberdeen
Department of Social Work
King's College, Old Aberdeen AB9 2Ub

First published in the United Kingdom in 1993 by
Jessica Kingsley Publishers Ltd
116 Pentonville Road
London N1 9JB

Second impression 1996
First paperback edition 1996

British Library Cataloguing in Publication Data
Child Abuse and Child Abusers: Protection
and Prevention – (Research Highlights in
Social Work Series)
I. Waterhouse, Lorraine II. Series
362.7

ISBN 1-85302-133-4 hb
ISBN 1-85302-408-2 pb

Printed and Bound in Great Britain by
Athenaeum Press, Gateshead, Tyne and Wear

Contents

Part 2: Responding to Child Abuse

Foreword

In recent years, there has been a mounting concern over the 'child abuse industry'. Academics, it is suggested, have used this distressing phenomenon for their own advancement. They fly to conferences all over the world, fares paid, to deliver papers which will (perhaps) redound to their glory and may (who knows?) add to the chances of promotion. Why yet another book on child abuse? Have we not got enough? Paradoxically, this book makes the case for yet more. By its scholarly quality, it raises a host of questions remaining to be explored. Indeed, the 'case of child abuse' can be used to illustrate fundamental issues of research, policy and practice more generally. Readers will select from this book food for their own thoughts. For me, there were three issues which stood out.

The first of these concerns the use of research by practitioners. There is some very useful discussion of research methodology, with clear acknowledgement of the ethical dilemmas which arise. Roberts and Taylor, for example, in describing their work with abused children, show how hard it is both to obtain reliable data in such circumstances and to draw sound inferences from it. (They conclude that, despite this, 'the children know what hurts and tell you', a timely warning to those who get bogged down in research minutiae.) Glasgow, on research in relation to perpetrators, shows clearly how the underlying assumptions of the researcher affect their work and how complex this work is to evaluate.

How should practitioners use research? Many are increasingly sophisticated and are keen to utilise the research which is available. One message from this and other books is 'it's all more difficult than you think', which may lead to increasing scepticism. This, however, may be a necessary stage in a process. There are real dangers, ultimately affecting adults and children involved, in a too ready acceptance of what may have become research myths. For example, Dobash et al. found that the majority of perpetrators (about 77%) had not been abused themselves. Even allowing for the possibility of under-reporting, this is a salutory reminder that caution is needed in using this as an indicator. However, healthy scepticism is not enough. The volume and complexity of the research emerging on child abuse is simply not accessible to the majority of practitioners whose time is so constrained and whose ability to pick their way through it varies (and this is no reflection on their professional skill). It seems to me that it is the responsibility of those who create and support structures in which child protection is practised to incorporate into these facilities for the distillation, clarification and dissemination of research findings. An example of research about which practitioners 'need to know' is in the chapter by Farmer. Her discussion of how the parents she interviewed reacted to attendance at case conferences blows some fresh air through the present uncritical rhetoric and has useful implications for those who are involved in this.

A second issue of interest, mirrored in this book, is that we may be moving towards a more international perspective on child abuse. Several chapters, for example those by Hallett, Christopherson and Clark, refer to law, policy and practice in other countries. Their interest to the British audience is considerable, for they challenge some of our assumptions as to what constitutes 'good' intervention. Specifically, the role of the police and the extent to which child abuse is 'criminalised' are fertile areas for further debate. It is very healthy that we are made increasingly aware that definitions of, and actions taken about child abuse are deeply contested and vary greatly in different societies. Indeed, as Hallett points out, the usefulness of 'child abuse' as a unifying concept may be reaching its end.

There is a third aspect of the book which I warmly welcome. As the title suggests, there is material here on both the abused and the abuser. For too long, despite the work of certain specialised practitioners, there has been a split amongst professionals between those who focus upon the abused and those who focus on the abuser. I well remember at a day conference organised by the British Association of Social Workers after the Cleveland Inquiry that there was no speaker on the implications for 'perpetrators'. I wondered what the row of Probation Officers present felt about that. The structural and professional divisions have encouraged a division of thought, as well as of practice, which is profoundly unhelpful and increasingly is seen as artificial. It is therefore refreshing to see the two areas brought together.

The range and depth of the matters here considered set child abuse in a wide context; social, legal and professional. We are reminded that it starts at the most intimate personal level and ripples outwards so as to call in question fundamental assumptions about the nature of our sexuality and about family life. It is a debate in which emotions operate powerfully, sometimes blocking genuinely rational discussion. Indeed, the hidden assumptions and beliefs of academics, as well as practitioners, may play their part in distortion of evidence. (This is to be distinguished from overt acknowledgement of theoretical assumptions.) There is much in this book which affords us a valuable opportunity to stand back and reflect critically on where we stand.

Olive Stevenson
Professor of Social Work Studies, University of Nottingham

Introduction

Lorraine Waterhouse

Despite the significant contributions which research and practice have made to understanding the causes, prevalence and variation in child abuse, the contributors to this book make it abundantly clear that there is still a great deal to learn and, perhaps, to relearn. The opening chapters by Jacqui Roberts and Cathy Taylor, Elaine Farmer and Harriet Dempster reveal the often neglected perspectives of children and young people, mothers and fathers directly affected. Their three studies, drawing on first hand accounts of children and parents, highlight the acute anxiety which sexual or physical abuse causes many children and young people; the grief of mothers who learn that their children have been hurt and misused by a partner with whom they have lived in good faith; and the exclusion which parents and children may experience during professional investigation and follow-up. It is important to stress that contrary to popular opinion these researchers found that most children welcome professional involvement and that most mothers whose children are abused take active steps to get help for them.

Decision-making in child protection is at the heart of good professional practice. Several of the authors point out the importance of basing decisions on clear and fair criteria. Joe Thomson, in his study of the Orkney case, stresses the important part which the law has to play in holding an acceptable balance between the State's powers and family autonomy in the protection of children. Robin Clark finds in her review of child abuse registrations in Australia that being poor and already known to the social services are two major factors likely to be associated with a decision to register the child as abused or at risk of abuse. Tom Pitcairn and I found that a significant proportion of registered cases in Scotland did not involve any specific incident of physically damaging aggression to the children. So far little is known from research about the position of children from diverse ethnic origins and how they fare in the decision-making processes.

Similarly, comparatively little is known about those who, either individually or collectively, abuse children. For this reason it has not been possible to include research on abuse in institutions, although the possibility of this has been made clear through recent scandals which report the apparently compromised handling of relations with troubled and troubling young people in residential care. Yet understanding who abuses and why is fundamentally important for the protection of children. David Glasgow traces through the exploration of different research traditions the potential origins of exploitative sexuality and suggests that men who abuse may have begun abusing when they were children or adolescents. Russell Dobash, James Carnie and I found in our study of individuals convicted of sexual offences against children that men feature predominantly, that violent criminal backgrounds are not uncommon, and that many but, importantly, not all the children were known to the men. Being harmed by a stranger remains a real threat for some children.

Helping children, women and men cope with the consequences of child abuse begs imaginative yet realistic solutions. Christine Hallett makes an important point in her study of professionals working together in child abuse when she argues that while inter-disciplinary practice is much valued by professionals, it remains largely uncosted. Who should bear the major costs of child protection? James Christopherson points to the growing recognition of abused children's rights in this and other European countries. Siobhan Lloyd turns to the importance of self-help as one means of responding to those who have been abused. David Gough ends this book by looking at the potential contribution of prevention in combatting child abuse.

Finally, as the title suggests, there is a need to develop policies and practices which recognise the importance of protecting children when harm has befallen them and the significance of preventing such harm in the interests of children, women and men.

Part 1
Perspectives on Child Abuse

Chapter 1

Sexually Abused Children and Young People Speak Out

Jacquie Roberts and Cathy Taylor

'It will never go away. It is like a never-ending story. It still worries me.'

'I think about it frequently. An experience I wish I could forget. It's not on my mind 24 hours a day, but always at the back of my mind.' (Two Scottish children speaking)

Introduction

The literature describing the immediate and long-term effects of sexual abuse draws mainly from adult accounts. First, there are the moving testimonies from adult survivors (mostly women) about the longer term devastating consequences of sexual abuse. A powerful example is from Maya Angelou, who describes her own elective mutism as a result of sexual assault. She illustrates clearly how sexual abuse compounded her suffering from racism (Angelou 1984). This story and others, such as Jacqueline Spring's Cry Hard and Swim (1989), reveal the long-term effects of sexual abuse and have been confirmed by research studies such as that of Stein, Golding, Siegel, Burnham and Sorensen (1988) who compared adults who had been sexually abused with controls and demonstrated an association between psychological difficulties in adulthood and childhood sexual abuse. Without survivors' courage and decision to tell, the secrets of sexual abuse of children may not have been so convincingly exposed. Yet most of these adults did not disclose the abuse in childhood.

Second, adults have reported what children have said to them during different stages of treatment, as exemplified by Finkelhor and Browne (1985), who describe 'traumatic sexualisation, stigmatisation, betrayal and powerlessness' as the core of psychological injury which make the trauma of sexual abuse unique and different from other childhood abuses (p.530). It remains unclear whether children, asked directly about their experiences, would trace the same themes.

Third, even when researchers have attempted to use standardised measures of childhood distress, such as Friedrich, Urquiza and Beilke (1986), the reports still rest on the adult caretakers' perspective. A recent review of research into the short-term effects of child sexual abuse by Beitchman, Zucker, Hood, da Costa and Akman (1991) reported on 42 publications using children or adolescents as subjects; in none of these were victim interviews, self-report tests and standardised measures used with the same subjects, and in only a few were any combination of these methods used.

It is important, therefore, neither to generalise from adult survivors' accounts nor to suppose that adults' views of the impact of child sexual abuse accurately reflect the children's views. The research reported here seeks to fill a recognised gap in research into child sexual abuse; namely, that not enough attention has been paid to the victim's own perceptions and/or attitudes about the abuse experience (Beitchman *et al.* 1991, p.552).

This chapter is based on a Scottish research study on the impact of sexual abuse on children and their parents, at the time of referral and one year later. The study began as an evaluation of a specialist child sexual abuse clinic based in a Dundee department of child and family psychiatry (Will 1983, p.229). When only 26 children who had attended the clinic in the study year were recruited, a further 119 Tayside children and young people who had been reported as sexually abused and referred to a child protection case conference were identified and included. Eighty-four of these children agreed to take part in the research and form the group of children discussed in this chapter. The research was an attempt to improve on previous studies by using a combination of sources of information about the children; gathering information from the children themselves directly in the form of semi-structured interviews and standardised self-report measures and adding that to parents' information about their children.

The strength of the study is that 67 of the 84 children contributed directly to at least one part. The results of the standardised measures are reported and the children's and young people's own words are used to describe how they felt about the abuse, the abusers and the consequences for them of the experience of abuse.

Methodological considerations

A further abuse of power?

Recent literature on child sexual abuse stresses the misuse of adult power over children for sexual purposes. Asking children questions about the abuse and their subsequent experiences could, if not carefully handled, constitute further abuse of power. Emphasis was placed on the children and families having the choice whether and to what extent they wished to participate in the research.

The research process therefore began by the social worker or sexual abuse clinic staff asking the family whether they would agree to meet the researcher. A positive response was followed by a home visit to explain the purpose of the study and what would be done with the results. With the children in particular, the researcher spent time explaining that there were a lot of questions and if they thought any question to be silly, upsetting or too difficult, then they should let the researcher know. The children were encouraged and shown how to stop the interview at that point and were also encouraged to add anything that they thought was important, in case they were asked the wrong set of questions. Many children did take control of the interviews and many, through positive encouragement, asked the interviewer similarly personal questions. Throughout the process the researchers did their best to be sensitive to verbal and non-verbal cues, which would lead to giving the option of withdrawing or changing the subject.

Maintaining this potentially empowering research process was the priority. Consequently, different numbers of children answered different questions. There is not a neat list of results. Nevertheless, this outcome has been justified by the honesty and clarity with which the children and young people spoke. They were committed to taking part as they hoped that their stories might help others. For them it was vital to find something positive out of what seemed an overwhelmingly negative experience. Others wanted to know exactly to what use any information would be put. Would something they said be important enough to go into a book? Could they be guaranteed absolute confidentiality? It is hoped that by producing this chapter in this way we have fulfilled our part of the bargain. The children and parents who spoke to us would take heart if they thought that what they had to say was influencing research, practice and policy for sexually abused children (Dempster 1990).

Gender

The conceptual framework underpinning this research was that child sexual abuse is an abuse of power, mainly male power, with many variables contri-buting to the enhanced vulnerabilty of some victims and the increased opportunities for some abusers (Finkelhor 1986, p.119). It was therefore decided that the gender of the researcher should be female, particularly as the majority of children and their carers were female, and all but one of the abusers was male. Nevertheless, this has raised a question about the ability of the male children to participate fully in the research. As shown in Table 1.1, 58 per cent of the girls were interviewed at both points in the research process, whereas only seven (37%) boys were interviewed at referral and five (26%) boys at follow-up. Also, smaller percentages of boys completed the standardised measures. Although many girls were obviously comfortable talking to a woman and complained about, for example, male medical and police personnel, in retrospect an opportunity to ask the boys for their views may have been missed. Nevertheless, it has been noted by Nasjleti (1980) that adolescent boys are extremely reluctant to talk about their abuse in therapy, irrespective of the therapist's gender.

Table 1.1 Number of children participating in research process

Time of referral	Self-esteem measure	Depression questionnaire	Direct interview	Total no. of children
	63% (n=12)	47% (n=9)	37% (n=7)	19 males
	81% (n=53)	71% (n=46)	58% (N=38)	65 females
Time of follow-up	Self-esteem measure	Depression questionnaire	Direct interview	Total no. of children
	31% (n=6)	31% (n=6)	26% (n=5)	19 males
	69% (n=45)	69% (n=45)	58% (n=38)	65 females

Incomplete and conflicting information

Information about a sensitive topic like sexual abuse is likely to be incomplete. It cannot be certain how representative any sample is of the total population of sexually abused children. In order to provide background information, a frequency study was completed of all incidents of child sexual abuse reported to Tayside police department in 1989, the mid-year of the research study (Roberts, Dempster, Taylor and McMillan 1991). Two hundred and sixty-five children and young people under the age of 17 years were identified. Not all these children would have been referred to a case conference because, for some, their safety was not in question. It is not known how many other children were sexually abused during the same time period, but whose abuse went unrecognised or unreported. There is general agreement in research studies that only a proportion of sexually abused children ever tell anyone of their experience; those whose case reaches legal, health or welfare services are an even smaller proportion. Much of this information is, however, based on retrospective surveys of adults who never disclosed as children (Haugaard and Reppucci 1988, p.40–51).

The information for this study came from various sources and, with careful cross-checking, it soon became evident that so-called 'facts' about the circumstances surrounding the child and the abuse conflicted with the 'facts' reported by others. Part of the problem is the timing of the information-gathering. For example, a single parent could be reported as such a mere two days after being officially recorded as a two-parent family. Other 'facts' are open to different interpretations by different people, and might not be directly verifiable, such as the age of the child at the onset of abuse, the type of abuse, the duration of abuse, the child's relationship to the abuser and whether the mother 'believed' the child. If the possibility of conflicting or variable information is added to incorrect assumptions and simple recording mistakes, it becomes clear that any research into sexual abuse based entirely on one source of written records is of questionable validity. As stated in a comprehensive review of research into the subject,

> 'data on the variety of aspects that warrant study will probably improve in quality but remain flawed…The consequence is that we must always incorporate research findings with a knowledge of their limitations. Researchers who claim that they have discovered the answers to the questions about child sexual abuse will in all likelihood be overstating their case.' (Haugaard and Reppucci 1988, p.374)

Control groups

The study began at a time when research reviews were calling for more careful systematic research into the consequences of abuse. For example, Finkelhor (1986) wrote that sexually abused children should be compared with another group of non-abused children in treatment. In their review of the research into short-term effects of child sexual abuse, Beitchman, Zucker, Hood, da Costa and Akman (1991) strongly recommend the inclusion of normal non-abused controls and a 'control group of psychologically disturbed individuals…to best test for specificity effects' (p.552).

Attempts in this study to obtain a psychologically disturbed control group, matched for age and sex, were unsuccessful because the control group gradually diminished when we asked if the 'control' children had been sexually abused: a significant proportion had. This unexpected finding has been reported elsewhere (Dempster and Roberts 1991), and calls into question the validity of some other reported control groups. The search for scientifically validated abuse-specific consequences therefore continues, although it needs to be asked whether such research will really explain more than the children themselves tell us. They know what hurts and why; if practitioners can get in touch with these children's feelings, the helping services may improve.

Standardised measures

Haugaard and Reppucci (1988) have suggested that a large population study, giving children batteries of psychological tests and recording changes as they relate to the occurrence of sexual abuse, is the only effective way of obtaining a study of the consequences of sexual abuse. The possible abusive effects of such a research process, with testing and re-testing and repeated questioning about abuse cannot be denied – there would also be problems with parental agreement. An alternative is to ask identified sexually abused children to complete questionnaires that have been standardised using whole populations of children. Such a process was favoured by this research study, with the acknowledgement of the limitations of measures standardised in populations from different cultures.

Clinical and empirical literature and practice experience guided this research towards testing for levels of depression, self-esteem and reported behaviour problems in the children who had been sexually abused. Although depression has been located in the clinical literature, figures have rarely been given to suggest that it is particularly notable in victims of child sexual abuse. Whilst acknowledging that the recognition of childhood depression as a diagnostic entity is still a matter of controversy (Birleson 1980), it was thought important to examine whether depression may be evident in this sample.

More recent literature suggests that there may be a constellation of problems which could be grouped under the heading 'post-traumatic stress disorder' including 're-experiencing phenomena' such as sexualised behaviour and nightmares, 'avoidance/dissociative phenomena' such as regressed speech, enuresis and encopresis, depression and loss of interest and 'symptoms of autonomic hyperarousal' such as irritability, aggression and difficulty concentrating or sleeping – such a constellation of symptoms being hypothesised to be a direct consequence of sexual abuse (Deblinger, McLeer, Atkins, Ralphe and

Foa 1989). It is still a matter of debate, however, as to whether such a 'syndrome' is peculiar to sexual abuse. A different study would need to be designed to answer this question.

The results of the standardised measures in this research are presented in two ways: first, as a broad picture of the level of problems in a sample of sexually abused children as compared with large populations of children; and second, to give some impression of relative improvement over the 12 months from referral to follow-up.

The sample

The sample includes 84 children living in Tayside Region, Scotland, who were officially identified as 'sexually abused' and whose case was referred either to a child protection case conference convened by the social work department or the sexual abuse clinic based in the Department of Child and Family Psychiatry at Dundee Royal Infirmary during the period August 1988 – December 1989. There was a potential sample of 145 children: 84 children from 78 families agreed to be interviewed and/or complete questionnaires. The definition of sexual abuse for the purpose of the study was in line with that used by Tayside Social Work Department:

> 'sexual abuse includes incest, rape, sodomy, intercourse with children, lewd and libidinous or homosexual practices or behaviour towards children, indecently assaulting children, taking indecent photographs of children and encouraging children to become prostitutes or look at pornographic material. Any child below the age of consent may be deemed to have been sexually abused when any person, by design or neglect involves the child in any activity intended to lead to the sexual arousal and gratification of that or any other person. This definition holds whether or not there has been genital contact and whether or not the child initiated the behaviour.' (Tayside Regional Council 1990, p.51)

Gender

There were 65 girls and 19 boys. The preponderance of girls (77%) was not unexpected, but it is significant that seven out of the 17 in the 0–5 age group were boys (41%). This raises a number of questions about the relative likelihood of boys disclosing abuse after a certain age, and corresponds with findings from paediatricians in Leeds who believed that the ratio of boys to girls is higher than previously thought, because of the 2.2:1 girl:boy ratio in pre-school children in 1986 (Hobbs and Wynne 1987).

Race

Two out of the 84 children were known to have one Asian parent. The rest were white. The expected percentage for children in Tayside to be from all ethnic minorities would be 1.6 per cent (CRC information for 1991).

Children with disabilities

Seven children were known to have learning difficulties. Four other children had disabilities such as hearing loss, epilepsy and poor vision at the time of the research. This could be an under-estimate because this information was systematically collected for only 74 children whose social workers completed the relevant questionnaire. Some children with learning difficulties were able to complete the questionnaires with appropriate help. Most of them could express their views very well in the interviews. Regrettably, research designs like this one often omit considering applicability of data collection methods to people with disabilities, as well described by Kelly (1991). Much more research is needed on the relative risks of sexual abuse for children with disabilities.

Age of children

The age range of the children at the time of referral was 2 to 17 years. At the onset of abuse they were aged 2 to 15 years, as shown in Table 1.2.

Table 1.2 Age of children at time of referral

Age of children	No. of boys	No. of girls
0–5	7	10
6–10	4	22
11–15	8	29
16–17	0	4
Total	19	65

Duration and type of abuse

For 33 children (41%) where the duration of abuse was recorded, the sexual abuse was said to have continued for over six months. For 31 children only one incident of sexual abuse was reported. This is likely to be an under-estimate for some children judging from their statements at later research interviews.

At the beginning of the study assumptions were made that it would be possible to grade the severity of the type of sexual abuse suffered by the children. This was in line with many previous researchers (Beitchman *et al.*

1991) who categorise penetrative abuse as more 'severe'. The interviews with some of the children, however, made us acutely aware that the details of the abuse were, at times, far too difficult to describe to an adult. This is in line with clinicians who contend that the actual abuse which children suffer is often greater than that initially disclosed. See for example Friedrich (1988, p.176–7) and Morrison, Will and Roberts (1987) who describe the often faltering and incomplete process of disclosures.

Table 1.3 Abuse of 84 children

Abuse	Number of children
Fondling genitals	49
Abuser exposes self to child	17
Abuser penetrates vagina with penis	14
Abuser makes child touch his genitals	13
Sucks/kisses/licks child's genitals	9
Abuser fondles child's breasts	9
Simulates intercourse	7
Anal penetration	5
Attempted anal penetration	5
Abuser ejaculates into child's mouth	5
Child shown pornography	4
Digital penetration of vagina (attempted)	4
Attempted penile penetration of vagina	4
Digital penetration of vagina	3
Ejaculation onto child's body	3
Abuser makes child suck/kiss/lick his genitals	3
Attempted anal penetration with object	1

Categorisation according to severity might also ignore the cumulative effects of multiple abuses. How does one classify, for example, the abuse of an 11-year-old who was kissed and licked in the vagina, had her genitals fondled, her breasts fondled, her vagina poked by fingers and who was made to expose herself and touch the abuser's genitalia? This child felt violated, yet if severity of abuse were related to penile penetration, her experiences would not have been included. The known abuses are listed above, without making any judgement on the severity of level of assault on the child's person.

A summary of findings on the standardised measures

The main findings on the standardised measures are reported below. More detailed analyses, along with an evaluation of the specialist sexual abuse clinic in Dundee, are provided elsewhere (Roberts, Dempster, Taylor, Bonnar and Smith 1992).

Depression

In order to find out the children's self-reported level of depression, the Child's Depression Inventory, which is derivative of Beck's depression scale (Kovacs and Beck 1977) was used. Thirty-six of 55 (65.5%) children over the age of six years reported themselves to be experiencing some degree of depression at the time of the first research visit.

By the time of follow-up, 12 months later, 28 of 51 (55%) children continued to show some degree of depression. The proportion was less than at the time of the first research visit, but it is important to note that six out of the 28 'depressed' children at follow-up had not reported such symptoms at the first visit. While no comparison could be made for 38 children who did not complete one or both questionnaires, and although 12 children scored as 'more depressed' after 12 months, the overall improvement in depression scores for this group of children at follow-up was statistically significant (Wilcoxon's matched-pairs signed-ranks test: $p < 0.01$).

Self-esteem

As a measure of self-reported self-esteem, the children completed the Culture Free Self-esteem Inventory (Battle 1980). Twenty-four of the children (37%) scored as having lower than average self-esteem. The estimated population percentage falling into this category is 33 per cent (Battle 1980). By the time of the second interview, 33 per cent of the sample were measuring as below average on self-esteem. This sample of children, therefore, did not demonstrate any striking short-term effects on their self-esteem, as found in another recent research study in the USA (Mannarino, Cohen, Smith and Moore-Motily 1991). It could be postulated that any effects on self-esteem are more long-term and therefore more likely to be reported by adults. It could also be suggested that those children with higher levels of self-esteem would have been more likely to take part in the research, or that those identified and receiving help would have a higher self-esteem. The comparison of scores between referral and follow-up was not statistically significant.

Behaviour reported by the parents

The parents were asked to give information about their view of the children's behaviour, by completing the Rutter Scale (A), a standard research instrument used for this purpose in UK studies (Rutter 1965; Rutter, Berger and Yule 1975). At referral, 69 per cent of the children were reported by their parents to have behavioural/emotional problems: this proportion had reduced to 49 per cent at the time of follow-up. All but four of these children had been reported to have problems at the first visit. It is important to note that, at the time of the first research visit, young children seemed especially vulnerable. Fourteen (82%) of the children aged five or under were reported by their parents to have either emotional or conduct problems according to the Rutter Scale (A); at the time of follow-up this proportion had fallen to 50 per cent (n=8).

Forty-seven of 70 children had improved scores after a year, five the same and 18 worse scores. As a group the overall improvement was statistically significant (Wilcoxon's matched-pairs signed-ranks test:p<0.01). No comparison could be made for 14 children where one or both questionnaires were not completed.

In summary, there were worrying levels of self-reported depression and parent-reported behaviour problems at the time of referral. By the time of follow-up there had been significant improvements on both these measures. The interpretation is that time and some form of intervention may help many children.

Mediating variables?

There have been regular attempts to assess the relative influence of variables associated with the sexual abuse on the outcome for the child. Findings have been conflicting. Beitchman *et al.* (1991) have provided the most recent summary of different research studies and have come to the conclusion that findings concerning age of onset, sex of child, duration and frequency of abuse are unclear, but that factors associated with severity of abuse, force/violence and closeness of the relationship between victim and abuser have consistently been related to 'greater trauma in the victim'. A review of research on the sexual abuse of boys, however, has concluded that 'the common sense expectation that the worst outcomes are associated with increasing severity, frequency and duration of abuse, requires further substantiation' (Watkins and Bentovim 1992, p.239).

The most recently reported American research study, using measures similar to those used in our study, has not found any clear association between abuse variables and outcome for the victim, apart from some indication that more emotional trauma reported later is associated with penetrative abuse (Mannarino *et al.* 1991). It must be stressed that most of the variables are interrelated to some extent: for example, the gender of the victim could relate to the type of offender, which could relate to the age at onset of abuse, which could relate to duration, which could relate to the use of force and so on. It is not surprising therefore, that little association was found in this study between problems in the victims and abuse, abuser, family or child-related variables. However, two results stand out. Using the <0.05 level of significance, two variables appeared to relate to the degree of depression reported by the children. These were whether or not the child disclosed to a parent and whether the mother 'believed' the child, as reported by the social worker on interview. Statistically, significantly more children who were not depressed at the time of the first interview did disclose to a parent (chi-squared test: $p < 0.05$), as shown in Table 1.4.

Table 1.4 Children's depression at first interview according to disclosure to parent

	Did not disclose to parent	Did disclose to parent
Not depressed	7	12
Moderately depressed	12	4
Significantly depressed	15	5

The meaning of this finding is open to interpretation. Are children who do not disclose to a parent more troubled because they did not disclose, or are they less supported by the parent in general, which makes them less likely to disclose and more prone to depression?

It is important to stress at this point that only nine of the 48 mothers for whom we had this information were reported not to 'believe' their child's disclosure of sexual abuse. Similar rates have been reported in other studies (see Dempster 1993). Nevertheless, it is statistically significant (chi-squared test: $p < 0.05$) that 95 per cent of the children who were not depressed at follow-up had been 'believed' by their mother, compared with 69 per cent of the children who reported themselves as depressed (see Table 1.5). Recent experiences working with these mothers and Dempster's in-depth analysis of interviews with women have shown that the simple label 'belief' is insufficient to capture the struggles some women undergo in coming to terms with the fact that their child has been sexually abused (Dempster 1993). It could be that the greater the woman's struggle, the more vulnerable their child is to emotional problems on follow-up.

Table 1.5 Children's depression on follow-up according to whether the mother was reported by the social worker to have believed

	Mother believed	*Mother uncertain*
Not depressed	21	1
Depressed	18	8

The boys

As already stated, the use of a female researcher may well have compounded the reasons for fewer boys than girls participating in the research. It is difficult to draw conclusions about gender-related outcomes for our sample, given the small numbers. Nevertheless one or two aspects need to be highlighted.

Eleven out of the 18 boys (61%) for whom a Rutter (A) Scale was completed at the first interview scored as having a behaviour problem by their parents. This percentage is less than for the girls (70%). However, the reported behaviour problem rate at follow-up for boys (57%), is higher than that for the girls (47%).

Only five boys completed the depression questionnaire at both first interview and follow-up, but three out of these five boys scored as more depressed by the time of follow-up. Given the small numbers, it is not possible to control for other influencing factors, but our limited findings add to the conclusion that the effects of abuse on boys are serious and perhaps more so in the long term (Watkins and Bentovim 1992, p.239). It is clearly important to support these authors' call for further gender analysis in research into victims of child sexual abuse.

What the children and young people said during the interviews

Forty-five children (seven boys) spoke to the researcher at the time of first interview, 43 children (five boys) at the time of follow-up. No semi-structured interview was held with children under the age of six years. The ages in brackets at the end of the following quotations indicate the age of the child or young person at the time of the interview. Boys' comments will be indicated as such.

The children's responses to the interviews form the remainder of this chapter and shed light on the complexity of their experiences, their fears, their anger and their hopes for the future.

Ambivalences, contradictions and inconsistencies

Sexual abuse of children is a complex phenomenon. Children's responses are varied and unique to each child. The responses are likely to be child- and family-related as much as abuse-related. Child sexual abuse is also a sensitive subject. There is a depth of experience which can be tapped only by a combination of words, expressions and gestures, rather than by responses to stark and structured questions. The children painted pictures in words of their feelings about the abuse – pictures that could never be captured in a questionnaire.

Asked whether sexual abuse still worried her and in what way, one girl replied:

> 'Just at times, when I'm worried – cracking up – it pours into my head – out of control'. (16)

Another, in response to being asked whether she still thinks about the abuse, said:

> 'Yes, I still think about it a lot – when it's in the press or on TV it flashes back – makes me scared. It's like a black pitch. It's a thing you can't forget'. (15)

One child explained the difference telling about the abuse had made to her:

> 'Cleared things up for myself – no black blur on my brain when people talk about sexual abuse'. (15)

Confusions, contradictions and mixed feelings

Standardised measures do not allow for the ambivalence which the children felt about the different parts of the experience of sexual abuse, towards the abuser and towards themselves. When the children spoke, their different and mixed feelings became apparent: they gave explanations for their conflicting thoughts. They often tried to express a jumble of mixed feelings and at any one stage they could feel unusual, frightened, angry, sad, embarrassed, dirty, guilty or inert, and yet still OK. They are confused by their own responses:

> 'I'm angry that I only sat there and froze and didn't do anything to stop it. I feel stupid – that I should have done something'. (14)

The children's parents spoke about their children's behaviour problems at length, whereas the children hardly mentioned their symptoms and overt problems. Instead, they described their direct feelings and thoughts, thereby far more effectively explaining the impact of sexual abuse on them. It seemed to us as researchers that these children needed adults to be in touch with their confusion, contradictions and mixed feelings, and that that in itself would help reduce the incidence of overt behavioural problems. The predicament for younger children is that they often do not have the words to express their confusion, and so resort to acting out their feelings, leaving the adults with 'behavioural management' problems, which can reduce patience and an ability to respond to a child's emotional needs.

Several children expressed ambivalence towards the abuser:

'He's a little bit nice. He gave me juice. Then he was bad to me.' (7)

The children know that this ambivalence is not always tolerated or even understood by the adults in their lives:

'It's difficult to say I miss him. People don't want to hear that.' (12)

'I'm sad about not seeing him. I used to play with him. I want Dad to live with me again.' (6)

The children often worry about the consequences of their disclosure for the abuser and for them:

'I did not want him to be punished, but it proved I was not a liar when he was found guilty.' (13)

'I'm glad I told, but also I'm not glad. I'm glad it stopped, but not glad. I miss him.' (12)

'I wished I had not told, then I would have none of all the bother, though I'm glad he got caught.' (12)

On follow-up, some of them explained how their feelings changed over time. One child expressed relief:

'...even though it [telling] was awful. At first I wished I hadn't. Now I'm glad.' (13)

Fear

Even after a year, the fear connected with the abuse and the abuser was palpable for many children. It is important to emphasise this part of the children's own responses because the system will not be able to respond effectively to the children's needs if the depth of the children's fear is not understood.

The children were deliberately asked an open question about what had been the worst part of what had happened to them. This was to allow them to choose whether it was the abuse itself, or any other part of the experience such as telling their mother or the system's response after disclosure.

Thirty-five children answered this question. Seventeen of them stated that it was the abuse itself that was the worst thing. From the following quotations, it becomes clear that it was the fear and uncertainty connected with the abuse which mattered most.

'The worse part was it actually happening.' (14, male)

'He said he would deny it. I was very frightened in case my Mum would batter me for doing it. They gave me money and sweets not to tell. I didn't want it. They made me.' (8)

'Sometimes it comes back – what happened and the fear of it happening again.' (12)

'It's scary – disgusting what he did – what made him do it? I don't know.' (15)

'I can't really describe it…just horrible inside…I did scream once…he said be quiet…I just said to myself, let him do it and then he will go…I dreaded going to bed.' (13)

'I was too scared to tell because X was living with us and he did it lots of times.' (8)

'I was frightened and wanted to cry but I couldn't…I'm frightened of men. I won't sleep with my light off…he threatened to kill me…he put his hand over my mouth when I tried to scream.' (17)

'Thought about telling Mum. Tried to tell – difficult to find the words. Didn't – frightened.' (13, male)

'I keep seeing him in the street. It's scary to see him. It makes me wet the bed.' (9)

'I was worried, scared. I had the courage to run, but he'd locked the door. I feel a bit better now that he can't come in the house at night. The door's locked. My nightmares are getting better.' (11)

It doesn't go away

Analysing the many variables that could have effected outcome for these children has produced little insight. The interview responses, however, of those children (18 girls:1 boy) who reported moderate to severe degrees of depression at both referral and follow-up suggest some common patterns. These children did not share the same concerns, but did seem to be particularly disturbed by one or more aspects of the abuse itself.

One child, who was still significantly depressed at follow-up, was concerned about seeing her abuser, who was not a member of her family:

> 'I see him from time to time as he lives locally. I saw him the other day. I walked faster. I was scared to walk past him. I walk the other way usually. Will there be a time when I can just walk past him? It should be him who looks down, but he's confident because he's got off with it.' (14)

One child was depressed because of threats of serious violence from the abuser who wanted her to retract.

The feeling of being different and needing to be normal is echoed by the following two children:

> 'I would have grown up different. It did change my life – made me wake up to the violence outside.' (15)

> 'I just wanted to be a normal family. When the police got involved, I was frightened they would put my Dad in prison.' (14)

For some children there were the many aspects of the abuse and what followed that continued to make them depressed:

> 'The whole thing was a nightmare. Police report, investigation and medical just as bad. They didn't consult me about whether I wanted to report it or would have a medical...just turned up.' (15)

> '...went on for four years. I wanted it to stop. It was sore.' (13, male)

One boy was experiencing problems because he was abused by a man and this had raised issues of his own sexuality and relationships with girls. He said:

> 'It's causing problems in relationships. Girls give me up when they find out...I think girls are wary of me. Boys tell them about me and they think "danger" and walk.' (16, male)

The number of questions, the invasion of privacy and the need to repeat what had happened many times was a recurrent theme. But so was the personal, physical and private damage done by the abuse. One 15-year-old, who had bled following the assault, said 'I was worried about maybe being damaged' and was experiencing a general fear of 'being in the dark and on my own. I'm scared, especially if someone walks behind me'.

One of the most common themes in the interviews of the children who were depressed at both times was the fear or reality of not being believed. This included other people in addition to their mother, other relatives, brothers, sisters and people like social workers, police and doctors:

> 'I would like my social worker to believe me and stop saying it was someone in the family. I don't like that, them having been accused.' (14)

> 'no-one would believe me.' (15)

Nor was it just a question of whether the children were believed initially, but that they needed to hear continued messages of belief, otherwise they became very unhappy. For example:

> 'She sees him [now] so she must believe him more…it makes me feel funny inside. I can't understand why she says she loves him. It makes me shiver.' (13)

The fact that it doesn't go away is well expressed by one young man:

> 'wrecked us…people don't talk, speak to me, because of what's happened. My mates think it's funnny – laugh at us – hurtful.' (16, male)

Anger with the law

The children in this study described well the many conflicting feelings they experienced as a result of the abuse. Anger was not often mentioned. When it did occur, it was likely to be aimed at the response of the criminal justice system to the abusers, even though there were conflicting feelings about the abuser being punished. For example, one child's reaction to her abuser being fined was to say that she was glad he was found guilty, but that:

> 'he should have been hung.' (12)

Similarly, a teenager talking about her abuser:

> 'I've seen him. I shall kill him. I felt like it. He got two years probation. Everyone thought he should have got jail. I feel he should have got jail. I feel angry, hurt, let down.' (16)

> 'I don't like them [abusers]. I feel like killing them.' (16, male)

Another says:

> 'It was a not proven. The procurator fiscal told me they knew it was true, but that wasn't any consolation. I was so angry I couldn't sleep'. (15)

I'm glad I told

All the children were asked at follow-up how they felt about having told about the abuse. Of the 38 children who responded to this question, all but three felt positively about having told. They acknowledged mixed feelings about telling and experiencing a change over time. They explained why they were glad they told and why they had been reluctant to tell.

The most obvious reason was:

> 'it's good to tell, if you're not taken away, because it stopped.' (12)

> 'I'm glad I told – stopping it was the most important.' (16, male)

> 'I'm glad I told because I would still be upset.' (12)

> 'Tell other children that if you don't tell you are put through more of it.' (13)

For some, the telling had a dramatic benefit:

> 'I'm happy I told. If I hadn't said something, I would have taken my life. Before I told, I was into glue/dope – a cry for help – everything was wrong. Once my mum believed me, it was OK.' (15)

> 'Judge and police were the most helpful 'cos they chased and stopped them – put them away – protected me and others.' (16, male)

Several children mentioned that their fears of the consequences of telling were not realised:

> 'I was scared at first to tell. I thought I might get shouted at. I feel a lot better having told. I've got it all out now.' (12)

> 'I thought I would have got into trouble – that it was my fault. I know it's not my fault. I felt better since telling.' (12)

Just three children wished they had not told: they felt they had been betrayed. For example:

> 'I would have preferred to tell my teacher in confidence. I did not want it to become public knowledge. I had no feelings of relief. I thought there would have been some.' (15)

For another, some very raw feelings were expressed at the first interview:

> 'I wish I'd kept my mouth shut. I get on worse with my mum now. She started ignoring me. She was that mad I had to stay at my sisters'. She thinks I encouraged him. Confused. Sometimes I wish I was dead. Everything's muddled. Nothing can get sorted out.' (12)

Messages for other children and young people – 'tell'

It was notable that the children and their parents often gave as a reason for wanting to take part in the research that it would be helpful to other children who are being abused. In order for them to have survived their ordeal they have been able to use in a positive way their own resources. They are, therefore, in a unique position to be able to give messages to other children about what is helpful. Rarely are the positive attributes of children, their altruism at an early age and their ability to use a negative experience for positive effects considered in the research literature in child sexual abuse. Yet children who have been abused may contribute towards other children's recovery. The children were asked what advice they had for others who had been or who were being sexually abused.

There was a good response to this question (n=33). Almost without exception they advocated that other children should tell someone about the abuse. Bearing in mind the very difficult time which some children have been through since they told, this message carries even more weight. We have quoted some of the reasons why it is best to tell, but also some children expressed the view that talking itself is therapeutic:

> 'Talking about it helped. I regret keeping it to myself.' (16)

> 'Talk – it set my mind at ease, getting my feelings out in confidence.' (14)

When talking may be too difficult, one girl suggests:

> 'Try to talk it through. Write it down if you can't say it. That's what I did.' (13)

A young man came up with the suggestion:

> 'speaking on an open line – speaking anonymously would help – might find it easier to express feelings.' (16, male)

The children stressed that there is a need to talk immediately. They suggested that it was important to tell other children to talk about the abuse straightaway, otherwise they would regret it:

'tell someone about it straight away. I regret waiting so long before telling. It makes it worse.' (14)

A message from one young woman sums it all up:

'Tell the nearest person straight away. I know it's hard, but you just do it. Don't back out. I know you go through problems, but it will turn out – but if you don't tell, you go through hell.' (15)

Other messages include staying away from the abuser, forgetting about the abuse and not blaming yourself.

Also, one girl said:

'don't let it beat you. Don't let it get you down. That's what I was doing. Now I realise.' (15) and:

'every time I felt depressed I kept thinking I must fight back.' (15)

Such statements serve to remind us that these children and young people are not simply the passive victims of a crime, with high rates of behaviour problems as a sign of their distress; they are engaged in an active struggle to fight back and deal with the consequences of the abuse and they feel strongly that other children could be helped earlier if they were able to seek adult help. Their messages for adults are these:

'believe what is said by children.' (12)

'don't blame the children.' (13)

'tell me it's not my fault.' (16, male)

'if they are teenagers, consult them. Don't just go ahead with the investigation…we've got brains and can make decisions. Take account of us. We are people.' (15)

Practice and research implications

Not only has the attempt to define sexual abuse as a distinct diagnostic category met with limited success, but so has the attempt to find which variables mediate the short and medium-term effects for children. This research study has been no exception. There are continuing problems of different methodologies which produce results open to differing interpretations. In this chapter a number of methodological considerations are highlighted such as conflicting and incomplete sources of information, lack of gender analysis, the elusiveness of meaningful control groups and the problem of relying on adults' perspectives for understanding the impact of sexual abuse on children.

The response to these various dilemmas in child sexual abuse research has been an appeal for uniformity and an attempt to refine techniques, hoping that this will lead to the 'true' and agreed upon effects of sexual abuse. The data from our study, backed up by the statements made by the children and young people, points to the need to challenge the assumption that clearcut explanations are awaiting discovery. The alternative is to focus on research strategies which allow for the exploration of diversities, rather than commonalities, and which begin with the assumption that there are differences rather than similarities in the experience. Part of the problem has been the drive from well-motivated practitioners, concerned with the pain they witness in victims of sexual abuse, to counter the omni-present denial or minimisation of sexual abuse as major child health problem by stressing an apparent uniformity in the experience.

It is clear that this research study, along with most others, has its limitations. Is the sample representative? Are appropriate measures and questions being used? It is now important to counter such challenges by making sure that, whereas other unidentified sexually abused children not included in the sample may have different experiences, this does not invalidate the experience of those reported here. Moreover, different methods for evaluating the effects of sexual abuse allow for different angles of the same complex issue to be shown. The responses to the interviews demonstrated that feelings from each individual can be multi-faceted and that different feelings are held by different children at different stages during the experience. It is important to emphasise the changes over time: most children were glad at follow-up that they had told about the abuse. Had they only been interviewed at the time of referral, this vital message may have been lost. Less optimistically, a group of children, including a small core of boys, felt worse at follow-up: the fact of sexual abuse does not go away and the adults in the individuals' lives need to know how to respond to that.

It is, therefore, important to bear in mind that, although the parents interviewed mostly empathised with their children and the effects of the abuse, their views were predominantly adult-centred. For example, the parents readily described the overt behavioural consequences for the children, often including sexualised behaviour. The children and young people emphasised their continuing feelings of fear of the abuser, a grave sense of injustice about the wrong that had been done to them and their conflicts over both good and bad feelings towards the abuser and others. It is clearly misleading to suppose that adults' views of child sexual abuse are accurate reflections of the children's views. A main message from the children is that many caring adults, within and outside the family, have difficulty getting fully in touch with how children do feel. Therefore the children seem to struggle on their own to deal with the emotional consequences of the abuse experience. It seems that the way forward is not to concentrate on the 'likely' consequences but to acknowledge fully with children that many conflicting feelings and thoughts are inevitable, that they are not going mad, that their conflicts are legitimate and that some adults, including their mothers, may not want to talk about it. By empowering children in this way they will be able to make sense of their emotions and thereby regain earlier emotional strength.

Both the results on the standardised measures and the comments made by the children confirm that the experience of sexual abuse has been a very painful one. The intensity of feeling during many of the interviews cannot be exaggerated. Although there are some negative remarks about the system's response to the abuse, many children who volunteered an opinion said that the abuse itself was the worst part of the whole experience; some children were obviously still living in fear of the abuser. Despite the fact that some had had difficult court appearances, an unpleasant medical or a negative peer reaction to the abuse, the overwhelming message to other children is to tell about the abuse.

This message is so important to convey to other children who are being sexually abused and who have not disclosed. It is also important that practitioners hear it, so that any inclination they might have to ignore a child's tentative hints about sexual abuse for fear that the results of telling might be worse than the abuse, will be dispelled. Thus, the children's main positive contribution to this research was their ability to evaluate for themselves the experience of sexual abuse and construct it in a way which might help other children. The significance of their views and feelings for them was that they were validating the feelings of other children who may be abused in the future: they were a means to offering advice, support and encouragement. In response, we have compiled a booklet consisting of these children's own statements to be made available publicly throughout Scotland; this is a way of helping children communicate positively some painful experiences for the benefit of other children. It is hoped that this will be one small contribution towards these young people's battle against the abuse of adult power they have already experienced.

Acknowledgements

The research was funded by the Child and Family Trust Ltd, Glasgow. We would like to thank the children and young people for their bravery, kindness and candour.

References

Angelou, M. (1984) *I Know Why the Caged Bird Sings.* London: Virago.

Battle, J. (1980) *Culture-Free Self Esteem Inventories for Children and Adults.* Seattle: Special Child Publications.

Beitchman, J.H, Zucker, K.J., Hood, J.E., da Costa, G.A. and Akman, D. (1991) 'A review of the short-term effects of child sexual abuse'. *Child Abuse and Neglect 15,* 537–556.

Birleson, P. (1980) 'The validity of depressive disorder in childhood and the development of a self-rating scale: a research report'. *Journal of Child Psychiatry 22,* 73–88.

Browne, A. and Finkelhor, D. (1986) 'Initial and long term effects: a review of the research', in Finkelhor, D. and associates *A Sourcebook on Child Sexual Abuse.* London: Sage.

Deblinger, E., McLeer, S., Atkins, M., Ralphe, D. and Foa, E. (1989) 'Post-traumatic stress in sexually abused, physically abused, and non-abused children'. *Child Abuse and Neglect 13* 403–408.

Dempster, H. (1990) *Child Sexual Abuse Research: A Further Abuse of Power?* Paper presented at 8th International Conference on Child Abuse and Neglect. Hamburg, September 1990.

Dempster, H. (1993) 'The aftermath of child sexual abuse: women's perspectives'. (Chapter 3 in this volume).

Dempster, H. and Roberts, J. (1991) 'Research into child sexual abuse: a methodological quagmire'. *Child Abuse and Neglect 15(4),* 593–595.

Finkelhor, D. and Browne, A. (1985) 'Initial and long term effects: a conceptual framework', in Finkelhor, D. (ed) *A Sourcebook on Child Sexual Abuse.* Beverly Hills: Sage.

Finkelhor, D. (ed)(1986) *A Sourcebook on Child Sexual Abuse.* Beverly Hills: Sage.

Friedrich, W.N., Urquiza, A.J. and Beilke, R. (1986) 'Behavioral problems in sexually abused young children'. *Journal of Pediatric Psychology 11* 47–57.

Friedrich, W.N. (1988) 'Research with child victims', in Wyatt, G.E. and Powell, G.J. (eds) *Lasting Effects of Child Sexual Abuse.* London: Sage.

Haugaard, J. and Reppucci, N.D. (1988) *The Sexual Abuse of Children.* San Francisco, London: Jossey-Bass.

Hobbs, C. and Wynne, J. (1987) 'Child sexual abuse: an increasing rate of diagnosis'. *Lancet ii* 837–842.

Kelly, L. (1991) *Disability and Child Abuse – What we know and what we need to know.* Paper presented to the first International BASPCAN Conference. Leicester, September 1991.

Kovacs, M. and Beck, A.T. (1977) 'An empirical clinical approach towards a definition of childhood depression', in Schulter-Bradt, J.S. and Raskin, A. (eds) *Depression in Children: Diagnosis, Treatment and Conceptual Models.* New York: Raven.

Mannarino, A., Cohen, J., Smith, J.A. and Moore-Motily, S. (1991) 'Six and twelve-month follow-up of sexually abused girls'. *Journal of Inter-personal Violence 6(4)*, 494–511.

Morrison, J., Will, D. and Roberts, J. (1987) 'Twenty myths that justify not tackling child sexual abuse'. *Social Work Today. July 20* 9–11.

Nasjleti, M. (1980) 'Suffering in silence: the male incest victim'. *Child Welfare 59*, 269–275.

Roberts, J., Dempster, H., Taylor, C. and McMillan, B. (1991) 'A study of the frequency of reported child sexual abuse in one Scottish region'. *Child Abuse Review 5(1)*, 3–6.

Roberts, J., Dempster, H., Taylor, C., Bonnar, S. and Smith, C. (1992) *Research Report on Sexually Abused Children and Families in Tayside.* Glasgow: Child and Family Trust.

Rutter, M. (1965) 'Classification and categorisation in child psychiatry'. *Journal of Child Psychology and Psychiatry 6*, 71–83.

Rutter, M. et al (1975) 'Attainment and adjustment in two geographical areas: 1. The procedure of psychiatric disorder'. *British Journal of Psychiatry 126*, 493–509.

Spring, J. (1989) *Cry Hard and Swim.* London: Virago Press.

Stein, J.A., Golding, J.M., Siegel, J.M., Burnham, M.A. and Sorenson, S.B. (1988) 'Long-term psychological sequelae of child sexual abuse: the Los Angeles epidemiologic catchment area study', in Wyatt, G.E. and Powell, G.J. (eds) *Lasting Effects of Child Sexual Abuse.* London: Sage.

Tayside Regional Council (1990) *Child Abuse: Protecting Children from Abuse and Neglect. Operational Instructions for Social Work Staff.* Tayside Regional Council.

Watkins, B. and Bentovim, A. (1992) 'The sexual abuse of male children and adolescents: a review of current research'. *Journal of Child Psychology and Psychiatry 33(1)*, 197–248.

Will, D. (1983) 'Approaching the incestuous and sexually abusing family'. *Journal of Adolescence 6*, 229–246.

Chapter 2

The Impact of Child Protection Interventions
The Experiences of Parents and Children

Elaine Farmer

Historically, public concern to avert infant deaths has been a force in shaping professional responses to child protection in this country from the 1870s onwards. The current child protection system in England and Wales stems directly from that devised after the inquiry into the death of Maria Colwell (Secretary of State 1974). The emphasis past and present has been on setting up reliable procedures to identify children at risk and to maximise inter-professional co-ordination.

It took the Cleveland Inquiry (Secretary of State 1988) into the alleged sexual abuse of children to bring about a major shift in public concern to include the rights and wrongs of professional intervention in family life. The parents of the children concerned had formed an effective lobby. The resulting inquiry took up their views and criticised the way that both parents and children had been dealt with by social services departments and other agencies. In particular, it was recommended that parents should be informed and consulted by professionals at each stage of the investigation, and that children should not undergo repeated interviews and medical examinations, nor be subject to precipitate removal from their families. The concern to avert child tragedies moved to include the concern that the child protection system should not compound the abuse which children may experience.

Since then, changes have been made to meet these criticisms. Within child protection the system of investigations of abuse jointly undertaken by police officers and social workers has become commonplace and further changes in practice are to be expected following the introduction of the 1989 Children Act.

How well is the system now working? To answer this question the perspectives of children and parents who have been involved in allegations of abuse need to be considered.

While a body of literature now exists in the UK on consumer views of social work and child care (Mayer and Timms 1970; Sainsbury 1975; Sainsbury, Nixon and Phillips 1982; Fisher, Marsh, Phillips with Sainsbury 1986) until recently little had been published on consumer views of child protection. A study by Celia Brown in 1984 was based on interviews with 23 parents of physically abused children, held some time after the abuse, and Brian Corby's study Working with Child Abuse (Corby 1987) included interviews with ten parents whose children had been subject to child protection intervention. In addition, David Gough's study of physically abused children under five who were registered in 1982–83 included interviews with 29 parents (Gough 1989). A more recent study by Lorraine Waterhouse and Tom Pitcairn has also added to our picture of consumer views on the need for child protection interventions (Pitcairn, Waterhouse, McGhee, Secker and Sullivan 1993) and this is reported on in chapter 4. Research attention has recently been directed to the impact on mothers of the discovery that their child has been sexually abused (Hooper 1989 and Roberts, Taylor, Dempster, Smith and Bonnars 1992), and details of the latter study appear in this book. Further, there has been considerable interest in parental participation in child protection case conferences and a number of studies which include parent views have been conducted with a view to developing ideas for improving practice in this area (for example, McGloin and Turnbull 1986; Shemmings and Thoburn 1990; Burns 1991).

This chapter will explore the views of parents and children about the initial stages of child protection intervention, and examine the extent of match and mismatch between the perspectives of social workers, parents and children at the various stages. Understanding what happens early on is vital if ideas of good practice are to be tested against the views of those whom they are intended to protect. It is not only the perspectives of participants which we need to understand, but also the interactions between social workers and family members because it is out of these interactions that the stage for later work is set. What happens in this early period may determine whether professionals and family members can act constructively to protect the child and further the child's best interests.

The study

This analysis is based on findings which are emerging from a current study of decision-making, intervention and outcome in child protection work which is being conducted by the author and Morag Owen at Bristol University. The research has been funded by the Department of Health as part of a programme of research in child protection, and uses data on 44 children on the child protection register. The sample was drawn from 73 newly registered cases after attendance at 120 initial child protection case conferences in two local authorities. The parents, older children and key workers were interviewed after the initial case conference and it is on these interviews that this chapter will draw. By the time that the study is completed the same participants will have been re-interviewed 18 months on in order to trace developments over time. This will also provide information about whether the effects of the early stages of intervention persist or decrease and what impact they have on outcome.

With the exception of their ethnic backgrounds, the children in the study represent a fairly typical cross-section of cases registered by social services departments: concerns centred on physical abuse in a third, on sexual abuse in another third, and the remainder were divided between cases of neglect and those deemed to constitute emotional abuse. Two-fifths of the children were under five, a quarter were aged five to ten, and a third were aged ten or over at the time of the initial case conference. Since no black or ethnic minority children were picked up in the sample reported here, the study has subsequently been extended to include them, and this part of the research is still in progress. The research has spanned a period of considerable change: the first interviews took place before the implementation of the 1989 Children Act and the follow-up interviews afterwards.

Forty-four mothers were interviewed and also, in a third of cases, the father, stepfather or male partner when there was one. At the time of the abuse or neglect which led to the investigation, the children had been living with both parents or in a reconstituted family in almost two-thirds of the cases and with a single mother in over a third. All the suspected perpetrators of sexual abuse were male (mostly fathers or stepfathers and a few older boys), whereas the physical injuries had been meted out in similar numbers by father figures in two-parent households and mothers who were living alone. In a few cases there was continuing uncertainty amongst professional agencies about the source of abuse. In cases of neglect and emotional abuse the concern of professional agencies had sometimes focused on one, and sometimes on both parent figures.

The parents interviewed included mother and father figures, abusers and non-abusers. In spite of these differences parents had a good many experiences in common. They will therefore be treated here as a group, and when important differences emerge, for example between abusing and non-abusing parents, or along gender lines, attention will be drawn to these differences.

The crisis of investigation

The first major stage of intervention for the children was that of the investigation. In many ways this was a time of crisis as social workers and police officers had to decide what steps to take and family members found themselves subject to intense scrutiny. The details of the investigation were often etched into the memories of the participants. For social workers this had generally been a very stressful period, principally characterised by a high degree of uncertainty about what had taken place combined with the imperative of making swift decisions on which the child's safety might depend.

The start of an investigation was also a time of crisis for parents and children. Allegations of physical, sexual or emotional abuse or neglect arose in a number of ways. In some cases of sexual abuse the child had purposefully made a disclosure, whilst in others the abuse was uncovered by people outside the family, such as school teachers or neighbours. Some children, then, having initiated action, were expecting a response, whilst others had no forewarning. The same was true for non-abusing parents. When children found ways to tell their mothers that they were being abused by fathers or stepfathers, the mothers had set off the process of investigation (see also Faller 1989, and Bagley and King 1990). However, when children shared information about their predicament outside the family – often at school – the allegations were in the public arena before the mother knew anything about it. Similarly, allegations that a child had suffered a non-accidental injury could be unexpected for parents, as could allegations of emotional abuse or neglect. In other cases, parents presented their injured child to a GP or hospital with some awareness that they or their partners might become the focus of suspicion.

For over a third of the parents (36%), then, the first that they knew of the allegations was when one or more police officers arrived at their door. As one mother said:

'The first I knew I had two CID blokes and a policewoman turn up on the door to say that Lucy had gone to school at 2 o'clock and said that my husband had been sexually abusing her.'

Mothers who heard in this way of their child's sexual abuse experienced shock, bewilderment, anger and the onset of profound feelings of loss. Some felt guilty that they had not guessed what had been going on or that the child had been unable to confide in them. In cases of sexual abuse mothers quite often discovered that their child had already been interviewed and they had been neither informed nor involved. This had also occurred in some cases of suspected physical and emotional abuse, for example when social workers had talked to the child in school without consulting either parent. In such cases non-abusing mothers, who were struggling to assimilate the notion that their partners had violated their children, found that the children had been encouraged to talk about the abuse to professionals while they themselves had been excluded. Consequently, the conduct of the investigation could marginalise non-abusing mothers and replicate their experience of discovering that their child had been abused without their knowledge. This exclusion could also make them feel angry and distrustful about the investigation.

Once non-abusing mothers had been brought into the investigation they also became the subject of scrutiny. Judgements were made about mothers who were often in a state of shock. If they did not react in the way that the investigating team expected they were sometimes held to be unable to protect their children. In one case a mother was kept at the police station for five hours with her two young and fractious children while her husband was questioned about bruises on the baby. Her reaction was to become upset and aggressive which so disquieted the investigators that the children were summarily removed, even though no-one was suggesting that she had abused them.

When, as was often the case, perpetrators protested their innocence, mothers could be torn between their child and their partner, caught in a position where believing one meant losing the other. As one mother put it, when allegations of sexual abuse were made against her ex-husband:

> 'It was ten years of my not knowing that I find very hard to believe. Especially of a man that I'd loved and deep down I still love now. I still find it very hard to think that he would do such things. My ex-husband is maintaining he's done no wrong. But the two girls are both saying, "Yes, these things have happened". So I feel as if I'm in the middle of a see-saw.'

Such mothers badly needed help in dealing with their feelings about what had happened. However, an exclusive focus on mothers as secondary perpetrators rather than as secondary victims of the abuse of their children often led social workers to judge them as non-protective mothers and to withdraw support. In the absence of such support some women remade an alliance with the abuser and excluded the child. The conduct of the investigation affected the way in which family members reacted, and to whom they turned for comfort and help.

It was, in part, on the basis of these reactions that decisions were made about removing the child, prosecuting the abuser and whether a parent figure – usually the mother – could keep the child safe from harm.

During the investigation alliances were formed between the social worker and child or parents, and between family members themselves. These set the pattern for the subsequent course of events. The process of investigation is often one where one parent is suspected of harming the child and the other is not. If the child is to be protected it is important that the benefits for the child and family of bringing the abuse to light outweigh the costs. This is a delicate task and one that is extremely difficult to perform in the present climate of child protection. When investigations were experienced as invasive or blaming, parents sometimes formed a defensive alliance against outside agencies. In the case of physical abuse cited above where the children were removed and the mother's distress compounded, the mother maintained her silence about her husband's alcohol problem. This was one way to retain control over an escalating situation and she may have considered the apparent threat to the family from the agencies as greater than that presented by her husband's conduct. Parents' reluctance to talk about such problems as marital violence or alcohol or drug addiction appeared to have been increased by their fear of the consequences of such revelations and in a number of cases to have led them to minimise or conceal such problems from professionals during the investigation stage.

In cases of sexual or physical abuse, the actions of the investigators could be crucial in setting the scene for the exclusion of the abuser or of the child from the family. When efforts were not directed at strengthening the alliance between the child and non-abusing parent, children were sometimes unnecessarily removed from their families or even left in families with the abuser present. An example may help to illustrate this. A 15-year-old girl revealed at school that she had been sexually abused by her father and expressed apprehension about her mother's reaction. She was interviewed and moved to a friend's family without her mother's involvement. The mother was not given an opportunity to hear her daughter's account of the abuse or to offer support. This set a pattern for the separation of the mother and daughter which the father was able to use to his advantage in discrediting the daughter's disclosure and regaining his place in the family, where he had ready access to the girl's younger sister.

Both parents and children spoke of feeling swept along by the investigation without being consulted or, in some cases, informed about what would happen next. Children who had revealed their experience of abuse had told because they wanted the abuse to cease. Sometimes they spoke out because they wanted to protect a younger brother or sister who they thought was next in line to be abused. Yet they had no idea what telling would set in motion. One child described how, after she had told her tutor at school about her sexual abuse, no-one had explained what would follow. She was taken to the police station and found herself 'going down a corridor and not knowing what was going to happen next'. This uncertainty could serve to magnify the sense of powerlessness which was already a central experience for abused children, as well as for mothers when they discovered what had happened.

The investigation stage was stressful for social workers, parents and children alike. For social workers the stress was somewhat reduced when and if they were able to form a positive alliance with the police officers with whom they worked. When this did happen, social workers could start to feel increasingly in control of events and this helped to relieve the anxiety of the investigation. In contrast, the stress for many parents and children continued at high levels and they often felt unable to affect the course of events. During this stage, decisions were taken which would profoundly influence the development of the case. The way the investigation was managed shaped the attitudes of parents and children and the alliances they formed or failed to form. By the end of the investigation decisions and interventions had crystallised which were likely to determine future child care outcomes.

The public arena of the case conference

The second major stage of the child protection process was that of the initial child protection case conference which was convened to determine what risks children faced and to decide whether their names should be placed on the child protection register. Here, the gap between the experiences of social workers and parents could become wider. While social workers generally approached conferences with some anxiety, knowing that their assessment would come under the spotlight, they were often fairly positive about the role which these conferences played. They saw the conferences as helpful in bringing together a group of professionals who could pool information so that informed decisions about risk could be made. They also saw conferences as spreading responsibility for these decisions. As one social worker said:

> 'It's useful to have had a conference, because you feel somewhat less exposed, having had that backing from different professionals.'

On the whole, social workers were fairly satisfied with the decisions and recommendations made at the conferences. In general, agencies had collaborated to further the tasks of the conference, and had ended by endorsing the view of the investigating social worker. Facts were assembled and case conference members agreed on whether to construe these as amounting to neglect or abuse and what the broad pattern of subsequent intervention might be. In many cases, uncertainty for the social worker had begun to diminish.

For parents, however, the situation was very different. In 41 per cent of cases neither parent had attended the initial conference, either because they had not been invited or were invited too late to attend, or because their social worker had suggested it would be too upsetting for them. In only five cases had parents chosen not to go, mostly because of previous bad experiences at such meetings. Parents who had not been invited were unhappy at being excluded from such an important meeting. In the remaining cases parents had attended but they were allowed in for only a part of the meeting. Discussion about how to construe the information presented to the conference had taken place in their absence. They felt that their attempts to voice an alternative interpretation fell on deaf ears. One theme which parents referred to time and time again was their feeling that decisions had been made in advance. As one mother put it:

> 'My feeling was that they'd already decided what they were going to do when we got into that room. And it didn't matter what we said, it would not have altered the decision – which it didn't.'

Parents often had a very different view of what had happened to the child and who was responsible from that held by case conference members, but they got little chance to express these views or to challenge those of others. They were grateful when they felt that they had been given help to say what they wanted.

Throughout this study, parents who had been invited to attend conferences were present for only a part of the conference and they withdrew while decisions about risk and registration were made and protection plans were drawn up. They felt very strongly about being excluded from part of the conference. As one mother said:

> 'In that conference room my whole life was talked about by "experts" and it just annoys me... I felt like kicking the door and saying, "Look, I am going to say my say now", but you can't do things like that.'

It was very important for parents to know what it was that others knew. Current moves to enable parents to attend the whole conference will certainly improve their situation and this has been a rapidly changing area of practice since the introduction of the Children Act 1989. The fact will remain that family members are alone in the presence of what may be a large group of professionals and on

unfamiliar territory. Social services departments had often involved others like
the county solicitor to assist them, but parents had rarely been encouraged to
bring others as supporters or advocates. In some cases they had been told that
they could not. Only one parent was accompanied by a solicitor. Some parents
had not known what to expect or who would attend and were often confused
and uncertain about why agencies such as the police or probation were present.

The experience of attending conferences was described by the parents as
intimidating, embarrassing and humiliating. Joining a roomful of professionals
was difficult no matter how well you were treated. As introductions were made
round the room, one mother pointed out that when it came to her turn:

> 'To actually say, "Jane Hall, mother" without shrinking down about three
> foot is a really hard thing to do.'

Parents did not know the 'rules' about when they could speak and had to guess
what to say to further their cause. Sometimes they had not understood what
was going on:

> 'I didn't understand what they were saying, because they were all talking
> upper class... I mean as far as I know they could have been talking about
> putting him in care, for all I know.'

They felt that what was being judged was their moral adequacy and fitness as
parents – as indeed it was. It was not uncommon, therefore, for parents to fear
that their children might be taken into care if they put a foot wrong even when
this was not being considered. They sometimes likened the experience of
attending a case conference to that of going to court.

Moreover, parents disliked feeling that their private life was being made
public to such large numbers of professionals, and felt embarrassed about this
later in contact, for example, with school staff. One mother said:

> 'It bothered me a bit, their knowing all my personal life and what was
> going on. I've really got no privacy left now.'

The conference stage was one where social workers generally felt their overall
view had been validated and that shared understandings had been developed
about how the case would be framed. In contrast, conferences could serve to
make parents feel that their views had been discounted and to underline their
position of powerlessness in the face of a large group of professionals. In spite
of this, parents had generally been glad that they had attended and upset when
they had been excluded.

Of the 120 initial conferences reviewed in this study, in 61 per cent of cases the children were registered. There was, therefore, a substantial group of parents and children who underwent the experience of investigation and conference but were not drawn at this stage further into the official child protection system. What were the views of participants when the conference decision was to register the child?

The stigma of registration

Social workers had been, with a few exceptions, in favour of the decision to register a child since they saw it as offering potential benefits in their manage-ment of the case. It gave them leverage in making demands of parents and in ensuring a degree of compliance, as well as legitimising surveillance of the child. It also raised the status of the case and occasionally released a scarce resource such as day care or the involvement of child guidance. This fairly positive view of registration, however, was in stark contrast to the views of most parents, although it was shared by some non-abusing mothers who welcomed the offer of help in the aftermath of the exclusion of their sexually abusing partner. At this point the gap between the views of parents and practitioners could become even wider, although it should be noted that some practitioners had a keen appreciation of the strength of feeling that registration might generate in family members.

The majority of parents reacted strongly to the news that their child's name had been placed on the child protection register. They often felt blamed and stigmatised and saw it as a judgement that they were unfit parents. They also experienced it as a breach of their privacy. Many mothers said that after the children were registered they felt that they had to let social workers and other professionals into their house at will, and also that they had to be able to account for every bruise that the child had sustained. In contrast, some men accused of physically abusing the child reacted by opting out of disciplining the children – and pushed this responsibility entirely onto the mother.

The experience of stigma was so great for some single mothers that they felt under increased pressure and their ability to cope with their children suffered. One lone mother described the effect of registration on her after some minor but unexplained bruising was found on her baby:

> 'Every time I go to the doctor's surgery I feel that they all know – you know, behind reception. They probably don't, but I feel that they're looking at me or whispering, and I feel that they all know. I mentally cut myself off, because otherwise I get so uptight.'

Parents knew that the use of the register meant that they were on warning, and that the warning was underpinned by the sanction of removing the children. One mother said:

> 'They are using it so that if another...bruise is put on them [the children] they have got the right to take them...so we take every bruise to the GP.'

Some parents were unclear about the reasons why their child's name had been placed on the register, particularly if it had been as the result of a cluster of small concerns rather than as the outcome of one more dramatic incident. This was especially true in cases of emotional abuse or neglect. As one father commented in confusion:

> 'I wanted to know what they meant, "very grave concern", and things, but nobody would say actually outright or straight what it was about.'

Registration was often interpreted by parents in terms of a court order – a 'Protection Order' as they called it. And since their frame of reference was that of care proceedings, it was not uncommon for them to assume that the children's names would stay on the register until they reached the age of eighteen.

Children had very rarely been invited to attend case conferences and sometimes felt, as one girl put it, 'as if everyone was talking behind my back'. It was usually only sexually abused teenagers who knew they were on the register and they often saw the decision positively as a pledge that social services would offer them care and protection. Registration was not always seen as supportive and some children were very embarrassed at being publicly singled out, as they saw it, and were afraid that their friends would hear about it.

At this early stage of the child protection process, it can be seen that case conferences which had generally validated the views of social workers were experienced by many parents as discounting their perspective; registration which found favour with most social workers was generally experienced as highly stigmatising by parents. Children had mainly been excluded from both of these processes. What is crucial about the ways in which parents experienced conferences and registration is that they had a major impact on their response to subsequent intervention.

Social work intervention after the conference

After the conference it was usually the social worker appointed as key worker who was expected to provide the main service for the child and family, and frequently no new resources had been released. At best, a health visitor might have agreed to regular visits. It was striking that while at the investigation and initial conference stage a number of agencies were involved, after the conference social workers were often virtually on their own with the responsibility of protecting the child. The advantages for social workers of collaboration with other professionals at the previous stages had melted away. Indeed, these former advantages could now have become costs since the work of the key worker took place in the context of the negative impact on parents and children of the previous stages of the process.

As we have seen, parents had not been involved in decisions about risk, registration or the protection plan. This had been a significant omission, since the views of parents about risk and the appropriateness of registration were often rather different from those of conference members and when this was the case, the task of dealing with these differing views fell on the social worker alone. As one social worker put it:

> 'I think, at the end of the day, it's the person working with the family who has to confront all the really difficult issues. So there's a certain amount of help, but ultimately you're more or less on your own.'

Agreement and disagreement between parents and professionals

Disagreement between parents and professionals about the findings of abuse or neglect had far-reaching consequences for attempts at social work intervention after the initial case conference. The greater the agreement the more possible it was for the social worker to form a working relationship with the parents and child. Disagreement between social workers and parents varied along three dimensions: first, that of commission (who had perpetrated the abuse or neglect), second, that of culpability (who was to blame), and third, risk (whether the child was still at risk). There were just eight cases out of the 44 in our follow-up sample (18%) where there was agreement between at least one parent and the social worker on commission, culpability and risk, as can be seen in category one in Table 2.1. In six of these cases the mother of a sexually abused child had accepted that the child had been abused, that their partner was to blame, and agreed with social services that the abuser should be out of the household as he presented a risk to the children. In one other case relatives were clear that the child they were looking after had displayed sexually abusive behaviour and was responsible, and they agreed with social services that only vigilance would enable her to remain in the household and reduce risk to their children. The eighth case was a self-referral for physical abuse by a mother who accepted responsibility for hitting her children and wanted help to stop.

In six cases (or 14%) as shown in the second category, there was agreement between parents and professionals about commission and culpability but disagreement about risk. These were situations where a parent, usually the mother, acknowledged that another member of the family had sexually or physically abused their child (for example, a grandfather, stepbrother, divorced or separated father) and was responsible for their actions. They disagreed, however, with professionals about future risk to the child since they believed that the child would be safe with the abuser either because he had 'learned his lesson' or because of the protection they themselves could offer the child.

Table 2.1 Percentage of cases showing agreement or disagreement between parent and social worker on three dimensions

	Commission	*Culpability*	*Risk*	
Category 1	Agreement	Agreement	Agreement	(18%)
Category 2	Agreement	Agreement	**Disagreement**	(14%)
Category 3	Agreement	**Disagreement**	**Disagreement**	(34%)
Category 4	**Disagreement**	**Disagreement**	**Disagreement**	(34%)

In a third and larger group of 15 cases (34%) shown in category three there was disagreement on two out of the three dimensions: parents and professionals agreed about commission but disagreed about both culpability and risk. In these situations parents accepted that they themselves had been the agents of the incidents of concern whether these had been taken to constitute physical abuse, neglect or emotional abuse. Nonetheless, they advanced a variety of reasons to absolve themselves of culpability and to claim that the child would not be at risk in the future. The justifications they put forward for their actions included non-intentionality (a bruise or burn had happened accidentally – it was not abuse); provocation (the child's behaviour was so difficult he or she had provoked a beating); atypicality (the incident was a one-off outburst of temper which was out of character); normalisation (hitting the child was normal chastisement); and minimisation (the son's sexual abuse of his sister had done little harm). These were mostly cases of physical abuse, with a smaller number of neglect or 'emotional abuse' by parents. They also included three cases of sibling sexual abuse where parents minimised the harm the abuse had caused.

In all the cases in this group the justifications advanced for the incidents of concern were accompanied by a view (not shared by social workers) that the children would not be at risk in the future.

In the last group of 15 families (34%) shown in category four there was disagreement on all three dimensions. These were mostly cases of physical or emotional abuse, or neglect. Where a child had sustained an injury the parents had said it was not caused by them – they had no idea how it had happened or someone outside the family must be responsible. In the other cases, parents defended the way in which they were bringing up their children, and hotly disputed the view of the case conference that they were neglectful or emotionally abusive parents. Since commission was denied, it follows that parents did not see themselves as responsible for the child's situation and denied that the child was at risk.

In less than a fifth of the cases, then, was there agreement between the social worker and parent on all three dimensions. Where agreement prevailed there were relatively few problems for social workers in establishing a workable relationship with parents, and in most of these cases the practitioner was involved with a non-abusing mother. Importantly, in the remaining 82 per cent of cases there was disagreement between the parties about risk, and often also about culpability and commission.

The effect of disagreement on social work intervention

These disagreements affected social work intervention in a number of important ways. First, in some cases parents fundamentally questioned the legitimacy of child protection intervention. This was especially true for cases in which a number of general concerns about a child had been constituted by a conference as amounting to neglect or emotional abuse. Sometimes case conference members or social workers had not conveyed their concerns clearly to parents and at other times parents disputed this interpretation of their parenting.

Second, at the stage of the investigation and case conference, assumptions were made by professionals about possible areas of disagreement with parents about risk and culpability and these had then shaped the ways in which agencies had dealt with families. For example, at the investigation stage a mother who was thought likely to side with the abuser rather than the child might not have been informed about the investigation or involved in discussions about placing the child. Moreover, parents who were known to be critical of social services or who disagreed with professional views had sometimes not been invited to case conferences or, on one occasion, were kept waiting throughout the conference and not invited in. For these and other families the experience of official scrutiny and its outcome had sometimes been so alienating that the investigating social workers had very little chance of establishing trust no matter how well-intentioned they were towards family members. This was never the case when there was agreement about risk. It was sad to find that a third of the parents in the follow-up study actively disliked and distrusted their social worker as a consequence of their experience of the investigation, and not a few had requested a change of worker. In only one case was this request accepted. An impasse between social worker and parents was taken to confirm the parents' intransigence.

Third, planning how best to intervene – short of removing the child – was a daunting task for social workers, accountable to a tight procedural system and faced with disputed information about risk and responsibility for the abuse. Abusing and non-abusing parents in contention with professionals could easily feel themselves the cause of frustration, uncertainty and in some cases disapproval. Not surprisingly, parents in conflict with the social services tended to share as little information as possible with the worker. Indeed, the effects spiralled, since the more control or censure that family members felt, the more likely they were to deny responsibility. Sometimes parents looked for other alliances, for example with the abuser, with a trusted friend or, occasionally, with another professional. The child protection system itself may unwittingly fuel this process, since the conference has the job of determining responsibility for harm to a child and responsibility can readily be translated into blame.

The contagious effect of blame

It is important to note that issues of censure are not restricted to parents considered to be abusing or neglectful. There appears to be a contagion effect where imputations of blame spread quickly to encompass non-abusing parents (mainly mothers) who do not act to protect the child in the ways social services departments or others expect of them, and to parents who remain attached to their abusing partners. These issues, individually and together, affected the likelihood of a workable coalition being formed between the parent and social worker, and between the social worker and child. Sometimes, social workers moved swiftly to ally themselves with an abused (usually sexually abused) child, while disapproving of the actions of the non-abusing mother. Although older children were initially grateful for the support and understanding they received, the gains that could be made were limited if the social worker had been unable to make an alliance with the mother. When parents were negative about the worker, children either accepted parental attitudes or experienced a conflict of loyalty in relation to their parents and the social worker. Such a rift was not conducive to building bridges between parents and children and served to undermine the already precarious relations between parents and their children.

The following example from the study illustrates the way in which the early stages of intervention can affect later child protection work and the way that disagreement about risk can continue to influence interaction between professionals and family members as time goes on. In this instance an inexperienced social worker had become increasingly concerned to find that a young mother was unwell and having difficulty coping with her 18-month-old daughter, who was quite withdrawn. The bruise which the worker noticed on the little girl was discussed not with her mother but with a senior colleague who activated child protection procedures and made arrangements for a doctor's appointment. The subsequent arrival of the worker and her senior colleague to take the child to the doctor left the mother feeling alarmed and angry. She was living with a violent partner and was distressed about the difficulties in her relationship with her young daughter. Help might have been acceptable to the mother if it had corresponded more closely with her view of the needs of her family, if she had been consulted and if events had not escalated so rapidly. Circumstances worsened when, at a poorly chaired conference, the mother felt on trial. Her request for a change of social worker was refused. The case conference decision to register left her feeling discredited. As a consequence of these interventions the mother did not feel able to risk getting closer to her daughter for fear of the distress this would cause to herself and her daughter should social services subsequently decide to remove her child. The original problem had been compounded by child protection interventions which had paved the way for a further deterioration in the child's relationship with her mother.

Decision-making and interventions are linked at each stage of the child protection process, and early decisions and interventions play a large part in shaping the course of subsequent events. A child protection system in which at the formative stages parents feel that the balance of power has been heavily weighted against them and that they have been excluded from crucial parts of the process can leave social workers in the unenviable position of carrying responsibility for a child's safety when at the same time opportunities for forming effective working relationships with parents have been severely constrained.

Implications for practice

While some of the issues described here may be inevitable by-products of any child protection service, the views of parents and children suggest a number of areas where changes in practice might improve outcomes. It would be useful if, at the outset of an investigation, professionals considered how best to intervene strategically in order to try to strengthen the support given to the child. This will often mean mobilising the resources of confidence in the non-abusing parent and strengthening the alliance between this adult and the child. Recent research has shown that children have the best prognosis for recovery when they are believed and supported by a parent (Conte and Schuerman 1987; Wyatt and Mickey 1988; Berliner 1991). In cases of sexual abuse women would benefit from feeling that their experiences of stress, self-blame and loss were acknowledged and if they were able to receive help in their own right. Women who do not immediately reject an abusing partner may be able to sort out their painful and conflicting feelings with appropriate help, and assume responsibility for protecting their children (Macleod and Saraga 1988; Faller 1989).

The 1989 Children Act has emphasised the importance of informing and involving children and their parents in agency processes. While this is far from straightforward to enact in child protection work, this study underlines the impact that a lack of involvement can have on participants, the resentment of professionals that can build up for parents, and even that in some cases a wedge may be driven between children and non-abusing parents (see also O'Hagan 1989). Exclusion from decision making can leave children fearful and uncertain about what will happen to them. Much work is now being directed in local authorities towards increasing the level of participation of family members and it is clear that practice may vary along a continuum from token involvement towards much more participatory models (Thoburn, Lewis and Shemmings (forthcoming); Marsh and Fisher 1992). Our research emphasises the importance of eliciting the views which parents hold not only about the incidents of concern to professionals, but also about risk and harm to the child. This is not to say that professionals should allow parents' views to usurp their own, but greater understanding of both points of view would make planning for the child and family members more productive. Parents' concerns about the welfare of their child may be different from those of professionals, yet, they may at times be equally valid. In a number of cases of physical abuse to teenagers, parents saw the central issue to be their difficulty in controlling the child, and the abuse as a by-product. Professionals, on the other hand, had seen the issue of control as secondary to that of abuse.

Moreover, time spent discovering parents' and children's views about what the child and other family members need will be repaid later. It is these understandings which should inform decision-making before, during and after the case conference if viable plans of action are to be made. While major disagreements between parents and professionals about commission, culpability and risk may be difficult to bridge, it may well still be possible to find enough common ground to fashion a protection plan which addresses the child's needs and is acceptable to the parents.

Involvement of parents and children in child protection conferences is one part of this dialogue. Whilst greater parental involvement might lead to more disagreement being aired at conferences, this is likely to be beneficial in the long run. There are a number of ways in which practice in this area could be improved. The study shows the crucial importance of parents attending for the whole conference whenever possible, and that anxieties about attendance are somewhat eased if arrangements are made so that they can be settled before the professionals start to arrive. An informal chat with the chair before the conference is also likely to prove helpful. Tokens of welcome such as the offer of a cup of tea are appreciated, and full advance briefing and preparation is needed for parents about the conduct of the conference, their role in it and who will attend, as well as a copy of the agenda. The use of name plates or the wearing of tags giving name and profession will also help family members identify individual participants, and encouragement for them to bring a friend, relative or advocate to give them support would be welcomed.

It is also important that clear explanations about the reasons for registration are given to parents and children. The new Working Together guidelines (Home Office *et al.* 1991) specify that simple, written, factual information about registration should be made available and this could correct some of the current misperceptions. Information about parents' rights would also be useful. The dropping of the 'grave concern' category should also have helped to sharpen the focus of conference members on the reasons for wishing to register a child. It would be helpful if consideration were routinely given at case conferences as to whether the investigating or current social worker is the best person to work with the family or whether a change of worker would be beneficial. It needs to be made clear that this does not reflect in any way on the practice ability of the workers involved. Referral to other agencies such as a family centre or child guidance may also be important, in order to separate out the 'coercive' and 'helpful' agencies where this would be productive. There may also be occasions when there is a case for separate workers for the child and the parents, when their needs are in conflict.

Interviews with parents and children 18 months after registration suggest that the impact of the early stages of intervention is often enduring. Nonetheless, there are mediating factors which allow social workers to carry out their child protection responsibilities effectively, even in quite difficult circumstances. In some cases workers have been able to adopt an open and non-blaming approach with parents who have not admitted to abusing their child, and common ground has been found which has formed the basis for constructive work. In other cases, feelings of bitter resentment and hostility on the part of parents have given way to acceptance with the advent of a new social worker who was able to show understanding for the parent's point of view and patiently fashion interventions which were acceptable to parents because they incorporated the parents' own goals and catered for their expressed needs.

Clearly there are very real dilemmas inherent in a child protection system in which help is offered within a stigmatising framework, which also includes the possibility of criminal proceedings. Up until now the majority of procedural and practice advice has concentrated on the identification and investigation of 'at risk' cases. It is important that, in future, efforts are made to deepen our understanding of what contributes to making subsequent professional actions effective. Clearly, we must try to ensure that the operation of the child protection system no longer works against itself by placing professionals and parents in positions of mutual antagonism. Over and above this, there is a real need for more detailed analysis of the interactions within families as well as those between practitioners and family members which shape the outcome of professional interventions.

References

Bagley, C. and King, K. (1990) *Child Sexual Abuse*. London: Routledge.

Berliner, L. (1991) 'Interviewing families', in Murray, K. and Gough D.S. (eds) *Intervening in Child Sexual Abuse*. Edinburgh: Scottish Academic Press.

Brown, C. (1984) *Child Abuse Parents Speaking: Parents' Impressions of Social Workers and the Social Work Process*. School for Advanced Urban Studies, University of Bristol.

Burns, L. (1991) *Partnership with Families: A Study of 65 Child Protection Case Conferences in Gloucestershire to which the Family were Invited*. Gloucestershire County Council Social Services.

Conte, J. and Schuerman, J. (1987) 'Factors associated with an increased impact of child sexual abuse'. *Child Abuse and Neglect II* 201–211.

Corby, B. (1987) *Working With Child Abuse*. Milton Keynes: Open University Press.

Faller, K.C. (1989) *Child Sexual Abuse, An Interdisciplinary Manual for Diagnosis, Case Management and Treatment*. London: Macmillan.

Fisher, M., Marsh, P., Phillips, D. with Sainsbury, E. (1986) *In and Out of Care. The Experiences of Children, Parents and Social Workers.* London: Batsford.

Gough, D. (1989) *A Longitudinal Study of Child Abuse in Glasgow, Vol. III, The Families of the Children Registered.* Social Paediatric and Obstetric Research Unit, University of Glasgow.

Home Office, Dept of Health, Dept of Education and Science, Welsh Office (1991) *Working Together Under the Children Act 1989.* London: HMSO.

Hooper, C.A. (1989) 'Alternatives to collusion: the responses of mothers to child sexual abuse in the family'. *Educational and Child Psychology 6*, 22–30.

Macleod, M. and Saraga, E. (1988) 'Challenging the orthodoxy: towards a feminist theory and practice'. *Feminist Review: Family Secrets Child Sexual Abuse*, No.28 Spring 1988.

Marsh, P. and Fisher, M. (1992) *Good Intentions: Developing Partnership in the Social Services.* York: Community Care Into Practice.

Mayer, J.E. and Timms, N. (1970) *The Client Speaks.* London: Routledge and Kegan Paul.

McGloin, P. and Turnbull, A. (1986) *Parent Participation in Child Abuse Review Conferences. A Research Report.* London Borough of Greenwich.

O'Hagan, K. (1989) *Working with Child Sexual Abuse.* Milton Keynes: Open University Press.

Pitcairn, T. Waterhouse, L., McGhee, J., Secker, J. and Sullivan, C. (1993) 'Evaluating parenting in child physical abuse'. (Ch 4 in this volume)

Roberts, J., Taylor, C., Dempster, H., Smith, C. and Bonnars, S. (1992) *An Evaluation of a Service for Sexually Abused Children and their Families.* A Research Report, Child and Family Trust, Glasgow (forthcoming).

Sainsbury, E. (1975) *Social Work with Families.* London: Routledge and Kegan Paul.

Sainsbury, E., Nixon, S. and Phillips, D. (1982) *Social Work in Focus. Clients' and Social Workers' Perceptions in Long-Term Social Work.* London: Routledge and Kegan Paul.

Secretary of State for Social Services (1974) Report of the Committee of Inquiry into the Care and Supervision Provided in Relation to Maria Colwell. London: HMSO.

Secretary of State for Social Services (1988) *Report of the Inquiry into Child Abuse in Cleveland 1987.* Cm 412. London: HMSO.

Shemmings, D. and Thoburn, J. (1990) *Parental Participation in Child Protection Conferences: Report of a Pilot Project in Hackney Social Services Department.* Social Work Development Unit, University of East Anglia.

Thoburn, J., Lewis, A. and Shemmings, D. (forthcoming) *Family Participation in Child Protection.* Report for the Department of Health, University of East Anglia, Norwich.

Wyatt, G.E. and Mickey, M.R. (1988) 'The support by parents and others as it mediates the effects of child sexual abuse: an exploratory study', in Whatt, G.E. and Powell, G.J. (eds), *Lasting Effects of Child Sexual Abuse.* London: Sage.

Chapter 3

The Aftermath of Child Sexual Abuse
Women's Perspectives

Harriet L. Dempster

The vast majority of child sexual abusers are found to be men, yet it is women who bear the burden when their children are violated (Herman 1981; Dobash and Dobash 1979). Not only are women left to pick up the pieces of their own lives but, as mothers, are charged with the responsibility of repairing the hurt in their children's lives and protecting them from further abuse. The reactions of women to the sexual abuse of their children have been largely neglected, despite their central importance to the wellbeing of their children before and after professional intervention.

This chapter begins by reviewing current literature related to the responses of women who have experienced professional investigation into the alleged sexual abuse of their children, highlighting a gap in existing research. Findings are then presented from an exploratory study which attempts to bridge this gap. These findings demonstrate that discovering your child has been sexually abused has a profound impact on women and the processes women go through are complex and prolonged. Common elements in women's experiences are distilled to suggest a common basis for understanding their reactions to the problem of child sexual abuse.

Review of the literature

Women have been much maligned in research and clinical literature (Lustig 1966; Matchotka, Pittman and Flomenhaft 1967; Meiselman 1978). The prevailing view is one of inadequate mothers who respond poorly to the knowledge that their children have been abused. Frequently, mothers are accused of colluding with the sexual violence and failing to protect their children (Wattenberg 1985). Rather than recognising the potential women have for helping their children overcome the effects of abuse, there is evidence that social workers tend to hold on to preconceived notions that blame mothers for the abuse (Deitz and Craft 1980).

In this context women have been identified as failing. They attract blame on three counts: their inadequate personal make up; their dereliction of motherly and wifely duties which leaves their male partners 'no choice' but to turn to their daughters for sexual favours; and their failure to protect their children from this abuse (Nelson 1987). Far from being passive, women apparently actively resist the recognition of sexual abuse (Goodwin 1982). Do these accusations stand up under close examination?

The early studies

Early studies examining the responses of mothers to the sexual abuse of their children underline two points. First, the tendency to criticise women when abuse occurs originates from the structure of our patriarchal society which places the interests, rights and needs of women below those of men. Second, much of social work theory is rooted in sexist ideology which serves to perpetuate the status quo and the inequality of women (McIntyre 1981).

Much of the early published research was conducted by psychiatrists who were influenced by a family systems approach to the problem. This theoretical perspective views sexual abuse as a symptom of family dysfunction (Furniss 1984). The responsibility for the abuse does not rest solely with the abuser but with all family members. Most notably, the woman is deemed to be failing to fulfil her part of the bargain in the marital and parenting relationship. A lack of female sexual compliance or responsiveness plus insufficient attention to the children or home are seen as likely explanations which account for the sexual abuse. The man's behaviour, in this context, is interpreted as a solution to other problems in the family. It is not surprising, therefore, that the image portrayed by the studies quoted above is one of the woman as collaborator of child sexual abuse. It needs to be stressed, however, that much of this research is based largely on anecdotal evidence drawn from very small clinical samples, all of which were restricted to intrafamilial sexual abuse (Lustig 1966; Matchotka, Pittman and Flomenhaft 1967; Meiselman 1978). To draw sweeping conclusions from them seems unjustified.

Later studies

Recent studies employing larger samples suggest a different picture. Only a minority of mothers may not respond supportively to their children on the disclosure of sexual abuse. Figures appear to vary depending upon whether the study is confined to abuse by a family member or whether it also takes account of abuse by someone outwith the family.

For example, samples of children abused by their mother's partner or a family member highlight women supporting their children in 56 per cent of cases (Myer 1985) to 78 per cent of cases (Sirles and Franke 1989). In studies inclusive of extrafamilial abuse, the figures range from 69 per cent of mothers supporting or believing their child (De Jong 1988) to 80 per cent of mothers taking some protective action towards the child, to 90 per cent of mothers being defined as demonstrating a moderate degree of concern (Gomez-Schwartz, Horowitz and Cardarelli 1990). The lack of consistency in the results between these groups can be explained by examining what is defined as protective action by the mothers and by examining the researchers' methods of establishing belief and non-belief. Research measures employed ranged from the researcher making a judgement on the basis of maternal responses to a questionnaire to clinical judgements. Definitions of protective action included establishing whether the mother believed the child, or had made a report to the police, to whether the woman separated from and/or divorced the abuser (De Jong 1988; Gomez-Schwartz, Horowitz and Cardarelli 1990; Mannarino and Cohen 1986; Pellegrin and'Wagner 1990; Sirles and Lofberg 1990).

Gordon, in her review of case records of agencies in the USA between 1880 and 1960, highlighted that both women and children initiated actions and sought help frequently to stop sexual violence within the family (Gordon 1989). Women as mothers continue to be one of the main sources of referral to agencies about the sexual abuse of their children (Bexley Social Services Department / Metropolitan Police 1987; Waterhouse and Carnie 1990).

Reviewing all the published research in chronological order, Hooper (1992) suggests that more mothers are believing their children. This trend is attributed to hightened public awareness of child sexual abuse and a more sympathetic agency response influencing mother's responses (Hooper 1992). This may reflect a move away from explanations of causation which stem from family therapy. McLeod and Saraga delivered a powerful and convincing feminist critique of the inadequacy of the family systems explanation of abuse (McLeod and Saraga 1988). This was followed by one of the original champions of family therapy declaring his doubts about the model and suggesting its application to the causation of sexual abuse is dangerous for children (Will 1989).

Little more can be gained from repeated research studies examining the proportion of women who believe their children without beginning to examine whether certain factors mediate a mother's response in these circumstances.

Mediating factors

It would seem that women are less likely to believe and be supportive to their child when the abuser is their current partner (Sirles and Franke 1989; De Jong 1988; Faller 1988; Erenson et al 1989; Gomez-Schwartz, Horowitz and Cardarelli 1990).

The type of abuse and mother's whereabouts at the time of abuse have proved also to be significant. Mothers seem more likely to believe if the abuse fell short of actual intercourse and if reports indicated they were out of the home at the time of the abuse (Sirles and Franke 1989). The age of the child may also be influential in determining the maternal response as studies have shown that the younger the child, the more likely it is that the mother believes him/her and the more likely she is to divorce her abusing partner (Sirles and Lofberg 1989). It has been noted that women's reactions may be shaped in part by the gender of the abused child (Hooper 1992).

Economic factors have largely been ignored by researchers. One study, however, found that women in employment were more likely to support their children. Conversely, children who were received into care as a consequence of abuse were more likely to come from families where the mother was unemployed (Pellegrin and Wagner 1990). The above findings have a parallel with research into domestic violence where women's lack of economic independence and choice force them to stay in violent relationships (Dobash and Dobash 1979).

The studies quoted above seem to assume a very restricted view of women concentrating on them as mothers. In the context of sexual abuse the different responsibilities women hold as wives and mothers often conflict. Ignoring this aspect has created an abstract quality in the analysis which obscures the reality of women's lives and experiences.

Believing or not believing are reduced to events as opposed to being understood as processes that happen in a personal and wider social context. Hooper acknowledges this inadequacy and highlights in her research the relative powerlessness experienced by mothers in the domestic family (Hooper 1988). Her findings suggest that women who discover their child has been abused by a partner or member of the family go through the trauma of loss. Rather than see the loss as analogous to bereavement, Hooper stresses the change in self-concept and threat to identity. This conceptualisation of women's response to their child's disclosure is important because it points up the acute feelings of distress that are involved and also offers an alternative to theories of collusion.

Little attention has been given to describing and analysing maternal responses to sexual abuse from within and outside the family. Regher (1990) presents data from 33 clinical cases of extrafamilial sexual abuse. No gender distinction is made between parents, which is an unfortunate omission as it denies the dynamics of sexual violence and the differential threat it places on men and women.

Description of research study

The purpose was to explore the emotional responses of women when they discovered their children had been sexually abused; and the meaning and impact of that abuse on the women as wives and mothers, taking account of their social and financial circumstances. This study, unlike much of the foregoing research, was not confined to cases where the child was abused by the woman's partner or a family member in order to discover whether women's responses differ between abuse from within or outside the family.

Methodology

A sample of 34 women took part in the study. Throughout a period of ten months between August 1988 and May 1989 women were recruited from two sources: referrals to a Child Psychiatry Specialist child sexual abuse team and referrals relating to incidents of child sexual abuse which were investigated by one local authority Social Work Department and later came to case conference.

At the first contact with the Department of Child Psychiatry or following the case conference the social worker approached the mother of the sexually abused child to ascertain whether she would be willing to take part in the research. A letter of introduction explaining the research and what it would involve was then given to the woman. If she agreed to take part an appointment was made to visit her at home where an in-depth interview was conducted.

The interview was loosely structured and the women were encouraged to talk in their own words about the sexual abuse of their child, the process of discovery, the events that followed and their feelings and reactions. This method seemed the most appropriate as a means of exploring attitudes and emotions. The format also offered flexibility to both respondent and interviewer to question, clarify and elaborate.

The women responded enthusiastically to this approach: they had stories they wanted to tell, despite the fact that the subject was personal and painful. Prompting was rarely necessary. For many this was the first opportunity they had had to be listened to and taken seriously. A number of the women viewed the opportunity of taking part in the research as a way of helping others. It was important to them to find something positive to come out of this overwhelmingly negative experience.

The women

The 34 women who took part in the research were all white. The absence of women from the ethnic minority community may be a reflection of the racism in our society. It has been suggested that a black child may find it harder to disclose because telling the authorities, which are overwhelmingly staffed by white people, may feel like an even greater betrayal (Droisen 1989). The women's ages ranged from 21 to 53 years. They came from differing social and educational backgrounds and lived in a wide range of housing in both urban and rural areas. Seven women had completed a further education course or had trained for nursing or teaching, ten women were in employment at the time of their child's disclosure and one ran a successful business. As a result of the abuse, two women gave up work to be at home with the child despite the adverse financial implications.

Twenty-two women were living with partners when the abuse was discovered whilst the remaining 12 were single parents. As a result of the child telling of abuse, the living situation for ten of the women changed.

These 34 women had a total of 102 children, of whom 51 had been abused at some time, 42 of these children were referred during the period of the research. The children were subjected to various types of abuse ranging from genital touching to oral sex to penetrative abuse. Some children experienced the abuse over prolonged periods. All the identified abusers were men. The ratio of intrafamilial abusers to extrafamilial abusers was 3:2. Fourteen of the 34 women disclosed that they had been sexually abused themselves as children.

Findings

The outcome in these 34 cases challenges notions about women colluding with abuse. All the women took some action toward ending the abuse and protecting their children when they found out about the abuse. For some this was done in the face of complete denial by the perpetrator, disapproval or even harrassment from the perpetrator's friends, from relatives and sometimes the surrounding community.

Nevertheless, none of the children concerned were received into care as a direct result of disclosure of sexual abuse. This study highlights that women are not only left to try and repair the damage and cope with the hurt their children feel as a consequence of sexual abuse, but also they are faced with their own personal pain. One of the key findings of this study is that discovering your child has been sexually abused is devastating for women. They feel shattered, shocked, frightened and isolated. Whether the abuse is by a partner, family member or someone outside the family the women universally experience a struggle to come to terms with the reality. The emotional and behavioural impact which can be long lasting mirrors what is experienced by the victims themselves.

The reactions of the women were complex. Discovery was much more like a process which was prolonged as opposed to a discrete event:

> 'The girls told me it had happened but that wasn't the end. It got worse and worse as all the details of what happened unfolded.' (The abuser was child's natural father)

The impact of the discovery was often debilitating. Coming to terms with the truth was always painful and frequently a struggle in the face of competing loyalties:

> 'I was devastated, I was shattered, I went completely to pieces. I just couldn't believe it. I thought "Oh, that's my son. How could he do that to his sister – my daughter?" I was in complete turmoil. When I look back I feel I let my daughter down. I didn't give her enough when all of this came out. I was so shocked I gave too much to my son. He's always been special to me. I love him but I hate him for what he has done to her, to all of us. It's affected the whole family, torn us apart. It was a nightmare that lasted for weeks. I just wanted to wake up and find it wasn't true.' (Abuser was child's older brother)

> 'He (my son) just told me out of the blue, I couldn't get my breath. I felt totally shocked. I believed him, I didn't doubt him but I had to find out is this true? I didn't feel it was real until the perpetrator admitted it.' (Abuser was the son of childminder)

The women expressed a need for support for themselves following a disclosure. Social workers were often perceived as focusing only on the children. Extended family were frequently experienced as unhelpful, offering advice when what

the women felt they needed was someone to listen and understand. Where women had met other women who had gone through the same experience they derived considerable support.

> 'She'd been through it – she was a great help. She understood and told me what to expect.' (Abuser was family friend)

Parallels are to be found between the experiences of these women and their children. The explanatory model developed by Finkelhor and Browne (1986) postulates that the experience of child sexual abuse can be analysed in terms of four traumatic factors. These include stigmatisation, powerlessness, betrayal and traumatic sexualisation. The factors which are central to the model are conceptualised as dynamic forces that alter the individual's cognitive and emotional orientation to the world. They create trauma by distorting the individual's self concept, world view and affective capacities. This, in turn, can create behavioural problems. The feelings expressed by the women during the research seemed to match those expressed by sexually abused children.

This model is used to explain the psychological impact and potential behavioural manifestations in women following the sexual abuse of their children. Direct quotes from the research interviews illustrate how this model can be applied and linked to some of the self-reported effects on women whose children have been abused.

Stigmatisation

Stigmatisation refers to the negative associations (about the experience) conveyed to the child. Ultimately, these feelings of badness, shame and guilt are incorporated into the child's self-image (Finkelhor and Browne 1986). Similar negative connotations are communicated to women whose children have been sexually abused. Like their children they feel shame and guilt but the reasons for this are different. Many women felt they must be bad mothers and these sentiments were associated with feelings of guilt and worthlessness about themselves:

> 'I thought, well that's it all gone for nothing. I can't be a good mother now when something like this has happened. I may not have been the best mother in the world but over the past 15 years I have struggled to do what's best for the kids. That won't count now.' (Abuser was mother's boyfriend)

One woman described how she was found wanting when she and her daughter appeared before a Children's Hearing.

'They told me I had failed to protect my daughter and she would have to go on supervision.' (Abuser was step-father)

Shame manifested itself in social isolation.

'When I walked down the street I felt everyone's eyes on me. I was worried we would draw comments. I was frightened. I felt like shutting myself away.' (Abuser was a neighbour)

Feelings of guilt prompted a number of women to give up work despite the fact that this had adverse financial implications for the family's standard of living.

Powerlessness

The dynamic of powerlessness occurs when a child's body is repeatedly invaded against his/her will. It is intensified if the child is threatened by the abuser or meets disbelief when she/he tells (Finkelhor and Browne 1986). Like children, women are relatively powerless in our patriarchal society. This is due in part to economic dependence, inadequate child care provision and a continued tolerance of the physical abuse of wives (Dobash and Dobash 1983). It is not surprising, then, to discover one-third of the sample experienced domestic violence. Already existing feelings of powerlessness are intensified when child sexual abuse is discovered. Sexual abuse is one more intrusion over which women feel they have no control. Just as in the case of their own abuse by men women feel powerless to stop the abuse of their children or undo what has been done.

'How was I supposed to know he would abuse the children? He didn't have any previous convictions. We had known him for 11 years. Abusers don't wear badges to tell you who they are.' (Abuser was a family friend and godfather to the child)

The consequences of disclosures were shown to have a psychological impact. Loss of control was felt after the matter was reported to the police. One woman reported she felt as if she were on a roller coaster and couldn't get off:

'A million police came and just marched in asking questions. I had no say in what happened.' (Abuser was child's father)

Others regretted the loss of privacy:

'I mean they sent a male social worker along, what good was that after something like this? She didn't want to speak to a man about it and neither did I, but we had no choice.' (Abuser was an uncle)

In the wake of the Cleveland publicity many women expressed very real fears that their children would be compulsorily received into care. A number of women recognised that the safety of children from the threat of sexual abuse rests upon the ability to change and manage men's behaviour. Strong and confused emotions were associated with this. Although a clear desire for punishment was not unusual there was a recognition that imprisonment alone was not the answer.

> 'He needs help.' (Abuser was woman's partner)

The fact that there were few programmes available to assist the men in working on their offending behaviour caused the women further frustration and increased their sense of powerlessness over the children's futures.

In two cases the perpetrator took his own life. The fact that nothing could reverse this outcome caused the women to experience intense guilt and self doubt.

Some of the women became depressed. Others complained of nightmares and eating disturbances. Not all women, however, remained overshadowed by events. Some women reacted to feelings of powerlessness by making choices. These may have been limited decisions but they were an attempt to gain some control over their lives. Examples of this included applying to move or moving house, seeking counselling, embarking on a course of study and joining a political party.

Betrayal

When children discover that someone on whom they have been dependent or for whom they care has manipulated them and caused them harm they feel cheated and betrayed (Finkelhor and Brown 1986). Similar feelings of betrayal were not uncommon for the women, nor were they confined to situations where the abuser was a member of the family, as this case of a woman who had nursed an elderly neighbour in hospital illustrates:

> 'I can't understand why he did it – I helped him and look what he has done to me.'

> 'I trusted him, he took a loan of *her* and me. He looked on her as a daughter so how could he do that? That hurt me.' (Abuser was the woman's partner)

The impact of betrayal was acute:

> 'I just felt like crying all the time. I cried and cried and cried for weeks.' (Abuser was natural father)

'I just don't know who I can trust now.' (Abuser was stepfather)

A loss of confidence in others was associated with these feelings of betrayal. This prevented some women going out in the evenings and leaving their children with a babysitter. Others felt very pessimistic about their ability to enter into another trusting relationship with a man.

Traumatic sexualisation

This is a process whereby the child's feelings and attitudes become adversely affected as a result of the abuse. A child becomes confused about sexual behaviour. His/her conceptions about what is and is not appropriate with regard to sexual behaviour are rooted in the actions and manipulations of the offender. Frequently, frightening events and memories become associated with sexual activity. The effects in children range from oversexualised behaviour and promiscuity to a complete avoidance of sexual intimacy (Finkelhor and Browne 1986).

Approximately half of the women interviewed remarked that they felt quite differently about sex as a result of finding out about their child's abuse:

'After it all came out my sex life with my husband was affected. I felt like a victim, like my daughter. If he came anywhere near me I just felt myself recoil.' (Abuser was an uncle)

'It's affected our sexual relationship. I don't want it to but it has. I go cold when it gets down to the nitty gritty. Part of me is saying yes, part of me is saying no.' (Abuser was brother)

In a couple of cases women described how they had nightmares where they kept dreaming abut what happened to their daughters but as if it was heppening to them. One woman, who had walked in while the abuse was happening to her son, was haunted by the thought of how much worse it might have been if she hadn't discovered it. In a further case a woman complained that since the disclosure she could not feel sexually aroused.

For the group of women who had been sexually abused themselves as children the effect was like a trigger unleashing painful memories of their own abuse. Some women reported that made them more aware of the problems they had with sex and how it had affected their adult lives.

'We had never had a good relationship (me and my husband) but after we found out she'd been abused it got worse and worse. It was like a double crisis. I realised then that some of the problem came from my own childhood and what happened to me. It got so bad I had to tackle it. I guess I decided to do something positive about something very negative.' (Abuser was a neighbour)

Although these women were struggling to cope with their own feelings about their own abuse they were very concerned for their children. They shared a conviction that it was much better to get the issue out in the open. Over half of them actively sought therapy for their children in the hope that this would spare them the hurt they had felt having to keep their feelings bottled up. This positive choice by these abused women may help explain why clinicians so often report that mothers of sexually abused children have also been victims.

Implications for practice

There are a number of implications for policy training and practice which flow from the above. There is a need to make a distinction between abusing and non-abusing parents. To date government guidance has only referred to parents failing to distinguish between the two (SWSG 1989; DOH 1988; DOH 1991). The importance of this is further underlined by research which has identified that one of the primary indicators used by social workers is assessing risk to a child is whether or not the mother believed her child (Waterhouse and Carnie 1991). Two benefits arise from this distinction. First, a clearer statement is made about where responsibility for abuse lies; and second, the opportunity to concentrate positively rather than negatively on women to enhance their maternal potential is brought into sharper relief.

Children and women are likely to place competing demands on a single social worker responsible for investigating child sexual abuse. Recent emphasis (London Borough of Brent 1985; Butler Sloss 1988) on the importance of being exclusively child-centred may work against an eventual positive outcome serving to alleviate and isolate the mother in her feelings of helplessness. A policy which advocates the allocation of two workers in order that the competing needs of child and mother may be handled may be expensive in the short-term but it is likely to bring considerable long-term dividends for both child and mother (Boushel and Noakes 1988). In order to promote a child-centred service it is necessary to ensure that practice is also woman-centred. The development of a woman-centred practice recognises the structural inequalities in society and the commonalities between women workers and clients (Statham and Hamner 1988; Phillipson 1992). This has implications for the gender of the worker involved. The advantages of a female helper in working with adult incest survivors and the issues for male helpers have been well documented (Hall and Lloyd 1989). It is also important to recognise the black perspective in work with sexual abuse (Bogle 1988). These issues may have equal relevance for women who discover their children have been sexually abused. Policy and practice need to take account of gender and race and afford women who discover their children have been sexually abused a choice of workers.

Child sexual abuse is an isolating and frightening experience for both children and women (Gomez-Schwartz, Horowitz and Cardarelli 1990). There is a pressing need for practitioners to recognise that women have to struggle to confront the sexual abuse of their children regardless of who has committed the abuse, and require support to do so. While there is a role for individual counselling the development of a group work approach which acknowledges the competing roles women have in society deserves attention. Many of the most successful support networks related to child sexual abuse have arisen out of the self-help movement. Professionals have a role to play alongside these developments, but there is a need to balance their involvement in such a way as not to obscure mutual support and the creative potential in women and children struggling to survive.

A more woman-centred practice might be encouraged to evolve if professionals did not frame women's experience as problematic. Although no suggestion is being made that sexual abuse is a positive experience individual women have used their disturbing experiences positively to help others.

Conclusion

This chapter highlights that discovering your child has been sexually abused has a profound impact on women. In facing the truth women experience confusing emotions, ambivalence and conflict.

If the helping professions are going to be effective in supporting women to be safe parents who can help their children overcome the trauma of abuse, there is a need to take account of the different perspectives of women, children and men. The concepts of stigmatisation, powerlessness, betrayal and traumatic sexualisation may promote a deeper understanding of the interplay of the different factors and possible effects on women who discover their child has been sexually abused. This could be used in training not only to help workers gain a better understanding but also might be developed to enable women to make sense of and manage their experience.

Finally, if social workers and other professionals are going to be of any support to women and through them help their children, there is a need to listen and learn from the women themselves and acknowledge the complexity and dynamics of their experience.

References

Bexley Social Services and Metropolitan Police Joint Working Party (1987) Child Sexual Abuse Joint Investigative Programme. Bexley Experiment – Final Report.

Bogle, M. (1988) 'Brixton Black Women's Centre'. *Feminist Review 28*, 132–135.

Boushel, M. and Noakes, S. (1988) 'Social services developing a policy on child sexual abuse'. *Feminist Review 28*, 150–157.

Butler Sloss (1988) *Report on the Inquiry into Child Sexual Abuse in Cleveland.* London: HMSO.

Deitz, C. and Craft, J. (1980) 'Family dynamics of incest, a new perspective'. *Social Casework, December 1980*, 602–609.

De Jong, A.R. (1988) 'Maternal response to the sexual abuse of their children'. *Paediatrics 81 (1)*, 14–21.

Department of Health (1988) *Protecting Children: A Guide for Social Workers.* London: HMSO.

Department of Health (1991) *Working Together, A Guide to Arrangements for Interagency Co-operation for the Protection of Children from Abuse.* London: HMSO.

Dobash, R.E. and Dobash, R. (1979) *Violence Against Wives.* New York: Free Press.

Droisen, A. (1989) 'Racism and antisemitism', in Driver, E. and Droisen, A. (eds) *Child Sexual Abuse: Feminist Perspectives.* London: McMillan.

Everson, M., Hunter, W., Runyon, D., Edelson, G. and Coulter, M. (1989) 'Maternal support following disclosure of incest'. *American Journal of Orthopsychiatry 59*. 2: 197–297.

Faller, K. (1988) 'The myth of the collusive mother; variability in the functioning of mothers of victims of intra-familial sexual abuse.' *The Journal of Interpersonal Violence.* 3.2: 190–196.

Finkelhor, D. and Browne, A. (1986) 'Initial and long term effects: a conceptual framework', in Finkelhor, D., *A Source Book on Child Sexual Abuse.* Beverly Hills: Sage, 180–198.

Furniss, T. (1984) 'Conflict avoiding and conflict regulating patterns in incest and child sexual abuse'. *Acta Paedopsychiatrica 50*, 299–313.

Gomez-Schwartz, B., Horowitz, J.M. and Cardarelli, A.P. (1990) *Child Sexual Abuse: The Initial Effects.* London: Sage.

Goodwin, J. (1982) *Sexual Abuse: Incest Victims and their Families.* Mass: John Wright and Sons.

Gordon, L. (1989) *Heroes of their Own Lives – The Politics and History of Family Violence.* London: Virago.

Hall, L. and Lloyd, S. (1989) *Surviving Child Sexual Abuse. A Handbook for Helping Women Challenge Their Past.* Brighton: Falmer Press.

Herman, J. (1981) *Father-Daughter Incest.* Harvard University Press.

Hooper, C.A. (1988) *Alternatives to Collusion: The Response of Mothers to Child Sexual Abuse in the Family.* Paper presented to the Annual Conference of the British Psychological Society, Leeds, April 1988.

Hooper, C.A. (1992) *Mothers Surviving Child Sexual Abuse.* London: Routledge.

London Borough of Brent (1985) *A Child in Trust.* A Report of Panel of Enquiry into Circumstances Surrounding the Death of Jasmine Beckford. London Borough of Brent.

Lustig, N. (1966) 'Incest, a family group survival pattern'. *Archives of General Psychiatry 14,* 31–40.

Matchotka, P., Pittman, F. and Flomenhaft, K. (1967) 'Incest, a family affair'. *Family Process 6,* 98–116.

Mannarino, A.P. and Cohen, J.A. (1986) 'A clinical demographic study of sexually abused children'. *Child Abuse and Neglect 10 (1), 17–25.*

Meiselman, K. (1978) *Incest – A Psychological Study of Causes and Effects.* San Francisco: Josey Press.

Myer, M. (1985) 'A new look at mothers of incest victims'. *Journal of Social Work and Human Sexuality 3,* 47–58.

McIntyre, K. (1981) 'Role of mothers in father-daughter incest: a feminist analysis'. *Social Work, Nov. 1981,* 462–466.

McLeod, M. and Saraga, E. (1988) 'Challenging the orthodoxy: towards a feminist theory and practice'. *Family Secrets and Child Sexual Abuse, Feminist Review 28,* 16–55.

Nelson, S. (1987) *Incest – Fact and Myth.* Edinburgh: Stramullion Press.

Pellegrin, A. and Wagner, W.G. (1990) 'Child sexual abuse: factors affecting victims' removal from home'. *Child Abuse and Neglect 14,* 53–60.

Phillipson, J. (1992) 'Practising equality – women, men and social work'. *Improving Social Work Education and Training No.10.* CCETSW.

Regher, C. (1990) 'Parental responses to extrafamilial child sexual abuse'. *Child Abuse and Neglect 14,* 113–120.

Sirles, E.A. and Franke, P.J. (1989) 'Factors influencing mothers' reactions to intrafamily sexual abuse'. *Child Abuse and Neglect 13,* 131–139.

Sirles, E.A. and Lofberg, C.E. (1990) 'Factors associated with divorce in intrafamily child sex abuse cases'. *Child Abuse and Neglect 14,* 165–170.

Social Work Services Group (1989) *Effective Intervention in Child Abuse: Guidance in Interagency Co-operation in Scotland.* HMSO.

Statham, D. and Hamner, J. (1988) *Women and Social Work: Towards a Woman Centred Practice.* Basingstoke: McMillan Education.

Waterhouse, L. and Carnie, J. (1990) *Child Sexual Abuse. The Professional Challenge to Social Work and Police.* Edinburgh: Social Work Services Group, Central Research Unit Papers.

Wattenberg, E. (1985) 'In a different light: a feminist perspective on the role of mothers in father-daughter incest'. *Child Welfare LXIV (3),* 203–211.

Will, D. (1989) 'Feminism – child sexual abuse and the long overdue demise of systems mysticism'. *Association for Family Therapy Newsletter, Spring 1989,* 12–15.

Chapter 4

Evaluating Parenting in Child Physical Abuse

Tom Pitcairn, Lorraine Waterhouse, Janice McGhee,
Jenny Secker and Cathleen Sullivan

Child abuse arouses public concern and causes personal misery for parents and children. Inability fully to protect children is highlighted in a succession of inquiry reports (see, for example, Colwell 1974). These reports give repeated emphasis to procedural failure, and therefore offer procedural solutions as the defence against fatalities. Yet at the heart of each case lies a professional judgement about the quality of parenting. The complexity of evaluating a parent's relationship with his or her child remains largely unexamined in child protection research. The purpose of this chapter is to outline a study which explores approaches to parenting through first hand accounts of parents whose children were registered as physically abused and how these compare with evaluations by social workers of the parenting.

Previous psychological research on parenting has concentrated on either defining the parental behaviour in global terms (such as permissive or controlling) and looking for effects in the short- or long-term on the child, or looking at the effect particularly of the type of mother-child attachment on later social and cognitive development. The work of Baumrind (1971) and Sears, Maccoby and Levin (1957) suggests that parents, over time, are reasonably constant in their styles of child rearing, whether they are warm or hostile, consistent or inconsistent in punishment, protective or neglectful or anxious or relaxed. Children themselves seem to be stable in the pattern of behaviour that they show to peers. In a study comparing peer relations in eight-year-olds with the same children ten years later (Huesman, Eron, Lefkowitz and Walder 1984), those labelled aggressive at eight were still so labelled at 18, and were also three times more likely to have police convictions. In contrast, those children rated as friendly and never fighting had very few criminal convictions. Given the absence of longitudinal studies in child abuse it is unclear whether this constancy in the behaviour of both the parent and the child would pertain.

Psychological research has also been concerned with the relation between parental style and the sociability of the child, although not specifically with the relation between the two when child abuse has occurred. In the studies of early mother-child relations the concept of attachment has been highly influential in the field, especially the work of Mary Ainsworth and her colleagues (see Ainsworth, Blehar, Waters and Wall 1978). She established the notion that some relationships were different from others, particularly in the dimension of the security of attachment for the child. This is a qualitative rather than a quantitative dimension, and insecurity (of whatever type, anxious or avoidant) leads to differences in the child's social performance with peers, with the securely attached child being more friendly, positive in relation to adults and more popular with the other children (Easterbrooks and Lamb 1979; Lieberman 1977; Waters, Wippman and Sroufe 1979). Ainsworth also described the maternal behaviours seen in these parents, with the mothers of securely attached children showing more interactions which were positive and supportive, with control exerted in a firm but caring way. Similarly, Manning, Heron and Marshall (1978) have shown that the type of aggression shown by preschoolers can be related directly to the sort of control exerted by mothers at home. They found that children were consistent in their type of hostility to peers. Specific hostility, which was short-term and limited to achieving a particular goal rather than being directed constantly at one or a few target children, was related to parenting which was relaxed and gave the child considerable freedom to operate on their own initiative. These mothers, however, did not simply ignore the child – their relationships were positive and supportive. Children who teased and harrassed others, however, had mothers who tended to be much more negative in speech and controlled their behaviour in a games situation very firmly, to the extent that the child had very little freedom of action.

Both highly punitive and highly permissive parents tend to have children who are highly aggressive (Sears, Maccoby and Levin 1957). If parents accept the child's behaviour in the early years and fail to set clear limits, the child's aggressive behaviour becomes strong and persistent (Olweus 1980). Patterson (1976, 1980) observed children with aggressive behaviour problems and found that their parents were hostile and lax in their enforcement of rules and limits. The mothers reinforced sometimes deviant behaviour, sometimes prosocial behaviour, and on other occasions ignored or punished either.

In a study on abusing mothers Oldershaw, Walters and Hall (1986) found that the mothers were more power-assertive and intrusive in their interactions with the child, and also more inconsistent in their use of parenting techniques. Abusive parents used more punitive disciplinary practices but their children committed more aggressive transgressions (Trickett and Kuczyinski 1986). In general, abusive mothers are found to be active and interfering, whereas neglectful mothers are uninvolved and passive (Crittenden and Bonvillian 1984). As might be predicted, the patterns of attachment in early infancy reflect these patterns of maternal care, with maltreated infants showing high levels of insecurity shown by their avoidance of the mother or their resistance to her (Lyons-Ruth, Connell, Zoll and Stahl 1987).

There are, then, clear and consistent effects of parental behaviour on the child. What has received little attention is the parenting style(s) of parents who have been accused of physically abusing their child, and the ways in which this parenting is evaluated by social workers.

Methodology

The study draws on a Scottish sample of 43 cases of physical abuse in three regional departments of social work. Sexual abuse cases were excluded as well as known cases of 'grave' concern. The teams from which the cases were drawn were divided between socially-disadvantaged inner city areas and outlying rural towns. Most cases, however, came from highly impoverished sections of each team's catchment area. New consecutive referrals which satisfied research criteria for eligibility were followed up. These criteria included type of abuse, index child 12 years or under and no current psychotic disorder in the parent.

Social workers notified the research team of each new referral, and initial case conferences were attended when possible. All professionals attending the case conference were asked, depending on the child's age, to complete a Rutter (1967) or Richman, Stevenson and Graham (1984) child behaviour check list. These check lists measure behavioural problems in the child and have considerable predictive value in discriminating children with neurotic or anti-social disorders. Parents were visited at home as soon as possible after the case conference and, while every effort was made to interview both mother and father, the mother was usually the main informant and will be reported on in this chapter. Parents also completed the Rutter or Richman check list. Social workers were interviewed in the area team offices. Follow-up interviews with both parties were conducted separately approximately four months later, and all interviews were taped and transcribed in full or part.

Semi-structured questionnaires were devised to collect biographical data and information on parenting, taking account of variables examined in the literature, and included questions about affection, control and discipline, physical care, protection, stimulation, and expectations. The emphasis was not on the main incident of abuse but on parental experience of the child and social work evaluation of child care. Although some questions asked for a yes or no answer, the majority called for a free response and were subsequently coded using a system of functional categories devised post hoc.

The outcome measures which were monitored at the four month follow-up were mainly subjective, relying on self-report from parent and social worker. These included changes in parenting within the categories outlined above, evidence of further injury, and expectations for the future. Reported here are the results from the first interviews with parents and social workers.

Sample

1. The parents

The majority of parents (72%) were born and brought up in Scotland, with 50 per cent living in the same town. Most mothers (75%) grew up in nuclear families, with a slightly lower figure for fathers (67%); 8 per cent with step-parents; 4 per cent (8% for fathers) in public care. Separation from their parents at some point in childhood was not uncommon, occurring in 57 per cent of the mothers and 25 per cent of the fathers, and a further 25 per cent of the parents were split up from their siblings. Thirty-three per cent of mothers and 25 per cent of fathers spent part of their childhood in care, usually a children's home. Marital breakdown and parental illness were given as the two most common reasons for family break up, with no parent reporting abuse as a precipitant factor.

Fifty per cent of both mothers and fathers said that, as children, they got on well with their parents; slightly more mothers remember poorer relations with their fathers than with their mothers, whereas for the fathers the picture is reversed. While half the parents, then, described their childhood as happy, 18 per cent were miserable. Thirty-three per cent suffered from health or emotional problems apart from normal childhood illnesses.

It is in the area of contact with the law that mothers and fathers in this sample mainly differ. Half of the fathers, but only 40 per cent of the mothers report being in contact with social workers as children, and the same 50 per cent of fathers appeared at a juvenile court (30% of mothers). Eighty-three per cent of the fathers had been in trouble with the law, with 50 per cent going to prison, borstal or both (35% and 13% for mothers). None of these offences were child related.

Although 90 per cent of mothers went to ordinary day schools, with 5 per cent attending special residential schools, for the fathers the figures were 50 per cent at day schools and 50 per cent at residential schools. Only two parents stayed on at school after 16 years and 73 per cent of mothers and 84 per cent of fathers left with no certificate. The mothers also had a higher percentage going on to some sort of further education or training (33%), the corresponding figure for fathers was 25 per cent. The majority of the training undertaken was short-term. Perhaps not surprisingly, then, the majority of mothers (83%) and fathers (75%) were unemployed at first interview, and most had been unemployed for the last year.

Current circumstances were thus rather bleak and further exacerbated by high levels of physical and emotional ill-health occurring in 60 per cent of the parents over the last year, as well as in the registered child. Fourteen per cent of parents admitted suffering from drug or alcohol related problems. Forty-two per cent of families had moved at least once in the preceeding year, with half of these families moving two or more times. According to the parents, these moves did not result in improved accommodation.

It is also important to note that the parents began bringing up children fairly young, with the median age at the birth of their first child being 18 for the mothers and 22 for the fathers. The median number of children in total is 2.2 for the mothers and 3.0 for the fathers thus far.

2. The children

There were 25 boys and 18 girls between the ages of one month and 13 years in the sample.

Table 4.1. Age distribution of the children

Age in years	Male $n = 25$	Female $n = 18$	Total $n = 43$
Under 1	4	6	10
1–5	12	7	19
5–10	6	2	8

The children, for the most part, represented a group of normal and wanted children. Seventy and seventy-five per cent of mothers and fathers respectively said the babies were wanted; and 80 per cent of the babies were full term and healthy. The most common complaint of illness was bronchitis. Of those babies born prematurely (22%), the majority were under four weeks. Six of the premature babies were separated at birth from four days to four weeks.

Despite generally good beginnings, only half of all the mothers in the sample reported being truly delighted with the baby once born and 20 per cent described feelings of some or prolonged ambivalence, including one mother who clearly rejected her child. Fathers remembered their feelings for the children as babies less clearly or were less willing to comment, but fewer apparently were delighted or ambivalent. Half the mothers recognised that their feelings for the abused child as a baby were different from those of their other children, although this difference was said to favour the child as often as not. That the child was premature was the main reason given for this self-perceived change in maternal attachment. It is important to note that 40 per cent of the mothers thought they were depressed after the birth of the index child with 13 per cent calculating the depression to have lasted over four months. Few sought help (8%) or received treatment (3%).

Of the 43 children, 39 were on the at risk register of the relevant region. The four unregistered children were reported originally as registered. Reasons for non-registration were; for two older children, despite acknowledged assaults on them, the focus of the problem was seen to lie in the child's behaviour; for one child, despite serious injury in a fire, the parents were seen as cooperating; and for the fourth child because complaints were unsubstantiated.

No specific incident was alleged in 12 out of 42 cases (in one case the precipitating cause was unknown). In those cases in which an incident was alleged, bruising or other minor injury was reported in 18 cases, no injury in three, and serious injury in one case. The apparently low incidence of serious injury clearly distinguishes these children from those reported on in high profile inquiries into physical abuse, but is much more representative of the everyday referrals to social work services.

Evaluation of parenting by the social worker

Surprisingly, given the nature of the referrals, parent and child relations are favourably assessed by social workers, with 83 per cent of the mothers said to have adequate to good relations with the index child. Evaluation of fathers' relations with the children (biological or step-children) was less positive. Overall, only two mothers and one father were seen as having very poor relations with their respective children. This global rating, while favourable, may be a product of the social desirability of presenting the parents in a good light, a pattern Dingwall, Eekelaar and Murray (1983) refer to as the 'rule of optimism'. When specific questions were asked about different aspects of parenting, the picture becomes increasingly negative. For example, social workers consider attachment of the children to be secure in only 50 per cent of cases. Similarly, parental awareness of the child's needs is seen as adequate in 62 per cent of cases and poor in only 25 per cent, and yet 50 per cent of parents were found in practice on a day-to-day basis to be unresponsive to their children, in part because 33 per cent spend little time with them.

Interestingly, once social workers had described in detail parental behaviour and then were asked to distinguish acceptable from unacceptable parenting, the responses suggest a greater willingness on the part of the practitioners to pass professional judgement rather than adhere to public social conventions. Overall, parenting was seen as good enough in 58 per cent of cases and unsatisfactory in 38 per cent. The majority of social workers claimed to use the same criteria when assessing the behaviour of parents referred to them professionally as they would with friends. Some, however, admit that they apply a lower standard of expectation to the sample families, suggesting that benefit of the doubt may inflate the number of positive responses still resulting in some overestimation of parental behaviour.

In order to move away from this global estimation of parenting, social workers were asked to rate the parents' behaviour towards their children along six dimensions which have been identified in the literature as important areas of concern. These were affection, physical care, protection, stimulation, parental expectations of the child and control and discipline. Table 4.2 lists the descriptions by the social workers in each of these areas according to whether the parents were rated as performing well, adequately, poorly or erratically. In very few cases was any distinction made by social workers between mothers and fathers in their behaviour towards the child.

If good and adequate responses are seen together as positive, contrasted with poor and erratic as negative, then the rank order of positive evaluation of the families among these categories of parenting is as presented on the table, with physical care at the top and stimulation and control and discipline at the bottom. The closest estimate, therefore, which corresponds to the global rating of good parent and child relations is in the area of physical care – provision of food and clothing, cleanliness, routines and medical care. It is also the category with the fewest don't knows. This suggests that social workers, when evaluating child care, are referring mainly to this practical care, which is both more observable and easier to make allowances for given the financial hardship in which the parents and children are living.

Table 4.2. Number of cases in each child care category, from 43 cases

	Good	Adequate	Poor	Erratic	Don't know
Physical care	20	13	7	1	2
Affection	14	10	6	6	9
Protection	10	13	12	3	5
Stimulation	6	13	13	6	7
Control and discipline	5	11	14	7	6

	Too high	Just right	Too low	Don't know	
Expectations	13	22	2	6	

Table 4.3. Statistics of the difference in the ratings of families who were all said to get on well with the child (n=33), but whose parenting was rated as either adequate (n=22) or not adequate (n=11)

	Chi-sq.	p
Physical care	7.82	<.01
Affection	<1	NS
Control and discipline	<1	NS
Protection	4.24	<.05
Stimulation	5.09	<.05
Expectations	3.09	NS

It is interesting to ask whether the quality of the maternal relationship with the child is seen as an important factor in deciding the overall acceptability of the parenting. In 22 cases when the mother is said to get on well with the child the standard of parenting is assessed as good enough, but in 11 cases, despite an apparently good relationship between mother and child, the standard is found wanting. This suggests that mothers getting on well with their children is not sufficient for social workers to be satisfied that the children are well looked after. The additional variables found to be critical in their evaluations include, as might be predicted from above, particularly the physical care as well as the protection and stimulation of the child. This would seem to be associated with neglect rather than direct hostility or aggression. Table 4.3 summarises these findings.

Within the categories listed above, specific areas were examined. In physical care the distinguishing factors (between parenting rated as adequate or not adequate) were not the provision of food, clothes or cleanliness, as the majority of families were rated as at least average on these items, but the medical care of the child and the establishment of routines (chi-sq. = 10.25 and 10.17 respectively, 1df, p<.01). In stimulation of the child the only significant factor was that of the mother's playing with the child, which was rated as poor in 75 per cent of the 'not adequate' group (chi-sq. = 6.21, 1df, p<.05). When the protection of the child was considered the most important factor of all was, not surprisingly, the protection in the house (i.e. provision of fireguards, removal of dangerous objects, etc. – chi-sq. = 13.15, 1df, p<.01), although the protection against siblings, strangers and known adults was also significantly low in the 'not adequate' group. Most importantly, protection was rated overwhelmingly as lax in this group (chi-sq. = 15.72, 1df, p<.001). Indeed, the only two cases of over-protective parents occurred in the adequate parenting group of families. This laxity corresponds well with the picture which emerges from these parents' strategies of control and discipline.

Control and discipline of the children presented the most telling information. It is usually assumed that physical child abuse involves damaging aggression to the child and inquiry cases (see, for example, The Beckford Inquiry, 1985) where fatal injuries have occurred contribute to this picture of the events behind abuse. Yet in this study control of the children was rated negatively (34% of cases) because it was lax in 22 per cent of cases rather than excessive as in only one case. It is important to note that both elements were considered present in 32 per cent of the families, further supporting laxness as significant in the approach to parenting. This pattern is consistent with the preferences attributed to the parents for disciplining their children. Social workers perceived parents to favour shouting to hitting and hitting to either reasoning or rewarding the child. According to the social workers, 53 per cent of parents apparently never rewarded or reasoned with the child and 25 per cent never relied upon physical punishment.

If parenting is as good as professional opinion would suggest from the findings reported above, then it might be expected that these children, who early in childhood had seemed to be a group of normal babies, would continue to do well. While some children had been separated from their parents, and then usually briefly, the majority (84%) remained at home with their parents, thereby reducing the likely impact of loss and separation on the children's psychological functioning. Two measures were taken of the social workers' and parents' view of the child. First, each was asked to rate the child on a series of bipolar dimensions such as easy/difficult. Second, depending on the child's age, either the Rutter (1967) or Richman, Stevenson and Graham (1984) child scale was completed. As suggested at the outset of this chapter, these check lists measure behavioural problems in the child and have considerable predictive value in discriminating children with neurotic or anti-social disorders.

On the Rutter and Richman scales (with a cut off of nine and eleven respectively for the non-disturbed population) only ten children were rated at a point below the 'disturbed' cut-off by the social workers, with even fewer (five) by the mothers. Social workers, then, rated slightly fewer children as disturbed and had a mean rating of 13.41 as opposed to 15.86 for the mothers (t=1.5, 28df, ns). Because the overwhelming majority of the children achieved scores from both mother and social worker in the disturbed category there appeared to be considerable agreement about which children are difficult. For those children, however, who were classified as non-disturbed by either mother or social worker there was very little agreement – of the 12 children in this category there was agreement about only three (Table 4.4). Furthermore, the correlation between mother and social worker on the absolute scores was very low (r=.20, ns).

Table 4.4. Scores by the mother and the social worker for the same child which fall above or below the disturbed threshold (based on Rutter and Richman scores)

		Social worker	
		Disturbed	*Not disturbed*
	Disturbed	18	7
Mother			
	Not disturbed	2	3

These Rutter and Richman scores are a compound of answers to a series of specific questions about the children's developmental difficulties. The parent or social worker was not asked to rate the child as disturbed or non-disturbed, which is a threshold score assigned by the researchers. When the parent or social worker was asked to evaluate the child directly on the bipolar scales, the

General Ref

BELFAST

description given was much more positive. Overall there was a slight tendency for social workers to rate the children more highly than either mothers or fathers but this was non-significant (chi-sq. 1.29, 2df., ns). There seemed, therefore, to be a reasonable degree of concordance until a cross-tabulation was made of the social workers' and mothers' rating of particular children (above one year old). Despite the high level of shared positive ratings the negative ratings were widely dispersed and thus non-significant (chi-sq. = 0.9, 1df, ns). Disagreement remained, then, about which children were difficult, aggressive or fearful. Fathers' responses here have not been analysed because of their small number.

These two measures of the child apparently elicit contradictory responses from both mothers and social workers. In the case of the bipolar scales, where the questions ask for qualitative judgements of the child on very general dimensions, the responses given were overwhelmingly positive. Yet with the Rutter and Richman scales, where the questions are directed towards specific behaviours in the child, the responses lead to scores which show a very high level of behavioural disturbance in this population. The difference may well lie in the reluctance of both mothers and social workers to label the child negatively, or to appear to blame them despite the high level of behavioural problems they do appear to have. There are two important outcomes of this similarity. First, the majority of the mothers do not appear to be hostile to the children. Second, it appears that an objective analysis of the child's behavioural problems and the significance of these for assessment and future help is not made by the social worker.

Parents' view of the child

The history of the relationship with their child as a baby was described by the mothers as mainly favourable. At least half the mothers said the babies were good sleepers, 60 per cent good feeders and only 10 per cent reported that the babies cried a lot. The mothers continued to think of the children as babies for a considerable length of time, 30 per cent still seeing them as babies at 24 months. Perhaps surprisingly only a small proportion (25%) admitted to feeling at the end of their tether with the child in the first year. Interestingly, for those families in which the index child was still a baby (under one year) at the time of the interview the responses were very similar, with the exception of the question about 'feeling at the end of your tether', where half the mothers reported such a feeling. These retrospective questions about the child as a baby seem to produce reliable information.

Despite the high frequency of feeling at the end of one's tether in the baby sample the mothers do not report losing control – only one case out of the ten did so. In the mothers of older children, however, loss of control became more pronounced, reported in 30 per cent of cases, and almost always (93%) resulting in hitting or shouting at the child. That this was seen as undesirable behaviour may be reflected in the 66 per cent of mothers who were upset by and regretted their actions. On the other hand, hitting and shouting feature routinely in the day to day management of the children. The parents were asked to describe the frequency with which they used particular types of control and discipline with the index child. These were hitting, shouting, isolating the child, withdrawing their affection, rewarding and reasoning with the child. Parents with children

Table 4.5. Parental account of frequency of different types of routine control and discipline

		Child		Baby	
		Frequent	Rare	Frequent	Rare
Hit	MO	53	30	20	70
	FA	12.5	50	25	75
Shout	MO	80	10	30	60
	FA	75	25	25	75
Shake	MO	-	-	0	100*
	FA	-	-	0	100*
Isolate	MO	30	57	0	100
	FA	12.5	75	0	100
Withdraw	MO	7	73	0	100*
affection	FA	12.5	75	0	100*
Reward	MO	70	27	30	70
	FA	25	62.5	25	75
Reason	MO	27	50	-	-
	FA	75	12.5	-	-
N	MO	30		10	
	FA	8		4	

Figures are percentages; the number of respondents in each group is given at the foot of the table. Child column is for cases where the index child was over one year at interview; baby where the index child was under one year.
Frequent = daily + 2/3 times per week
Rare = rarely + never
*in these cases all responses were in the never category.

under one year were also asked about shaking the baby, but not about reasoning. The frequency categories used were: daily, 2/3 times per week, weekly, monthly, rarely and never. Table 4.5 shows their responses as percentages of two superordinate categories, daily plus 2/3 times per week, and rarely plus never.The patterns of discipline and control of mothers showed remarkable consistency from babies to children (even though the absolute frequency of the behaviours was lower with babies), with shouting, rewarding and hitting as the most common controlling behaviour. Little use was made of withdrawal of affection and reasoning with or isolation of the child. Fathers, by comparison, report a different approach, making much more use of reasoning and less of rewarding or hitting.

This pattern of control by the father is counter-intuitive and one possible explanation might be that the fathers are less than truthful. However, it is notable that in the cases in which the child is a baby the pattern of responses of mothers and fathers is remarkably similar (admittedly based on a small sample), even on socially unacceptable behaviour such as hitting or shouting at the baby. In the case of the behaviour to their children, although reasoning (up) and hitting (down) go in the socially acceptable direction, rewarding does not as it is less frequent. Other possible explanations are that either the fathers have less contact, and hence less duties of control, or that they interpret the terms reasoning and rewarding differently from the mothers. For example, if a parent shouts 'I've told you not to do that a thousand times!', this statement could be interpreted either as shouting at or reasoning with the child. If fathers in this sample spend less time with their children, even though they were mainly unemployed, this may give them a greater reserve in dealing with the child, so that they may be less likely to hit.

Social workers' evaluations of the parents' patterns of control and discipline are very similar to that of the parents themselves, with shouting, hitting and rewarding featuring as the main methods used, and isolation of, rewarding and particularly reasoning with the child being used infrequently. This pattern seems to be no different from that in the general population of this social class (Newson and Newson 1965; Ghate 1991). Just as the social workers report laxity in control, rather than over-control, in the parents, about 60 per cent of parents themselves also report that they fail to discipline the child fairly frequently when the child is behaving badly.

This pattern of control and discipline needs to be put in the context of the general relationship between the parent and the child. The positive relationship reported by social workers is less clearly reflected in the parents' descriptions of how they get on with their children. As babies, including the sample who were still babies at interview, positive descriptions of their character were given by all fathers and 68 per cent of mothers. In the baby sample, 90 per cent of mothers and 75 per cent of fathers report being close to the baby, whereas for the child sample this figure drops to 63 per cent for both. Similarly, parents' descriptions of the character of their child contain more negative attributions, with only 50 per cent of mothers and 38 per cent of fathers speaking completely positively of the child. The picture is not uniform, but these findings do not suggest that these parents dislike and have always disliked their children. On the contrary, the vast majority of relations contain at least some positive elements.

Conclusions

1. This study was based on the accounts of parents and social workers, not on direct observation of parent/child relationships. The findings reported, however, are not simply derived only from the verbatim accounts of the parents; they are drawn by comparing mothers' and fathers' responses, and both with the reports of the social workers. There was considerable consistency in all these accounts reported here.

2. Social workers use physical care as a measure of parenting standards. Yet this is the area in which the families, according to social workers, performed best, with 81 per cent of parents rated as average or good. This is not as useful a discriminating measure for the majority of families as the emphasis given to it by social workers would suggest. It is comparatively easy to measure, but will reflect social deprivation directly. While it may reflect material neglect, although not emotional neglect, it bears little if any relation to the qualitative day to day handling of the child, surely the most important contributory factor to child abuse.

3. These routine cases in social work departments are not characterised by major violent acts resulting in severe injuries to the children. The problems faced by the families seem to be twofold; first deprivation, and second the problem of management of their children, namely, the problem of maintaining discipline within a positive relationship.

4. Child abuse is often attributed to aggression and over-control by the parents. The parents in this study did not seem to be predominantly hostile to their children, indeed they seemed to care for them relatively well according both to themselves and the social workers. What stood out was

the laxity of parental protection and control, with parents apparently unresponsive to their children and spending little time with them. Parents themselves admitted to failing often to discipline their children when they knew they should. Research quoted at the beginning of this chapter suggests that such laxity and inconsistency in parental handling leads to aggressive behaviour and behaviour problems in the children.

5. Despite the lack of serious injury to the children, they none the less constitute a group of highly disturbed children according to their Rutter and Richman scores. These behaviour problems were in the main not recognised by the social workers, and the children did not receive professional help. The children, therefore, are greatly at risk, but not perhaps for the reasons for which they were registered. The process of registration normally concentrates on an incident or incidents of harm to the child, whereas the major problems here seemed to rest in the normal, day to day, management of the child. This attention on incident focuses on what is done to the child rather than the well being of the child, with service provision dependant upon the likelihood of injury. The consequence of this may well be the withdrawal of professional involvement when the perceived risk of injury has abated, but before either the management problems have been sorted or the child's disturbance addressed. Whether the disturbance is outcome or cause of the poor management is not addressed in this chapter, but previous research findings would suggest it to be outcome.

6. As an aside which may be of direct relevance to practice, two points should be made. First, the practice of shaking an infant as punishment has long been noted as a very dangerous practice, one which can lead to extensive brain damage (Caffey 1972). The dangers of shaking seem not, however, to be generally recognised, and in an American study Showers (1992) found that an education programme was thought to inform over 50 per cent of a sample of normal mothers. In the sample of parents in this present study, with an abusing population, it is notable that all of the fathers and mothers reported that they never shake the baby. This may well indicate a higher awareness of the problem here, although the question about the dangers of shaking was not asked directly.

The second practice point concerns the frequency with which children are taken to medical services. When the children are under one year old the statutory services are so organised as to ensure that the children undergo regular medical supervision. As the children move outside this service provision, however, the parents in this study seemed to make less use of medical or dental services. Not only does this have potential consequences for the child's health, but also restricts the general practitioner's knowledge of the child, limiting the amount of information available for assessment for use by other professionals.

The majority of routine referrals for child protection, within this study at least, seem to reflect social and family problems rather than cases of serious injury to the child. Child injury is the symptom of a much larger underlying problem within the parent-child relationship, as evidenced by the behavioural disturbance of the children. Professional evaluation, to be fully effective, needs to concentrate not only on the pattern of injury to the child but also on the daily approach to child care and control within the family. Of particular concern is the lack of recognition of the severe behaviour problems of the children. This may arise because each of the problems is seen as a single event rather than as part of a pattern of disturbance which requires treatment. Parents and children need to be seen in relation to each other, not as isolated individuals.

The idea that the root of family problems may lie in the management of relations between parents and children is not new. Indeed, training in this aspect of behaviour as a therapeutic method is to be seen in many European countries. What professionals in Britain can do within a context of decreasing public expenditure remains open.

Acknowledgements

Many people were involved in this research, not least of all the families and social workers who so unstintingly gave of their time and their lives to help us when we could give so little in return. We wish to thank Dr. Sula Wolff and Professor R. Nicol, Consultant Child Psychiatrists, for their advice in designing the questionnaires. We wish to thank Douglas Howat for designing the computer format for analysing the data. The study was supported by a grant from the Economic and Social Research Council, no. R 000 1436.

References

Ainsworth, M.D.S., Blehar, M.C., Waters, E. and Wall, S. (1978) *Patterns of Attachment: A Psychological Study of the Strange Situation.* Hillsdale, New Jersey: Erlbaum.

Baumrind, D. (1971) Note; 'Harmonious parents and their preschool children'. *Developmental Psychology 4,* 99–102.

Beckford (1985) *A Child in Trust: The Report of the Panel of Inquiry into the Circumstances Surrounding the Death of Jasmine Beckford.* London Borough of Brent.

Caffey, J. (1972) 'On the theory and practice of shaking infants'. *American Journal of Diseases of Children 124* 162–169.

Colwell (1974) *Report of committee of enquiry into the care and supervision provided in relation to Maria Colwell.* London: HMSO.

Crittenden, P. and Bonvillian, J. (1984) 'The relationship between maternal risk status and maternal sensitivity'. *American Journal of Orthopsychiatry 54,* 250–262.

Dingwall, R., Eekelaar, J. and Murray, T. (1983) *The Protection of Children: State Intervention and Family Life.* Oxford: Basil Blackwell.

Easterbrooks, M.A. and Lamb, M.E. (1979) 'The relationship between quality of infant/mother attachment and infant competence in initial encounters with peers'. *Child Development 50,* 380–387.

Ghate, D. (1991) *Violence against children: How deviant are At Risk parents?* Paper to British Association for the Study and Prevention of Child Abuse and Neglect, Leicester, September 1991.

Huesmann, L.R., Eron, L.D., Lefkowitz, M.M. and Walder, L.O. (1984) 'The stability of aggression over time and generations'. *Developmental Psychology 20,* 746–775.

Lieberman, A.F. (1977) 'Preschooler's competence with a peer: relations with attachment and experience'. *Child Development 48,* 1277–1287.

Lyons-Ruth, K., Connell, D.B., Zoll, D. and Stahl, J. (1987) 'Infants at social risk: Relations among infant maltreatment, maternal behavior, and infant attachment behavior'. *Developmental Psychology 23,* 223–232.

Manning, M., Heron, J. and Marshall, T. (1978) 'Styles of hostility and social interaction at nursery, at school and at home. An extended study of children', in Hersov, J. and Berger, A. (eds), *Aggression and Anti-social Behaviour in Childhood and Adolescence.* Oxford: Pergammon Press.

Newson, J. and Newson, E. (1965) *Patterns of Infant Care.* London: Pelican.

Oldershaw, L., Walters, G.C. and Hall, D.K. (1986) 'Control strategies and noncompliance in abusive mother-child dyads: An observational study'. *Child Development 57,* 722–732.

Olweus, D. (1980) 'Familial and temperamental determinants of aggressive behaviour in adolescent boys: A causal analysis'. *Developmental Psychology 16,* 644–660.

Patterson, G.R. (1976) 'The aggressive child: Victim and architect of a coercive system', in Hamerlynck, L.A., Handy, L.C. and Mash, E.J. (eds), *Behaviour Modification and Families: I. Theory and Research.* New York: Brunner/Mazel.

Patterson, G.R. (1980) 'The unacknowledged victims'. *Monographs of the Society for Research in Child Development 45.* University of Chicago Press.

Richman, N., Stevenson, J. and Graham, P.J. (1984) 'Pre-school to school: A behavioural study', in Schaffer, R. (ed), *Behavioural Development: A Series of Monographs.* London & New York: Academic Press.

Rutter, M. (1967) 'A child's behaviour questionnaire for completion by teachers: Preliminary findings'. *Journal of Child Psychology and Psychiatry 8,* 1–11.

Sears, R.R., Maccoby, E.E. and Levin, H. (1957) *Patterns of Child Rearing.* New York: Harper & Row.

Showers, J. (1992) '"Don't shake the baby"; the effectiveness of a prevention program'. *Journal of Child Abuse and Neglect 16,* 11–18.

Trickett, P.K. and Kuczyinski, L. (1986) 'Children's misbehaviours and parental discipline strategies in abusive and nonabusive families'. *Developmental Psychology 22,* 115–123.

Waters, E., Wippman, J. and Sroufe, A. (1979) 'Attachment, positive affect and competence in the peer group: two studies in construct validation'. *Child Development 50,* 821–829.

Chapter 5

The Origins of Exploitative Sexuality
The Challenge of Conducting Useful Research

David Glasgow

Increasingly, the origins of sexual abuse and offending are being sought in adolescence and childhood. A primary theoretical assumption is that the exploitative sexual behaviour of adults has childhood precursors – perhaps in the form of personal characteristics or in the form of particular experiences, most notably having been abused or beginning to abuse. A less theoretical (but as yet unproven) assumption is that prompt intervention triggered by the identification of such precursors will be more effective than working with adults in whom the behaviour is well established and resistant to modification.

These assumptions expose the enormous pressure which exists to conduct research which is directly relevant to practice. On the other hand, they obscure, or at least do not make explicit, the gulf which currently exists between research and practice and the obstacles which exist facing those wishing to bridge it. On either side of the gulf, professionals are conducting work which, considered in its own terms and in isolation, is interesting and illuminating. However, there is a general failure to embark upon research and practical intervention together, each being an equal partner. Too often, one or the other is tagged on, post hoc, to 'the main project'. As a result, resources and personnel are inequitably and inadequately allocated to the project, leading to patently flawed work and results.

This chapter will attempt to give an overview and some analysis of the difficulties facing those who attempt to undertake research on the origins of sexual offending. While some of the difficulties are shared by many behavioural scientists, this area presents theoretical, ethical, systemic and methodological problems unmatched by any other field. It is inevitable, then, that what follows will be an incomplete account, but it is hoped that some of the more obvious pitfalls will be identified and that recommendations made will assist in the planning of future projects.

Theoretical issues

It is important to be aware of the basic theoretical perspectives which determine the various constructions of sexual offending. Yet it would be a mistake to assume this refers only to scientific perspectives restricted to the 'scientific community'. Indeed, some would find it offensive to isolate the so-called 'scientific community' from the wider community. A major failing of 'sexologists', certainly prior to the 1980s, may have been to ignore the impossibility of value free research and so fail to see that their work was distorted by cultural and gender-based biases. What is less frequently asserted and explored is the fact that the subjects of the research also have implicit or explicit theories which will strongly influence what the research 'discovers'.

A central theme of the contrasts and conflicts between different theoretical positions is the relative statuses of sexuality, individual behaviour, social behaviour, culture and politics. It would be a mistake to attempt to prescribe here which is or are superordinate to the others, although it is well worth pointing out that various hierarchies of relative influence are often determined by the (largely) unhelpful influence of the nature v. nurture debate. Sexuality is often claimed to be in the domain of that which is genetically or at least biologically determined. The degree to which this is held to be true determines the influence of psycho-biological accounts of sexual behaviour and sexual offending. This, in turn, has considerable implications for assumptions about the purpose and nature of research which is likely to be regarded as helpful. For example, important consequences arise from the influence of biological explanations, arguably more so than those which have been so thoroughly explored in the 'nature-nurture and IQ debate'. At the heart of this matter is differential allocation of resources based upon educational potential. With respect to exploitative sexuality, the degree of culpability and responsibility accorded and accepted by sexual offenders, and also the determination of appropriate ways of dealing with them, are the issues. It might be argued that these may be more serious but affect many fewer individuals than those associated with the IQ debate. This would be a very narrow view of the impact of the length or brevity of incarceration, compulsory or voluntary physical or psychological treatments of offenders on wider society, particularly on victims and potential victims.

Biological abnormality (albeit as yet unidentified) is central to the medicalisation of offending behaviour, a process which has gone much further in the United States than it has here in the United Kingdom. For example, a debate has taken place there as to whether rapists should be diagnosable as suffering from a symdrome primarily by virtue of their tendency to commit rape. In this country resistance to such a perspective is staunch and well established. This resistance is principally based upon the importance given to the offender taking responsibility both for his actions and for the commitment needed to bring about change. This alternative perspective is founded upon the belief that a 'diagnosis' can permit an unacceptable evasion of responsibility while offering no real 'treatment' of the 'disorder'.

The roots of this criticism of medicalisation lie in an increasingly influential theoretical position which emphasises individual responsibility for both behaviour and psychological processes related to sexual offending. The great strength of this position is that it involves no a-priori assumptions about the appropriateness of punishment and treatment. Responsibility for an abusive act may be diminished by disorder and/or disability, although this changes little with respect to the goals of intervention which are largely pragmatic and individualistic rather than theoretical and general: Can this person be accorded and accept responsibility for the offence(s)? Can they enter into a contract of active participation in a programme designed to change their own cognitions and behaviours believed to render offending more probable? The answers to these questions should then, in theory, determine the duration and nature of the management of the offender by the criminal justice system, allowing for a retributive component to the disposal determined by the court.

The pragmatism of this psychological approach offers the potential for improvement of, without demanding radical change to, the systems which currently deal with sexual offenders. To be critical, it is as yet an unproven assumption that the core questions can be answered with any reliability and validity. Even if they can, the requirements that the offender accepts responsibility for the act(s) and participates actively in work towards personal change begs the question of whether programmes effecting reduction in sexual recidivism actually exist. The absence of conclusive evidence that psychological treatments of sexual offenders are effective is not a reason to conclude, however, that the men cannot be treated.

When fundamental approaches to explaining and understanding sexual offending differ between the research and wider communities, there is a serious risk that bodies sanctioning and funding research will be slow to initiate and support appropriately innovative research. This obviously demands that, at least at present, research teams work hard to make their theoretical heritage and current position very clear, as well as providing some compelling arguments for modifying whatever orthodoxy is being challenged. This is an onerous task, but it could be argued that there are signs that significant theoretical and conceptual progress could take place soon which would reduce the 'theoretical inertia' which seems to exist at present. There is a progress towards a general consensus (of researchers) that simplistic biological, medical and political or cultural accounts have little to offer which is of direct, practical assistance to those working with the problem of sexually abusive behaviour. Fewer professionals now talk in linear terms, of cause and effect. The tendency is increasingly to adopt evolutionary terms with respect to the development of patterns of behaviour. This, in conjunction with the influence of cognitive-behavioural work with adult offenders, offers the prospect of identifying psychological factors which mediate and are modified by social and cultural factors. In this respect, Ryan, Lane, Davis and Isaac (1987) were among the first to describe in detail what they believe to be a non-linear process involving interactions between cognitions, behaviour and social experience, which describe an offender's passage from sexual offence to sexual offence.

Increasing emphasis on a developmental, non-linear, interactive understanding of the origins of sexual offending is without doubt to be welcomed. Perhaps it would not be too optimistic to anticipate that this would offer the opportunity for a non-hierarchical relationship to emerge between sexuality, behaviour, social behaviour and culture. Of course, making connections between individual development and socio/cultural development is scarcely new. Some early theorists saw sexuality as the energy which drove society both on a day by day basis and with respect to change at a social level: 'sex...and hunger...are the two original sources of dynamic energy which brings into existence...the most elaborate social superstructures' (Ellis 1936, p.3). Mechanistic metaphors are not without some currency today, although it is sincerely to be hoped that studying the evolution of sexuality and sexual behaviour in childhood, adolescence and adulthood will begin to reveal the actual rather than metaphorical interactions of intrapersonal, interpersonal and cultural factors.

This suggests it would be erroneous to assume that theoretical progress can be made simply or without the precipation of painful conflict and crisis. Insofar as adult behaviour is not biologically determined, the discovery of how and what children learn about sexual behaviour and what influences sexual development will also teach us about ourselves and the society in which we live. Unwelcome discoveries may be anticipated and perhaps even avoided. If actually discovered, it is certainly not unknown for researchers to face an uncomfortable choice between commenting upon the social implications of their research and risking public criticism, or restricting their reports to scientific commentaries to the research communities. Researchers should be aware of the emotional backlash which is likely to greet any evidence that social change is required to reduce the development of exploitative sexuality in children and adolescents. The message and messengers will elicit a particularly hostile response if change is indicated in any commercial exploitation of sexual interest to which children have access, such as telephone chatlines, magazine and video pornography and advertising.

Contrasting theoretical positions about adult sexual offending, whether primarily moral/retributional, biological/medicalising or psychological find a level of coherence in locating responsibility in the offender, even if this responsibility may be temporarily or permanently impaired. This coherence can be severely challenged, however, by both research and practice with children and adolescents, primarily because they cannot be automatically accorded responsibility for their actions. With the recognition that children sexually abuse other children or show early signs of becoming abusers (NCH 1992) there is a pressure to look beyond the child for the primary influences on their behaviour. Whether the possibility being considered is the influence of non-sexual familial experiences, previous sexual abuse or exposure to pornography, adults must, however reluctantly, own the responsibility for shaping and determining those experiences.

When the abuser reaches majority, alleged early influences on their behaviour tend to be regarded as an historical matter of regret (and some research interest). The pressure for change focuses on the individual rather than their environment and professional or scientific discomfort associated with the exploration of childhood experiences is far less (to all that is, but the individual in question). Why does this change happen? First, it is perceived that historical influences on an adult cannot be changed, whereas current influences on a child can, although this is confusing because the influences might be very similar or even the same. Second, there is a lack of understanding about the processes associated with transition from childhood to adulthood involving both the real and 'official' acquisition of responsibility. The former is a complex, poorly understood process which varies from individual to individual. The latter is an arbitrary age boundary enshrined in statute after which an individual is deemed criminally responsible for particular sexual offences. Experiences which may have shaped and rendered more probable sexually exploitative behaviour can be comfortably reconstrued by 'the system' as pleas for mitigation or mere excuses.

Methodology

It is important to have at least a passing familiarity with how knowledge about 'normal' and 'abnormal' sexual behaviour is acquired. To do this it is desirable to interpret 'methodology' in the widest possible sense in order not to exclude very influential sources of information and theory which might otherwise be missed. For this reason included for discussion are approaches to research drawn from psychotherapists, sexuality surveyors, and laboratory studies.

The psychotherapists

Psychotherapists and their clients can spend a great deal of time talking about sexuality, sexual relationships and sexual behaviour. Sexuality has a central theoretical position in almost all schools of psychodynamic psychotherapy. This would suggest that particular attention should be paid to hypotheses generated by psychotherapists regarding sexual behaviour in childhood, adolescence and adulthood. In fact the hypotheses are now of far less accuracy and interest than the clinical material which was generated by a meticulous idiographic approach. In other words, with respect to understanding, researching and modifying the sexual thoughts and behaviour of children, what little Hans said is of more interest than what Freud said about him. Similarly, Melanie Klein (1932) has done great service to researchers who are not psychodynamically active or even oriented by allowing access to what many young children had to say about sexual matters, irrespective of the emphasis on fantasy, phantasy and dynamic processes.

Of course, such material lacks a normative reference, other than that implicit in the abnormality attributed to the child by parents and therapist. This alleged abnormality permits conversations which would not be ethically acceptable with children who were not identified as 'patients' – and these conversations cannot be placed in the context of 'normal' children. As a direct result the generalisability of most clinically derived research data to a non-clinical population is always uncertain. What do the children patients have in common with other children? Or what is distinct about them?

There has been a resurgence of interest in qualitative research techniques, which might offer the prospect of a non-psychodynamic analysis based on a similar idiographic approach. It is uncertain what value would lie in conducting and analysing such detailed conversations with children and young people.

However, the ethical objections to the sorts of conversations permissable with 'non-client' children are largely culturally determined and therefore may not preclude detailed conversations with children about sex. It takes little to expose the hypocrisy involved in permitting the shallow and potentially misleading dialogue existing between children and the media but in preventing skilled and constructive interviews with children on sexual matters.

Both family therapists and sexual and marital therapists have also contributed to the struggle to understand sexually exploitative behaviour. The former has been unique in the close attention paid to the influences of family relationships on the behaviour of individuals throughout childhood, adolescence and adulthood. A strong tradition of compelling descriptions of family functioning as a system has been both positive and negative. Such descriptions might be creative, thought provoking, plausible, and yet remain post hoc and possibly misleading constructions of what actually takes place within a family. The point is not that they are necessarily so, but that it can be difficult to generate the evidence which confirms the formulation, a task rarely taken on by proponents of particular systemic processes. A good example of this is the formulation offered by Tilman Furniss (1991) of sibling sexual abuse which he calls 'The Hansel and Gretel Syndrome'. In essence, the argument is that the nature of parental relationships influences the function and quality, in particular the intimacy, of the sibling relationship. Whether this really happens, and if so, how often, is uncertain. Furniss goes on to argue:

> 'Adolescent boys in the Hansel and Gretel Syndrome must not be treated like adult abusers and girls must not be seen like other child victims abused by parenting figures. Although the relationship can look like an adult-child abuse the issue of responsibility and structural dependency needs to be addressed differently. Both children need to take equally the appropriate responsibility for their inappropriate sexual relationship'. (Furniss 1991, p.335)

This example illustrates one of the objections raised, sometimes unfairly, against systemic data concerning the attribution of responsibility. Systemic approaches emphasise the interrelatedness of cause and effect in understanding the behaviour of individuals in families. It is argued that systemic explanations allow the attribution of responsibility to be lifted from individuals and instead accorded to a 'pathological system'. This is not only inimical to the more psychological approach described above, it is also claimed to sometimes share blame inappropriately amongst family members other than the perpetrator. It is not difficult to raise theoretical objections to this line of argument, and many would wish so to do. However, it is impossible to demonstrate the hypothesis is false and its logical and practical sequellae mistaken, in the absence of rigorous research.

Nonetheless, the influence of systemic thinking on modern practice and research must not be underestimated. Family therapists have been posing non-linear, cyclical hypotheses for many years. The cycles described by Ryan *et al.* (1987) are slightly different principally because of the emphasis on cognitions and the only shadowy, implied presence of the offender's social world. Even if there is no direct or indirect systemic influence on the development of the work of Ryan *et al.*, there is clearly a convergence of thinking about the interactive quality needed in explanation.

To claim systemic work relating to sexuality and sexual abuse is rarely proven by research is misleading. Any systematic model, including those arising from family therapists and sexual and marital therapists can be a rich source of hypotheses which might be tested by researchers other than their originator. For example, the quality of the relationships described in the Hansel and Gretel syndrome could, in theory at least, be operationally defined such that parent/child and sibling relationships became measurable. A traditional group research design could then test whether different types of relationships were present in families in which sibling abuse had occurred compared with families in which it had not.

It is also important to appreciate that developmentally sensitive research is somewhat more complex than that which does not include a developmental component. The Hansel and Gretel research referred to above has no developmental component, therefore the research would be, relatively speaking, straightforward. This must be immediately qualified by the confession that the above research proposal was grossly oversimplified, perhaps even unfair to the hypothesis. Much sexual activity initiated by and between children is clearly abusive and exploitative, some much less so. Furniss restricts his model to circumstances in which the differences arising from psychological development, gender and physical development are not apparent,

> '...an equal sexual relationship in which both children try to give and to receive some distorted form of mutual satisfaction, comfort and care. The sexual abuse is a perverted and confused form of emotional care in which the sexual stimulation and arousal is a poor and sad substitute for absent parental emotional care.' (Furniss 1991, p.334)

Of course, the research itself could very usefully answer the question posed, but the design would necessarily be rather more complicated. Comparison of family relationships would need to be between cases of inter-sibling sexual behaviour divided into groups of 'high exploitation/coercion', 'no apparent exploitation/coercion' and 'no sexually inappropriate behaviour'. The hypothesis predicts an inverse relationship between degree of exploitation (which, like the family relationship itself, must be operationally defined and validly measured) and the presence of the family relationships alleged to characterise the 'Hansel and Gretel' syndrome. In fact, the comparison with the 'no sexually inappropriate behaviour' group may benefit from being even yet more elaborate. Frequency of non-sexual exploitation between siblings might be held constant in this group and perhaps also measured in the other groups (answering the question of whether bullying is correlated with abusive child-child sexual behaviour within the family).

Clearly this hypothetical research project has become considerably more complex. Complexity on paper almost inevitably indicates considerable problems realising the proposal in practice. How would the various families be found? Whose agreement would be required to undertake the research and to investigate the families and their circumstances? Exactly how can the degree of sexual and non-sexual exploitation/coercion be operationally defined and measured? Similarly, how can the alleged family dynamic be operationally defined and measured? The last two questions may involve utterly different processes and problems. The former involves measuring characteristics of discrete historical events of which it is very likely that different individuals will have different accounts. The latter relates to measuring a particular pattern of relationship which should pervade many if not all areas of family life. Family life is much disrupted by the discovery of inappropriate sexual behaviour between siblings, and careful thought would need to be applied to whether the pattern can still be expected to be detectable 'post-discovery'. If the family pattern is a robust one, a most telling prediction would be of a characteristic coping strategy to discovery itself associated with Hansel and Gretel families. However, a more direct measure of the relationships ought to be made, ideally including a retrospective, i.e. pre-discovery, component.

Sexuality surveyors

Moving more towards a 'mainstream' research approach, it is crucial to consider the methodology and influence of surveys of sexual behaviour. The fundamental principle of a survey is that a sample of individuals answer a range of questions intended to reveal something about the attitudes, beliefs and behaviours of part or all of the population at large. More thorough surveys are

designed such that the sample closely matches the epidemiological characteristics of the entire population.

In most respects the emphasis is on description of the phenomena in
question rather than establishment of causal links or the prescription of change.
Data arising from the Kinsey survey (e.g. Kinsey, Pomeroy and Martin 1948) is
often referred to and criticised, but the original report is rarely read. Although
it is, without doubt, seriously flawed in some respects, and out of date, Kinsey
set out to answer many questions which are still posed today. It is instructive
to see what answers he came up with, and also to consider how he set about
asking questions. He looked at developing sexuality in childhood and adolescence by simply asking children about their own sexual behaviour and asking
adults about the sexual behaviour of their children.

He quite clearly had a somewhat naive faith in the skills of his interviewers,
particularly with respect to interviewing very young children and adolescents
(Kinsey, Pomeroy and Martin 1948, p.58). The former demand particular skills
by virtue of their cognitive limitations and some degree of compliance and
suggestibility. The latter pose considerable problems because of the particular
emotional salience of sexual matters to that age group and their very variable
experience and understanding of sexual matters. At best, the data arising from
a survey which has paid insufficient attention to the special needs of children
will be transparently inconsistent or missing. At worst, the data will be inac-
curate and misleading without being obviously so.

An excellent example of the difficulties arising with a teenage group are
surveys reported by Knoth, Booth and Singer (1988). They found a very high
level of refusal to complete the survey, one third of children, and had to exclude
further data because it was internally inconsistent. While the survey reports
fascinating results on a range of phenomena and behaviour related to sexuality,
it is unclear whether apparent patterns in the data reflecting gender and age
differences are in fact artifacts. Similarly, Kinsey *et al.* (1948) report data about
children and young people which should be treated very cautiously, although
it would be wrong to dismiss it out of hand. In *Sexual Behaviour in the Human
Male* he poses and answers questions that are often studied today but as if the
question itself, let alone the results, was a new revelation. He certainly anticipated modern views of the high incidence of exploitative sexual acts committed
by teenage males, although this is rarely acknowledged. Again in *Sexual
Behaviour in the Human Male*, published 45 years ago, he claimed 'that 85 per
cent of the younger males could be convicted as sex offenders if law enforcement officials did their job as well as most people expect them to do'.

It is doubtful that a modern large scale survey of childhood sexuality would have a great deal to offer our understanding of the development of offending. It is also doubtful that consent could be obtained to ask children the questions posed in the Kinsey survey. In many respects this is an identical point to that made above with respect to the detailed interviews with children by Melanie Klein, and confirms the suggestion that cultural factors are very influential in the determination of what is and is not regarded as acceptable. Kinsey worked in a time when scientific enterprises had a very high status and evoked rather more deference and trust than is now the case. A difference in the status of children may also have helped make the survey possible at a time when less public concern about the rights of children was in evidence.

Laboratory studies

Many questions posed with respect to the sexuality of adults have been investigated in the laboratory and valuable data has been produced. However, even a passing familiarity with the literature leads inevitably to the conclusion that the techniques described could not, under normal circumstances, be used with children and young people. Dekker and Everaerd (1989) review laboratory studies of the psychological determinants of sexual arousal in adults using self report and/or physiological measures.

Problems with surveys which depend on self report have been discussed above. Laboratory paradigms designed to investigate sexuality have additional problems. Typically a comparison is made between different stimulus conditions or different groups of subjects. In principle this would be a very useful approach with respect to say investigating the pattern of arousal amongst adolescents to consenting and non-consenting stimulus material, or whether the responses of children who have committed no known sexually exploitative acts differ from those who have committed one, two, three or more.

The fact is that such experiments could hardly be seen as anything but sexually abusive of the subjects. The only possible case for the use of sexually explicit stimulus material with child subjects would be that the benefits of conducting the research warrant any harm concomitant with exposure to the material. Similar issues arise with respect to the method of measuring physiological sexual arousal, the penile plethysmograph. This device provides an ongoing measure of penile size which can be correlated with whatever stimulus material was presented at the time.

The consensus is that plethysmography and sexually explicit stimulus material cannot be used with 'normal' children. There is somewhat more of a debate with respect to their use with older children who have committed sexual offences. This technique is often used as a clinical assessment tool with adult sexual offenders, and is widely regarded as useful. By extension, the argument is that such a valuable assessment tool should be available for use with adolescent sexual offenders and, being sexual offenders, they are unlikely to be harmed by the process. This is by no means self – evidently the case, and this position was firmly rejected by the NCH Committee of Enquiry into Children and Young People who Sexually Abuse Other Children, who saw the use of the technique only justifiable with older children presenting serious risk to others (NCH 1992, p.12).

The fact is that even if the techniques can be used with children who sexually abuse, the laboratory paradigm relies on the use of comparison groups upon whom it could not be imposed. The prospects that laboratory studies will offer any real assistance in understanding the nature of sexual interest and behaviour in childhood are therefore very poor.

What research is possible?

The above offers a rather pessimistic view of the limitations and constraints of research methodologies. Some limitations are relevant to their application to subjects of any age, but many relate to the particular difficulty of researching developing sexuality in children. A common theme is that it is not acceptable to gather data from children on sexuality and sexual behaviour in ways which are or have come to be seen as acceptable with adults.

When children are identified as displaying unacceptable sexual behaviour, it is not unusual for a formal investigation to take place of the alleged perpetrator, the victim(s) and the general circumstances of the family. This does not constitute a research exercise, but a forensic one, the data gathered being used to make decisions within a legal framework about the nature of any interventions deemed necessary to protect children and assist and/or control the child perpetrator.

This offers the prospect of closely linking research projects with statutory processes, ideally to the benefit of both. An obvious benefit to the research is that it becomes firmly anchored in the real world and is more likely to have what is referred to as 'ecological validity'. Also, the research can operate at more than one level, that is, the actions of professionals can be studied as well as the information which arises about the children. The sample of children too will be more representative than most reported samples, which tend to be drawn from those referred to a clinic.

It would be foolish to imagine that 'ecological research' avoids ethical dilemmas, including those relating to what data it is acceptable to gather and from whom. Just because data is already gathered by social workers and police officers on many children does not mean it is that which is required or is in a form which can be analysed. Researchers face a question of how much they attempt to influence the data gathered by the statutory system. Research requires a rigorous standardised investigation producing reliable data which must not only further knowledge but protect children and detect offenders. Paradoxically, what researchers require of professionals are the very things which professionals hope that the results of research will guide them upon. It might be expected that this leads to an easy alliance, although in fact this is not the case. Data collection informed by the results of research is very different from that required by the conduct of research, in terms of quantity and quality. Consequently professionals often experience research as an unwelcome burden. It is incumbent upon a research team to understand this and do as much as possible to alleviate the burden, 'streamlining' data collection so that it is as quick and straightforward as possible.

One of the factors most frequently suggested to be significant in the evolution of sexually offending behaviour is the perpetrator's experience of having been sexually abused as a child. The hypothesis that one leads to the other is widely regarded to be, at least to some extent, true. Some have suggested that sexually abusive behaviour by an adult is necessarily a result of having been abused as a child. It is important to remember that those who adopt this position are not suggesting that all children who are sexually abused become abusers. This is obviously not the case because the majority of perpetrators are male and the victims female.

The position that all sexual offenders have been sexually abused must be regarded as an extreme one and no evidence can be offered to support it. Most offenders do not admit to having been abused, although of course, this does not necessarily mean they have not in fact been abused. Further, the hypothesised process by which such an allegedly close relationship between having been abused and becoming an abuser might be mediated remains unspecified. Clear hypothetical links are often drawn in particular cases, but with reference to all abusers the alleged process is rarely more clearly formulated than as 'an attempt to deal with their own abuse'. Scarcely a rich source of research hypotheses.

The extreme position remains sustainable, however, because of the absence of any compelling evidence against it, or indeed, the opposing position, that the incidence of childhood sexual abuse among perpetrators is no different to that of the general male population. The difficulty is that the evidence, such as it exists, arises from asking offenders whether they have experienced childhood sexual abuse. Even more than usual the results are likely to be determined by what question is asked, how it is put and when it is put. Offenders are notorious for their unreliable accounts of their own behaviour and experience. They are also likely to have idiosyncratic concepts of what constitutes abuse and what the implications to themselves might be, positive and negative, of declaring they have been abused. These factors considerably increase the caution with which retrospective data are (always) greeted to a point such that it is unlikely that continuing to ask identified perpetrators if they have been abused will ever convince a person whose *a priori* position does not accord with whatever answer is given.

So what might constitute a useful research project on the relationship of childhood experiences of sexual abuse and the later commission of sexual abuse? Theoretically it is possible for a child's development to follow several paths with respect to being abused and abusing. Children who have been sexually abused and those who have not been so abused may or may not themselves subsequently behave in a sexually abusive manner, first as children and subsequently as adults. In order to avoid the problems associated with retrospective data, the development of the children needs to be tracked, that is, the research must be longitudinal. However, the need to track development is far more than the need to identify events of being abused and abusing if either occur. Reference was made above to the complex interaction between a developing child and their social environment and, since it is known that most victims do not go on to abuse, other factors must be involved. In developmental psychology and psychopathology these factors are referred to as risk and inoculating factors. The most striking factor in this respect is gender (as stated above, most victims being female yet most perpetrators male), although it would be of little help to merely identify gender in the research. What would be much more exciting and significant would be attempting to systematically examine some of the social, physiological and psychological correlates of gender which are risk and inoculating factors. What a revelation it would be to discover that some characteristics generally associated with girls, when present in boys tend to 'inoculate' against displaying or developing abusive behaviour.

Returning to the longitudinal project, decisions must be made regarding what data will be gathered, the ages at which it will be gathered and the means by which it will be gathered. A significant dimension here is that of active and passive data collection. The former is when the researchers gather data by direct contact with the child or by contact with significant others, such as carers or teachers. The latter when professionals who already gather data from and about the child do this on behalf of the research team. Active data collection from both primary and secondary sources is enormously costly because of the time involved for researchers and the skills required to undertake interviews. However, it allows researchers to be confident that what they want to be asked is, in fact, being asked: It also allows the dataset to depart rather more in quality and quantity from that which the statutorily involved professionals might be expected to gather anyway. Of course this also increases the need to pay very close attention to the ethical issues associated with gathering such data.

The more complex the data and the larger the cohort of children, the less likely it is that researchers can be involved in much active data gathering from individual subjects or even secondary sources. These factors also influence data gathering intervals because longer intervals offer more opportunity to assimilate and undertake some preliminary analysis of the data gathered. With a large cohort and large dataset this interval may be more of a necessity than a luxury. So, for example, from the age of say ten, a cohort of children could be checked annually with respect to their developmental and social status and the likelihood of having been abused and abusing. Given the imminence of puberty, it would not be unreasonable to hope that differences between the abused and non-abused groups would begin to emerge within only a few years.

An alternative to data gathering at fixed intervals is to establish an alerting procedure whereby if certain pre-specified conditions arise, the research team is alerted and data gathering initiated. The hypothetical research project shows signs of needing both systems; a periodic gathering of developmental data and an abuse triggered data gathering.

Practical and ethical considerations once again arise and must be addressed. It is clear that the research team must have continuing liaison with and active cooperation of statutory and educational professions. Perhaps more significantly, the issue of parental consent for their child to be included in the cohort must be considered. If this is sought, along with active cooperation of parents throughout the study, then the risk is obviously present that this is likely to select out at least some of the children it is most important to include in the study. Parents who are or are at risk of abusing their children are presumably unlikely to consent to inclusion in the project at the outset, or may withdraw that consent when an alert takes place. The alternative, perhaps even more disturbing, is that an abuser, in the knowledge of the child's inclusion in the research, will increase the sanctions against disclosure of the abuse, effectively preventing detection and probably damaging the child more than otherwise would have been the case. Of most significance to the research itself is the fact that unless the probability of the child in question having been sexually abused by a parent is sufficient to trigger successful care proceedings, crucial loss of data is inevitable. The only way to avoid such a loss of data is to restrict the scope of parental consent to routine periodic data gathering and not to that triggered by an alerting procedure. The latter becomes increasingly acceptable the more closely the process is tied to the existing activities of statutory agents.

Reference to the probability of abuse occurring returns attention to methodological issues. So far, although different developmental pathways have been referred to, the assumption has been that at each 'stage' there are only two alternatives – inclusion in the abused or non-abused group. Reality can rarely be satisfactorily represented in a binary fashion, creating a need to identify a range of categories in which subjects might be placed which more closely reflects the real world. This is likely to increase the sensitivity of the research to, for example, the type of abuse or abuses and also allows the post hoc analysis of various combinations of categories. On the other hand, increasing the number of categories increases the complexity of the categorisation task and also increases the probability of misclassification.

With respect to child sexual abuse, the child protection and criminal systems already function as categorisation systems and the option obviously exists of adopting their categories. Unfortunately, this is not entirely satisfactory. The statutory categorisation process is both slow and somewhat unpredictable in terms of the criteria applied to inclusion of children in abused and non-abused categories. It is not unusual for criminal and child protection proceedings to conflict with respect to affirming the presence of abuse, nor is it unusual for professionals to strongly believe abuse has taken place but see no possibility of legal proceedings confirming this. Notwithstanding this, it is reasonable to identify a 'high probability' category, the children placed in which are either subject to a court order primarily or partly related to having been sexually abused and/or who have been confirmed as a victim of sexual abuse in criminal proceedings. It is important to be aware that this does not necessarily mean that a conviction has occurred. It is often not disputed by the defence that a child has been sexually abused, indeed it may be part of the case for the defendant that the child has been abused by another party.

These are relatively straightforward circumstances. But what of an allegation which arises against an itinerant or completely unknown abuser? or, perhaps, an allegation against a nine-year-old child outside the family who will not be subjected to child protection or criminal proceedings. Intuitively, it makes sense to include both in a high probability category and it is important to establish and make explicit rules which allow this to happen. At the opposite extreme, a 'no evidence' category is needed which assumes that the absence of evidence for sexual abuse is correlated with the actual absence of abuse. Of course it is logically false to assume that absence of evidence is evidence of the absence of abuse. Consequently, mis-categorisation may be detected when a child discloses abuse which indicated that they had been previously mis-categorised. From this it must be deduced that there will also be undetectable mis-categorisation; abused children who do not reveal abuse in the duration of the research.

Intermediate categories could correspond to the occurrence of an alert where evidence is sufficient only to proceed to interventions less severe than legal proceedings. These are likely to be difficult to define and use, so much so that little value would be gained from struggling with this option.

Of course, considerably more data than the presence or absence of abuse must be gathered. Measures must be taken of the impact of abuse and its sequelae on the children. This must involve looking at emotional and behavioural responses, as well as making some estimate of familial and other support. So, for example, indicators that the abuse was sexualising of the child could be identified and measured. Similarly, the duration and quality of support the child requests, receives and accepts could be measured, the obvious hypothesis being that children who show signs of precocious sexualisation and who do not receive post abuse support are more likely to become perpetrators. It is at this level that correlates of gender might be discovered to be of significance. For example, boys might seem to be generally harder to help and support post abuse, but those who share social and familial networks that correspond in their qualities to those characteristic of some girls' experiences might be less likely to subsequently abuse.

It is also important that other dysfunctional behaviours are monitored because it might be that the crucial issue is not whether a child becomes a perpetrator or not, but what determines the manner in which the impact of sexual abuse is expressed. What is clear is that the knowledge base relating to child development is of central significance. If research in this area is to make any sense at all, it must exploit the established research literature on child development and become much more closely united with established work on emotional, cognitive and social development. The ever more influential field of 'life span' psychology offers a framework within which this might usefully occur.

So far, no attention has been paid to research on treatment outcome. It is sufficiently important to demand some discussion, and also impinges on the above hypothetical research project such that it must be mentioned in that respect. The children being studied will not only be sources of data, they will be the subjects of interventions of varying rigour intended to shape the behaviour of the child. Interventions are very much ad hoc and variable with respect to what they consist of, the professionals responsible for them and to whom they are applied. A significant factor in this respect is the age of the child who has acted sexually against another child, an act which, if the child was older, would be regarded as an offence marking the 'official' acquisition of responsibility. A wise researcher will know that the impact of the responses of others to the child's behaviour may be as influential for the child as the abuse itself. Research is not assisted by the fact that (in English law) children are deemed criminally culpable for acts other than penetrative sexual offences at age ten. Children only months different in age, engaging in identical acts, experience enormously different consequences to their behaviour. In extremis, one abuser might become identified as a Schedule one offender, with all the long-lasting consequences this can have for relationships and parenting. This arbitrary 'watershed' of responsibility can certainly act as a confounding variable in research intended to monitor outcome of maturation and development. Children involved in criminal proceedings also become very difficult to include in research projects, partly because they are simply less accessible. It is also important to be aware that any data gathered on this child may be at best noted by, at worst distorted by the criminal process. Those working with children therapeutically are familiar with both the threat that they will be drawn unwillingly into criminal proceedings as witnesses or that the child will receive advice as to whether or not they should cooperate with a programme, and even what they should say.

In principle, working with child perpetrators in treatment offers the prospect of rather more satisfactory methodology than can normally be achieved with adults. Children are less autonomous than adults and are more closely supervised. They are much less likely to simply disappear from a treatment and research programme so that, even if they 'drop out', data may still be gathered on them and a follow up process continue.

However, major obstacles to effective treatment outcome research persist. Numbers in treatment remain a small proportion of those who, on the face of it, might be candidates for such treatment. This has two major consequences. First, research must cover many treatment programmes in order to have a sufficiently large sample size to detect anything other than the largest and most significant treatment effects. Work with adults suggests treatment effects are subtle, multiple and consequently easily obscured or distorted by random variability often present in small samples. Second, children are selected through a range of filters, intentionally and unintentionally, for inclusion in treatment. Of course, there is a clinical legitimacy to selecting individuals for treatment – after all, what is the point of treating those who will not benefit? The trouble is that the validity of whatever selection is being used is based largely on assumption. How can it be known who is more likely to benefit from a treatment when we have yet to demonstrate that it is effective at all?

It is also important to note that much of the selection procedure is not controlled by those running a particular treatment programme but by those who choose to refer or not refer children to it. This may not only be a matter of preference, but also of resources, since access to treatment may involve a considerable cost to a referring agent.

Two apparently similar programmes, then, might include children whose potential for recidivism is quite different. The selection for one group might prefer children whom practitioners identify as most needy, that is presenting more risk, and for the other, children they expect to be able to influence, i.e. those less well established on offending careers. Whatever the sources of selection coming to bear, non-random, non-explicit selection for treatment programmes is an anathema to outcome research because differences in recidivism detected may not be due to the treatments included. For research to have a chance of being effective:

1. referral to treatment must be routine;

2. selection criteria must be standardised and explicit;

3. allocation to active treatment or a comparison control group must be on the basis of matched subjects randomly allocated. This means there must be at least regional, preferably national agreement and coordination of these processes.

Analysis of typical treatments included in child perpetrator treatment programmes reveals another difficulty. Drawing on work with adults, the view is that the factors contributing to the occurrence of sexual abuse are many and complex. The most favoured approach is cognitive behavioural and it is, therefore, not surprising that treatment programmes tend to involve a variety of components targeted at a range of behaviours and cognitions.

An analogy with an outcome study of a drug treatment programme may illuminate this point. Although one drug usually has several effects (including placebo), what is likely to happen as a result of a given dose is much better understood than psychological interventions. Treatment groups for child perpetrators are much more analogous to several people creating, modifying and taking a cocktail of partially identified drugs over a period of time. Even if a very strong treatment effect is established, it will be very difficult to identify what is responsible for it, either in isolation or combination. The only option offering informative data is to identify the 'ingredients' which can then be systematically included and excluded from programmes on a nationally agreed and monitored basis. As a first step in this direction, it would certainly help to identify what is effective if the range of interventions, tasks and techniques was surveyed and reduced to a representative core, at least in the short term. Such 'core treatment' would offer the prospect of reasonable outcome research constituting a baseline against which the influence of 'additional ingredients' could be measured.

Beyond dismay

The above examples were not intended to deter individuals from becoming involved in research on understanding the evolution of sexual offending. The key is to understand that any one individual should be dismayed upon reading this chapter – if not, the enormous significance and challenge posed by the work is not understood. The task is beyond the traditional capabilities of individuals or research teams working in either child development or social science generally and begs a degree of coordination and co-operation between the different disciplines in the social sciences and between practitioners and researchers not previously realised.

It was never anticipated that this chapter could cover sufficient ground to enable research to be undertaken using the material as a sourcebook. However, a point has been reached at which the required performance characteristics of a research team can be specified along with some of the characteristics of the research plan itself.

1. The research team must be theoretically well informed, and spend time making explicit their preconceptions about the nature of sexual behaviour, sexual development and sexual offending. Conflicts and inconsistencies identified early are much less likely to threaten the research. It is important to recognise that these views are personally and politically as well as professionally and scientifically determined.

2. At least one member of the team should have particular expertise in research methodology, not restricted to surveys or laboratory work.

3. The team should include skills in direct contact with children and knowledge of child and adolescent development. These skills and knowledge may be used to obtain data directly, to devise an age appropriate protocol for data collection or critically appraise the methods used by others to generate data for the research team.

4. A sound understanding of the juvenile justice and child protection systems is necessary. Ecologically valid research cannot occur in the absence of a symbiosis with statutorily driven agencies. Unlike non-forensic medical and psychological research, the real authority to determine what happens to a child lies outside the research team. It is important to know and understand what is happening within the forensic system, partly to gather data properly and partly to obtain as much assistance and support from workers within the system. It may be that the system might make some adjustments to routine and often complex processes in order to facilitate research. An example of this would be an attempt to make responses less variable according to (very) local practice such that data gathered in adjacent districts becomes comparable. This requires not only knowledge and understanding but good contacts, good liaison and good social skills.

5. Ideally, members of the team will contribute to an extensive collective knowledge of the literatures on adult sexual offending, child development, gender and sexuality. Important hypotheses might be generated by very diverse source material, so it is a mistake to impose an orthodoxy of acceptable literature on a team. This is not the same as developing a workable theoretical consensus as described in the first point above.

6. The presence of at least one member of the team who works systemically is of enormous value. Such skills can not only be brought to bear on the development of sophisticated, systemic hypotheses, but also on the systemic processes occurring during the conduct of research. It also helps enormously to prevent the common failure to perceive the child within a family context, consequently missing perhaps the most significant influences on their development and behaviour.

7. The ethical dimensions of research should not be constrained to making a case which obtains ethical approval from whatever committee must be approached. The possibility of harming and/or distressing children and their families must be continuously appraised. In such a sensitive but important area, compromises are inevitable. They should be made con-

sciously and explicitly with as full an exploration of the potential ramifications of the research as is possible.

8. A recurrent theme above has been the importance of regional and national organisation. A research team must make every effort to connect with the wider community researching in similar fields; directly, through conferences and through relevant organisations.

References

Dekker, J. and Everaerd, W. (1989) 'Psychological determinants of sexual arousal: A review'. *Behaviour Research and Therapy 27 (4)*, 353–364.

Ellis, H. (1936) *Studies in the Psychology of Sex*. New York: Random House.

Furniss, T. (1991) *The Multiprofessional Handbook of Child Sexual Abuse*. London: Routledge.

Kinsey, A., Pomeroy, W. and Martin, C. (1948) *Sexual Behaviour in the Human Male*. Philadelphia: Saunders.

Klein, M. (1932) *The Psychoanalysis of Children*. London: Hogarth.

Knoth, R., Boyd, K. and Singer, B. (1988) 'Empirical tests of sexual selection theory predictions in onset, intensity, and time course of sexual arousal'. *Journal of Sex Research 24*, 73–89.

National Children's Home (1992) *The Report of the Committee of Enquiry into Children and Young People who Sexually Abuse Other Children*. NCH.

Piaget, J. and Inhelder, B. (1969) *The Psychology of the Child*. London: Routledge.

Ryan, G., Lane, S., Davis, J. and Isaac, C. (1987) 'Juvenile sex offenders: development and correction'. *Child Abuse and Neglect 11 (3)*, 385–395.

Chapter 6

Child Sexual Abusers
Recognition and Response

Russell P. Dobash, James Carnie and Lorraine Waterhouse

Few people must now doubt that the sexual abuse of children is a social problem of significant proportions. The media publicity surrounding the issue – Cleveland, Rochdale, Orkney – has shocked a concerned, though sometimes mystified, public. Child protection has been the focus of public and statutory attention. Social workers have had to shoulder criticism for intervening too precipitously – or for not intervening at all. Children have been portrayed as not only the victims of (alleged) sexual abuse, but also the victims of an insensitive welfare and criminal justice system which has added to their ordeal. Until very recently, though, little attention has been given to the part perpetrators play in this complex equation.

Recent research and growing clinical experience emerging from work with the victims and perpetrators of sexual offences sheds light on some previously held popular assumptions about the nature and consequences of child sexual abuse. Early thinking emphasised, for example, the significance of sexually untoward behaviour by strangers against children, the public rather than the private nature of the behaviour, the apparent passivity of women in protecting their children from abuse and the overwhelming predominance of girls as victims, and often stressed the minimal long-term psychological consequences for children (e.g. Schlesinger 1982). In the last decade there has been a significant shift in thinking. Current research suggests that most sexual abuse occurs within the family; that both girls and boys (albeit to a lesser extent) are the victims of sexual abuse; and that such behaviour may be detrimental to children's well-being as children and in the future as adults (e.g. Showers, Farber, Joseph, Oshins and Johnson 1983; Wyatt 1985; Schlesinger 1986; Nelson 1987; Finkelhor 1986; Hall and Lloyd 1989). Evidence also indicates that almost all abusers are males who are known to the victim, and that women in their role as mothers do not usually collude with incestuous perpetrators (Tamarck 1986; Russell 1986; Faller 1988; Horton, Johnson, Roundy and Williams 1990; Williams and Finkelhor 1990).

Increasingly, it is recognised that the offender needs to be considered in a more comprehensive effort to deal with the problem. Although still the subject of much debate, appropriate intervention strategies for perpetrators may help to minimise the risk of future abusive behaviour and be viewed as a form of child protection. Yet little systematic research has been directed at explaining the actions of perpetrators of child sexual abuse or investigating potential strategies of intervention to address their offending behaviour.

It needs to be stressed that research about perpetrators is comparatively embryonic. While there is a growing but still small British research base, most studies are based on American samples drawn from clinical or hospital populations (see Williams and Finkelhor 1990 for a review). Such studies, while often useful, are not necessarily representative of all types of perpetrators and these perpetrators may be atypical because of their involvement in treatment prior to or during the period of the research. Samples are generally small and tend to concentrate on formally identified cases usually of incestuous fathers excluding others who may abuse children. Definitions of abuse vary from study to study imposing limitations on the comparability of findings as well as influencing calculations of incidence and theories of causation.

This chapter will present some preliminary findings from a research study into the management of child sexual abusers in Scotland and will highlight their backgrounds and some dilemmas concerning intervention. Since the number of female abusers was found to be less than 1 per cent (3 out of 501 cases) male abusers only are the focus here.

The study

The research incorporated three main aims – to provide an analytical description of the characteristics of known perpetrators of child sexual abuse in Scotland; to examine the policies, professional practices and forms of management associated with such cases; and to investigate the context in which abuse occurs and the rationales offered by perpetrators for their behaviour.

Methodologically, the study was divided into two phases: a predominantly quantitative first phase involving analysis of documentary case records of child sexual abuse drawn from a range of social work, criminal justice and health service sources; and a second, primarily qualitative, phase consisting of taped interviews with 53 known perpetrators and 66 professionals involved in the management of sexual abuse and sexual abusers.

During the first phase of data collection a 33 page standardised research form was used to record information from agency case files. It should be stressed that this work was not intended to lead to estimates of the rates of child sexual abuse in the population (see Roberts, Dempster, Taylor and McMillan 1991), rather the research aimed to provide a 'characterisation' of known cases and of typical responses. As such, the study was oriented to gathering a wide range of information about the nature of the abuse, the perpetrator and the victim. For example, information was collected on family composition of the perpetrator, most common form of abuse, principal location of abuse, method of procurement, use of violence, and the criminal and social background of the perpetrator. Information was also gathered on the management of cases of abuse, including the number and nature of contacts with agency staff, engagement of the perpetrator and the nature of professional intervention.

Phase two which followed involved structured interviews with perpetrators and professionals. Perpetrators were asked about their childhood, schooling and general background; marital status and own children, if any; sexual development and awareness, including any episodes of childhood sex as a victim; adult sexuality; nature of offence committed and details of sexual acts perpetrated; perceptions and interpretations of the offence; perceptions of the victim and the context of abuse; experience of and reactions to imprisonment or probation; and responses to professional help offered and received. Interviews with professionals explored experiences of dealing with child sexual abuse; case management issues; objectives in sexual abuse cases; assessment criteria for measuring progress; methods of working with perpetrators; attitudes and perceptions of the problem; and ideas on future developments and initiatives. Phase two fieldwork was conducted in a wide range of agency locations and included interviews with social workers, prison officers, psychiatrists, psychologists, police officers, procurators fiscal (prosecutors) and reporters for children's panels.

In Scotland it is the responsibility of Local Authority Departments of Social Work to carry out the duties normally associated with the Probation Service in England and Wales. Social workers in Scotland perform a similar range of tasks to probation officers in England and Wales and may, for example, hold probation orders and provide reports for the court. For these reasons, the term social worker rather than probation officer is used throughout this chapter.

The sample

Reported here are findings derived from the first phase of the study which relied on an analysis of 501 documentary case files pertaining to sexual abuse. These agencies included Scottish Local Authority Departments of Social Work, the Scottish Prison Service, Police Forces, the Children's Hearing System and an adolescent unit in a psychiatric hospital. Figure 6.1 presents the proportion of cases examined from these different sources and shows that about half of the information was gathered from social work files.

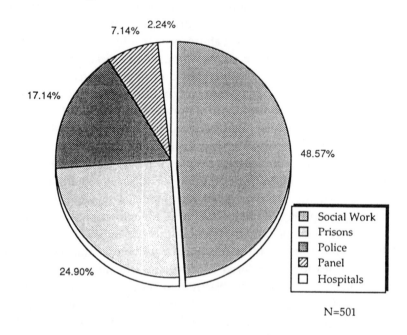

Figure 6.1: Sources of information

No definition of sexual abuse was imposed on the selection of case files. Providing the author of the record classified the case as primarily concerned with the sexual abuse of a child or children under 16 years of age, inclusion was automatic. In practice, then, a wide span of sexual behaviours ranging, for example, from the public exposure of genitals to violent sexual assault was included. This breadth in case file selection allowed for information about the nature of abuse, the perpetrator and the victims to be drawn from a range of disciplines not routinely sought in other studies of child sexual abuse.

Negotiating access and locating the files proved time-consuming and not always rewarding because of the uneven documentation of information within and between files. Despite these problems the results constitute a rich source of quantitative and qualitative information unique within Britain. While it is unclear how these cases of abuse known to public welfare and criminal justice agencies compare with those which fail to come to public and professional notice, a picture of the biographies of the men, their relationships to the children, and their methods of sexually involving the children nevertheless begins to emerge. Building on such a comprehensive sample may open the way to a better understanding of child sexual abusers, their recognition and the different responses by professionals.

The nature of information on file

Information contained in case files was uneven. Most of the social work area team files examined tended, not surprisingly, to focus on child protection issues with sparse attention being given to the circumstances of the alleged perpetrator other than to ensure that his whereabouts did not continue to pose a threat or danger to the child victim. More detail on the offender was to be found in dedicated Social Enquiry Reports prepared for court appearances, yet even these accounts sometimes skirted around the issue of the abuse itself, especially if the accused continued to deny the allegations.

By comparison, the nature and extent of abuse was usually clearly specified in the criminal charges of police files. The description, however, of some charges, such as 'lewd, libidinous and indecent practices' could be imprecise about the exact details of the sexual acts alleged to have occurred and in those cases where criminal proceedings were still pending information could be restricted lest it prejudice an accused's court hearing.

Medical reports on the perpetrator were scarce and usually confined to prison files. Supplementary details on the perpetrator were piecemeal, cited, for example, in occasional prison psychiatric and psychological reports.

Information from the different disciplines and agencies also appeared to be poorly coordinated in the written documentation. Important biographical facts such as the non-abusing parent's education, occupation, employment pattern, cultural background, personal characteristics and attitudes, and role in relation to the alleged abuse were missing as well as details about the perpetrator. The extent and nature of professional involvement with the offender was not always precisely recorded, nor, indeed, was the extent and nature of professional cooperation between agencies. Deficiencies such as these make it difficult for professionals to utilise file information when first encountering an offender. Lack of knowledge may mean delays in response and result in poorly coordinated intervention.

While the files provided an important source of information, the research revealed an unevenness in the reporting of even straightforward information about the circumstances of the abuse and the abuser. In some instances it was possible to collect very complete information, for example, reports on the perpetrator's living arrangements at the time of disclosure; only 6 per cent of all the files did not include this information. Conversely, information was not so complete in other areas such as the source of income in the household of the perpetrator; only 26 per cent of the cases yielded information on this issue. Problems such as these are frequently associated with the use of agency files and, while unfortunate, do not invalidate the wealth of information that is available (see Dube and Hebert 1988; Haugard and Emery 1989). It is important to recognise in the analysis presented hereafter that the calculation of any specific pattern or trend is based on those cases where information was available and not usually on the entire sample of 501 cases.[1]

Perpetrator characteristics

Males were the perpetrators in 99 per cent of cases. As can be seen in Figure 6.2 these males ranged in age from 10 to 81 and the most common age was 40. Most of the men were in unskilled manual or skilled manual occupations, with about one-quarter of them employed at the time of the offence. Another quarter were recorded as unemployed at the time of disclosure; the status for the remainder is not known. These employment patterns are consistent with other studies of offenders perhaps revealing more about those who find their way into the records of agencies of the state than about the characteristics of child sexual abusers.

More surprising, however, is the apparent stability of the childhood backgrounds of these men. In those 223 cases out of the total 501 where it was possible to ascertain the circumstances of their parental care, three-quarters or

---

1   These figures serve to highlight a dilemma which pertains to the presentation of statistics when information is missing from case files. The percentages may be calculated either as a proportion of the total sample, in this study 501 cases, or as a proportion of the number of cases in which the information required was recorded. In this study a large number of factors were investigated in a comparatively large number of cases. The files on these cases, however, often lacked the information needed for the research. Consequently, the base figure varies considerably from one question to another. The convention adopted in this paper, namely to present findings as a percentage of only the cases for which the information is available, seems to give the more accurate picture of what is actually known.

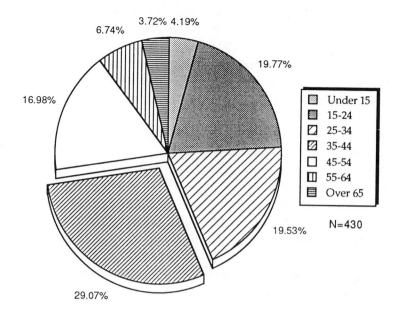

Figure 6.2: Age of perpetrators

167 perpetrators lived with both natural parents. The remaining quarter were raised either by one natural parent only, or by one natural parent and a step-parent, or by other relatives or foster or adoptive parents. Only a small proportion of the overall sample grew up in residential care. Little is known from these case files or other studies about the quality of relationships experienced by the men while growing up whether in their families of origin or in institutional care.

Files revealed that in 213 cases where an assessment was made, 5 per cent or 10 men were reported to have been both physically and sexually abused as a child; 6 per cent or 13 men had suffered physical abuse only, while 12 per cent or 26 men had been victims of sexual abuse only. This means that in the 213 cases where this information was noted, 23 per cent or 49 of the perpetrators had been the victims of sexual and/or physical abuse. A further 7 per cent of this group of 213 cases were assessed as having suffered emotional abuse and 3 per cent were reported to have suffered physical neglect. These results should be interpreted with considerable caution because of the limited number of cases for which an assessment was made. Findings suggesting, however, that a relatively small proportion of perpetrators experience abuse as children may challenge the supposed connection between victimisation in childhood and subsequent sexually abusive behaviour as an adult.

As adults, 109 perpetrators (224 out of 501 cases) were reported to be involved in some type of substance misuse, primarily alcohol. A small number were also reported to suffer from a physical disability (6%), mental illness (8%), or a learning disability (11%). Documented evidence was available on only 224 cases.

The 300 criminal files on the perpetrators suggest this is a group of people with a history of criminal offending with a reasonable proportion of the identified group having been convicted of past sexual or violent offences. Ninety of the 300 perpetrators had been convicted of property offences (30%) and 24 of these property offenders were also convicted of sexual offences. Another 37 or 12% had been convicted of only sexual offences. In all, then, there were 61 (20%) perpetrators who had been previously convicted of a sexual offence. Fifty-seven men (19%) were convicted of violent offences. These figures are, of course, much smaller if taken from the total 501 cases representing 12% and 11% respectively.

Relationships and abuse

There is considerable public concern about the assumed threat posed to children's safety from strangers. The results of this study point to the importance of understanding child sexual abuse as predominantly a problem of male perpetrators known to the victim. The vast majority of the male perpetrators were living in the home of the victim and were known to the victim at the time the abuse occurred. Where relationship could be determined in 459 of the 501 cases or nearly all the sample, just under one-half of the male perpetrators were biologically related to the victim. As Figure 6.3 indicates, the largest category in this group were 107 natural fathers who made up 23 per cent of known abusers. Children were also abused by uncles, grandfathers, brothers and cousins. Step-fathers and cohabitees also figured prominently as abusers, together they constituted nearly 23 per cent of the identified abusers. Only a tenth or 47 of the male abusers were identified as strangers.

The nature of abuse varied from obscene phone calls and public exposure of genitals (flashing) to vaginal intercourse, rape and murder (see Figure 6.4). The most frequent form of abuse in the 395 cases where the type of abuse could be identified was sexual manipulation of the genitals beneath or without clothing. This occurred in 38% or 150 of these cases. Nine per cent of the cases involved fondling of the genitals through clothing; and a small proportion (6%)

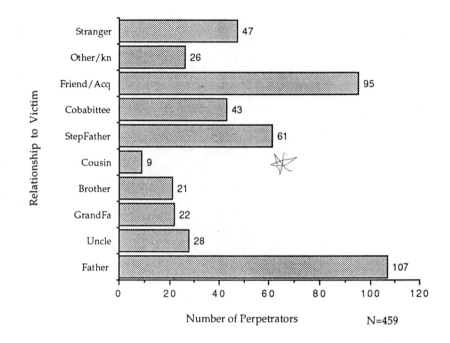

Figure 6.3: Relationship to victim

included voyeurism, verbal harassment or exposure. The nature of contact could vary from touching to masturbation and digital penetration and range from the transient to the prolonged.

With regard to the most serious forms of abuse,[2] a small proportion of perpetrators (4%) engaged primarily in oral sex with the child, while for a similar number (4%) sodomy was the principal form of sexual abuse. Fourteen per cent of abusers inflicted vaginal intercourse on their victim(s), and 7 per cent of the men raped their victim(s), sometimes repeatedly. In another 19 per cent of cases the form of abuse was unspecified and was subsumed in a criminal charge such as lewd and libidinous practices.

The most commonly used methods of securing sexual relations with a child were classified into four categories and included verbal bribes or inducements, coercion by indoctrination, verbal threats and physical force (see Figure 6.5). These categories, created by the researchers, seek to encompass and summarise

---

2   The categorisation of seriousness follows Russell's widely used definitions (Russell 1984).

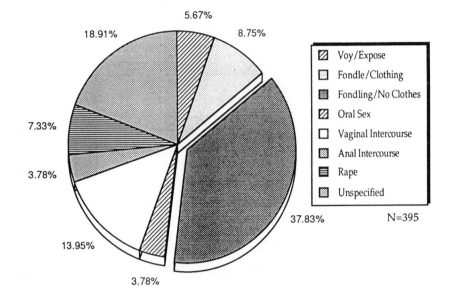

Figure 6.4: Nature of abuse

an extraordinary range and diversity of actions. Whatever the specific methods of procuring sexual relations with a child, they all involve coercive behaviour in which the victim is treated like an object denied of separate personal emotions to be used for the sexual gratification of the perpetrator (Foucault 1977; Dreyfus and Rabinow 1982; Rabinow 1984).

Even in the least physically intrusive forms of abuse, such as genital flashing, the child appears to play a part in the script of the offender. The child's fantasized or actual reactions to witnessing the public exposure appear to contribute to the perpetrator's sexual gratification. In other cases of abuse the perpetrator is clearly involved in coercing the child to participate in a more direct manner. Coercion can take many forms, ranging from direct violence to threats of revealing to others the child's 'misconduct'. Over a third of the cases examined in this study typically involved the use of physical violence and in another 10 per cent the child's participation was secured through verbal threats of violence.

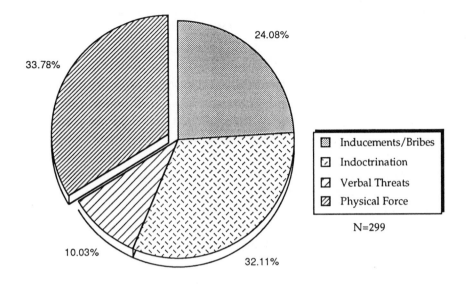

Figure 6.5: Method of procurement

In those cases where the abuse began at an early age and continued for many years – usually cases of father or step-father incest – the child was too young to resist in a meaningful manner and the offender was able to 'groom' or mould the child into a sexual object (Boon 1984; Christiansen and Blake 1990). In these cases the child is certainly treated impersonally, but the abuser aims to create an apparently 'willing' participant. Through encouragement, coercion, surveillance and constraint the child is made, in the eyes of the offender, a 'willing subject'. Participation of the child is usually secured over an extended period of time and may be the result of a process of normalisation whereby legitimacy is accorded the initial sexual overtures and subsequent sexual behaviour through the superior status of the adult and the exercise of his authority over the child. This process may encompass the child's entire personal and social identity, transforming her or him in the perception of the abuser and through the sexual experience into a purely sexualised entity. Although possibly less overtly coercive than other methods of procuring a child's participation, this process could be seen potentially as the most damaging, because the child is denied the possibility of developing an identity – an authentic self – apart from the desires of the abuser. The end product is the objectification of the child for the uses and gratification of the abuser. This extended process has been characterised by the researchers as 'coercion by indoctrination'.

The children

The overwhelming majority of the children, 360 (74%), were female; the remainder 125 (26%) were male. This proportion of boys, while numerically small, confirms the growing recognition that both girls and boys are potentially vulnerable to sexual abuse. In a small number of cases the gender of the child was not recorded.

Many of the children were living with their maternal mother and father when they revealed that they had been the victims of sexual abuse. Figure 6.6 details the living arrangements of the children at the time the offence was committed. These results suggest that children living either with mothers alone or with their natural mother and step-father/cohabitee appear to be at greater risk of becoming abused, although it cannot be assumed that the children are always at risk from those adults with whom they are living.

For many children abuse may begin early in their childhood, long before any complaint is made by them. A comparison of children's ages at onset and at disclosure reveals that the age of onset of abuse is usually very different than

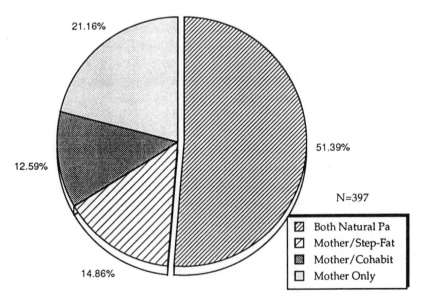

Figure 6.6: Living arrangement of child at time of abuse

the age of disclosure. The reasons for this difference may be complex and are likely to be influenced, for example, by the child's maturation, growing cognitive sophistication, expansion of relationships with others outside the family and possibly their changing confidence in the potential reactions of others to these events in their lives. It would be wrong, however, to infer from this delay that children do not experience anxiety and harm during this period of their lives.

The age of the index child at the time of disclosure of abuse was available in 425 of the 501 cases. Of this group of 425 children 13 per cent (30) were under the age of four, 21 per cent (90) were between the ages of five and eight, and 22 per cent (94) were between the ages of nine and 12. Another 38 per cent (161) were between the ages of 13 and 16. The remaining 5 per cent were over the age of 17 by the time professional agencies became involved.

The age of children at the onset of abuse was, on average, much lower than the age at time of disclosure. Information on age at onset of abuse was available in 363 cases out of the overall sample of 501. Over 70 per cent of these 363 children were under the age of 12 when the abuse occurred or began. By contrast, just over half of the children were 12 or less at the time of disclosure. In those cases where the child was under the age of 12 at the onset of abuse, 14 per cent (52) were under the age of four, 30 per cent (104) were between the ages of five and eight, 38 per cent (103) were between the ages of nine and 12 and the remaining 28 per cent (103) were between the ages of 13 and 16.

Other studies

The research results reported here are broadly in line with the findings of existing studies (e.g. Mrazek, Lynch and Bentovim 1983; Showers *et al.* 1983; Finkelhor 1986; Roberts *et al.* 1991; Gordon and O'Keefe 1988; Dube and Hebert 1988; Cupoli and Sewell 1988; Faller 1989; Kelly, Regan and Burton 1991). In contrast to previous understanding of the problem, however, these results indicate that the sexual abuse of children is serious and often involves the use or threat of physical force. The abuse is often highly intrusive to the children and when compared to physical abuse appears more frequently to be extreme (Waterhouse and Pitcairn 1991). This is not to suggest that the consequences for the children are necessarily directly determined by the apparent severity of the abuse. Children may react very differently to similar incidents.

Men known to the victim and often in positions of authority over the child are the most likely perpetrators. A significant finding, one repeatedly found in other studies, is that children are at considerable risk from their fathers, step-fathers and the cohabitee of their mothers. Consistent with a number of other studies, step-fathers and cohabitees are very much over-represented in these results (Russell 1984; Daly and Wilson 1985, 1988; Gordon 1989; Conte 1990). Although it is difficult to obtain reliable estimates of the proportion of children living with step-fathers and male cohabitees in order to make direct comparisons, on the basis of this research children living with step-fathers and male cohabitees appear to be much more at risk of sexual abuse than children living with both their natural parents.

The female and male children abused by the men in this study are mostly under the age of 12 at the onset of abuse. Other studies have uncovered even younger ages of onset. Cupoli and Sewell (1988) found that 42 per cent of the sexually abused children treated in the hospital referrals they studied were under the age of seven. Other recent studies confirm that abuse may begin long before children tell of their experiences. Results such as these point to the importance of distinguishing between the age of onset and age of disclosure. Practitioners and researchers should be alert to this discrepancy since disclosure may only occur after years of abuse when the child has the maturity and strength to reveal his or her victimisation to others.

Professional intervention

Social workers were most prominently featured as keyworkers responsible for the case management of the perpetrator although no indication was given in 156 files of who carried the main responsibility. Two-thirds, then, of the remaining 345 cases involved an area team social worker as the principal figure responsible for the perpetrator's casework; in 7 per cent of cases prison social workers took on this role. Psychiatrists and clinical psychologists, usually, although not exclusively, in the context of prison, were responsible as principal professionals in less than one-tenth of cases.

Contact between the abuser and psychiatrists and psychologists usually came later in the sequence of professional contact and was likely to centre on the perpetrator's mental state and rationale (if any) for his conduct. Depending on the offender's conviction and sentence contact might either be prison based or community based. Occasionally, for instance, psychiatric help was made a condition of Probation by the Court. Also psychiatric and psychological reports could be requested by the Court prior to sentencing in order to assist the Court in determining the most appropriate disposal. Most usually, psychiatrists and psychologists were involved in assessing perpetrators with only minimal involvement in therapeutic or management activities.

In the majority of cases a social worker interviewed the (alleged) perpetrator about the sexual abuse referral. The nature of the engagement could vary according to the timing and context of the interview – if conducted as part of an initial investigation the interview might confront the suspect with the allegation and attempt to elicit the perpetrator's own account of events; if conducted later in the proceedings, for example after a perpetrator's admission of guilt, the exchange might well focus on the abuser's conduct and offer some form of counselling depending on the offender's motivations and circumstances.

In most cases perpetrators were involved with social work as a result of routine case management rather than intensive specialised intervention. While information was present in only about half the cases, only one-third of abusers had received some form of individual counselling in respect of their abusive activities. Moreover, much smaller numbers, less than 10 per cent, appeared to have places on a specialist programme or were engaged in specialist group work. Contact with professionals primarily involved interviews and assessments associated with the demands and requirements of courts, prisons and statutory social services rather than specific work associated with the abuse.

Only a small proportion of abusers known to criminal justice and social services, then, were engaged in 'therapeutic' counselling for their offending behaviour although techniques for working with child sex abusers were being developed in both prison-based and community-based settings in Scotland. Such responses were usually ad hoc, established on the initiative of individuals who found their caseloads to contain an increasing proportion of child sex offenders. Despite this individuality common themes were invariably present in the approaches adopted. It may be helpful to look briefly at some of the common assumptions which appear to underpin such 'intervention'.

The nature of intervention

The basis for much of the recent developments in Britain stems from research and clinical work conducted in North America which questions the motivation of the offender: why is the abuser sexually aroused by children? why does he derive gratification from sexual contact with children? why is he unable to derive sexual and emotional gratification from more normatively approved sources? and why is he undeterred by conventional social inhibitions and taboos? Of major importance also is feminist analysis which stresses the unequal distribution of power between men and women and adults and children (Herman 1981; Russell 1986; Nelson 1987; MacLeod and Saraga 1987; Kelly,

1988; MacLeod and Saraga 1988). Feminist scholars criticise approaches such as the 'family systems theory' which emphasise the supposed importance of all family members in causing and in solving the problem of child sexual abuse, arguing that treatment based on principles of family therapy remove responsibility from the offender and locate it at least partially in the behaviours of women and children (Avis 1988; Lamb 1991). One of the significant contributions of feminist analysis is to emphasise the intentional aspects of abusive behaviour and to stress the need for offenders to take responsibility for their actions (Dobash and Dobash 1992).

Cognitive and behavioural approaches have also gained a significant foothold in the analyses and treatment of child sexual offenders. Here, emphasis is placed on techniques which will enhance and extend the offender's cognitions (understandings) of his own actions. Using group and individual work perpetrators are urged to reconstruct the sequence of events associated with particular incidents of abuse as a means of identifying motivations, justifications and rationales and encouraged to locate specific incidents within a wider context of objectification of the victim and normalisation of the abuse. These reconstructions of the specifics of abuse are intended to enhance self-awareness and to stimulate empathy toward the victim. The focal point of this sort of work is always the abuse, with offenders required to locate their emotions and reactions in a direct and concrete manner (Dobash and Dobash 1992, 243–250). Cognitive approaches explore the misinterpretations and misrepresentations of children's behaviours and motives which perpetrators may make and stress the restructuring of these distorted cognitions. Behavioural approaches emphasise the importance of dealing with events and actions and the introduction of alternative patterns of behaviour.

A common assumption across this theoretical diversity in addressing the offender is that sexually abusive behaviour is repetitive and deliberate. Rarely, if ever, is the sexual abuse accepted as a 'one-off incident', spontaneous and unplanned. Rather, the bedrock of intervention is the assumption that the sexual abuse was worked out well in advance and has certainly occurred on more occasions than the perpetrator is prepared to admit or accept.

Child sex abusers are habitually thought to deny their involvement in anything untoward, to minimise the seriousness of what has happened, and to deflect responsibility away from themselves, reactions which are also associated with physical violence against women in the home and the rape and sexual assault of adult women (Scully 1990; Dobash and Dobash 1992). The tendency to 'minimise' or to make the abuse seem like 'ordinary' behaviour stems from a self-justifying interpretation, often quite elaborate, of the circumstances, events and motivations which preceded the sexual abuse. Perpetrators usually deflect responsibility for their actions onto the victims by blaming them either for failing to prevent sexual involvement or for encouraging its initiation and continuation. This externalisation of responsibility in part originates in the offender's sense of his entitlement to children and women.

One of the main obstacles to be overcome in work with sexual abusers is denial. Denial can consist of an outright refusal to accept that any sexual abuse has occurred at all or it can take subtler forms where, although sexual activity is acknowledged, responsibility is shifted elsewhere. Perpetrators may blame others or shift responsibility onto other external factors such as alcohol or childhood experiences. The need to challenge perpetrators about their attitudes and actions to encourage a sense of responsibility for what has happened through the erosion of their denial and minimisation is seen by practitioners as the way ahead.

For a growing number of professionals working with abusers, denial and minimisation have to be confronted at the outset. Inevitably this can lead to tensions between professional and client as the contract for work is established. A dialogue with the abuser has to be established which concentrates on the offence, is challenging and confrontational, but not discriminating, aggressive or hostile. Child sex offenders' attitudes and assumptions which underpin their abusive behaviour need to be constantly questioned and challenged in a firm but sensitive manner while concentrating on the offence itself. This can lead to a contradiction for workers – on the one hand they must (try to) develop a positive and constructive relationship with the client to encourage dialogue and rapport, while at the same time indicating unequivocally that because of the nature of the offence and the associated tendency of self deception and the deception of others it will never be possible to 'trust' the offender entirely.

The initial task for the worker is to identify the (true) scale and pattern of the perpetrator's offending. Key questions in the assessment concern who has the client abused and over what period of time? has he focused on a particular type of victim? what does he fantasise about? how has he approached and engaged his victim(s)? what inhibitions (if any) does he have to overcome to carry out the offending? what sexual acts does he actually engage in? is guilt experienced after the abuse and how long do periods of guilt persist? in what way does he overcome his guilt in order to abuse again? and how does he legitimise his offending both to himself and to others?

For progress to be made in reducing an offender's risk to children, professional literature suggests that a perpetrator must first understand the motivations and stimuli which contributed to his offending. This provides a template against which offenders can measure their own feelings, thoughts and behaviour, allowing them an insight into the structural pattern of their offending. Individuals can identify times in their own past which correspond to these reconstructions and can begin to recognise the circumstances which preceded the abuse. Through this understanding it may then be possible for the individual to address perceptions and actions which will enable him to consider, develop and model new ways of thinking and acting which will avert future abuse.

Confronting sexually abusive behaviour usually combines a number of cognitive and behavioural techniques – 'brain-storming' events leading to the abuse; challenging and examining the use of language; attitudinal questionnaires; diary keeping; 'flow' charts outlining the cycle of behaviour; videos and focused group discussion. Developing and improving methods of self-monitoring are considered crucial to this sort of work. Although individual and group work is conducted, the small group format seems to be the preferred model. Groups can create a learning environment where revealing actions and beliefs becomes normative. Participants who are developing insights and changing cognitions can encourage and cajole others, creating a climate for exploring emotions and actions.

Examples from this research illustrate how offenders are being encouraged to address their offending behaviour. On one prison based specialist assessment programme, offenders are required to keep their own 'diary' as one means of improving 'self-observation'. While doubt about the authenticity of feelings might be raised, the following illustration taken from case notes illuminates the type of response which may follow intervention:

> 'EXCUSES – There are none, someone spoke to me not so long ago about reality, and I've given it a lot of thought, and the reality is that it's not anyone else's fault that I have abused a child. It's certainly not the child's and no matter what your circumstances are I don't think it's your partner's either. I have blamed everything from my partner to drink and unemployment, but the reality is down to me. Nobody else abused the child. I think I have always known this but it's taken me a long time to admit it to myself, I don't feel any better for admitting it to myself but now at least I can stop blaming other people for something I done.'

This example shows how, with appropriate guidance, abusers may gain insights into their motivations and possibly begin to accept responsibility for their sexual offending. Accepting responsibility, being accountable, is seen as a prerequisite for any positive intervention to occur. This acceptance is one of the criteria to be considered when deciding on the best use of resources. For those offenders who accept responsibility then the foundations for further work clearly exist. For those, however, who continue to deny either partially or completely, how much time and effort should be, or could be, spent in an attempt to make them recognise their accountability?

Sceptics argue that there is no evidence to date to suggest that any type of treatment has any effect whatsoever on sexual offending. Pessimistically, this school of thought sees little prospect of changing the motivations, predispositions and behaviour of abusers, arguing that the perpetrators' removal from the community is the only cast-iron guarantee that risk to children will be reduced.

More positively there are those who argue that imprisonment on its own will achieve nothing unless it is accompanied by some attempt to engage and confront the offender about his sexuality and his sexual offences. Even if change could be effected in only a small proportion of perpetrators, given the large number of children research suggests some perpetrators abuse (Fields 1988), then potentially many children could be saved from future harm. Viewed in this context work with abusers can be seen as a form of preventative child protection.

There are dangers however. Some may see in the perpetrators' reflective insights the desire to please those making the assessment by reproducing 'correct' responses. A superficial shift in attitudes which masks an underlying reticence to alter behaviour is a situation which professionals must guard against. Giving perpetrators a theoretical explanation for their sexually abusive behaviour may serve only to educate them to be more skilful abusers. While this always has to be recognised as a potential risk of intervention, it is perhaps less of a danger than no intervention at all.

Practice and policy highlights

The research presented in this chapter has revealed the paucity of information contained in some records on perpetrators. Yet good information is needed both to assist future research and to support practice and policy planning. Investment in good case records might aid practice if clearer documentation of the events surrounding abuse and the perpetrator's behaviour were available. This might provide a common starting point and thereby limit the scope for dishonesty or avoidance of the facts by perpetrators, assist in promoting inter-disciplinary collaboration and contribute to an economy of effort.

The findings point to the predominance of social workers in managing work with offenders. The aims of the different disciplines may at times be conflicting or complementary but evidence of co-ordination does not feature strongly in the case records. Information is not necessarily shared across disciplines which may ultimately contribute to offenders receiving inconsistent messages, potentially distracting from the overall effort to combat future abuse. Clarification of goals and methods of working with perpetrators may point the way ahead.

In considering future efforts it will be necessary to maximise the efficient use of resources when dealing with offenders. Their willingness to co-operate may be crucial in these efforts. In this study one-third of perpetrators reported in the records were judged to be willing to co-operate with professionals, while a quarter were reported as unwilling to co-operate. A further tenth were deemed to be insincere about seeking help and in the remainder of the cases the offenders were undemonstrative about their intentions. The question arises whether it will be possible in the future to discriminate between those who will never regard themselves as culpable and those who despite initial denial are able to respond to therapeutic interventions. This distinction may be important in deciding whether to concentrate resources on those more likely to respond. If so, what provision, if any, is made for those who appear ineligible for help?

The Scottish picture suggests a group of men who are over-represented in skilled or unskilled work which may be associated with educational disadvantage. Adversities such as depression, substance dependency or educational deficiencies may be important in their own right. This is not to suggest such factors are causal and should be used as reasons for excusing the behaviour or for denying the full responsibility of the perpetrator. Left unaddressed, however, they may delay or impede responsiveness to methods of intervention which seek to concentrate on the offending. Responses by professionals may also need to be better co-ordinated in the future with community health education drawing attention to questions of mutual interest concerning social status, health and sexuality. Improving knowledge about the relationship between these areas may help to combine in public health and social programmes an emphasis on personal responsibility for abusive behaviour and public responsibility to safeguard the interests of children by challenging and perhaps changing the men who harm them.

This study conveys the embryonic state of development of services for men who commit sexual offences against children. It confirms the need to direct more effort at offenders. Current policies and practices which concentrate on children protecting themselves from abuse by saying 'no' may not go far enough to achieve the goal of child protection. Such programmes have an important role to play in prevention. Yet the absence of good programmes for perpetrators may serve unintentionally to locate responsibility for managing the abuse in the children rather than the men.

Finally, in planning a national response to the problem of child sexual abuse many questions remain. Should men who act incestuously towards children be seen as distinct from those who were strangers to the children? Do professionals need to consider the impact of their own gender in implementing treatment? What are the appropriate forms of training for professionals? When should imprisonment be used? Allocating resources for 'work' with child sexual offenders is not universally popular. Ethical concerns about offenders' 'needs' being addressed when there is still so much to be done in providing support for victims may cause unease. In theory, helping one child abuser to change attitudes and behaviour may, by reducing and containing risk, safeguard other children from future abuse.

Acknowledgements

We wish to thank David Finkelhor and Linda Williams for allowing us to see their interview schedules and research instruments which assisted us in preparing our own. Our appreciation is extended to Liz Kelly who made a number of helpful suggestions on an earlier draft of this chapter. Finally, we are grateful to the Scottish Office and in particular Social Work Services Group for their generous support and continuing encouragement.

References

Avis, J. Myers (1988) 'Deepening awareness: A private guide to feminism and family therapy'. *Journal of Psychotherapy and the Family 3*, 15–46.

Boon, C. (1984) 'Betrayal of trust: Father-daughter incest'. *Tellus 5 (winter)*, 17–19.

Christiansen, J.R. and Blake, R.H. (1990) 'The grooming process in father-daughter incest', in Horton, A. et al (eds), *The Incest Perpetrator.* London: Sage, 88–98.

Conte, J.R. (1990) 'The incest offender: An overview and introduction', in Horton A. et al (eds), *The Incest Perpetrator.* London: Sage, 19–28.

Cupoli, M.J. and Sewell, P.M. (1988) 'One thousand fifty-nine children with a chief complaint of sexual abuse'. *Child Abuse and Neglect 12*, 151–162.

Daly, M. and Wilson, M. (1985) 'Child abuse and other risks of not living with both parents'. *Ethology and Sociobiology 6*, 97–210.

Daly, M. and Wilson, M. (1988) *Homocide.* New York: Aldine de Gruyter.

Dobash, R.E. and Dobash, R.P. (1992) *Women, Violence and Social Change.* London: Routledge.

Dreyfus, H.L. and Rabinow, P. (1982) *Michael Foucault: Beyond Structuralism and Hermeneutics.* Chicago: University of Chicago Press.

Dube, R. and Herbert, M. (1988) 'Sexual abuse of children under 12 years of age: A review of 511 cases'. *Child Abuse and Neglect 12*, 321–330.

Faller, K. (1988) 'The myth of the collusive mother: variability in functioning of mothers of sexually abused children'. *Journal of Interpersonal Violence 3(2).*

Faller, K.C. (1989) 'Characteristics of a clinical sample of sexually abused children: How boy and girl victims differ'. *Child Abuse and Neglect 13*, 281–291.

Fields, M. (l988) *Legal and Social Work Response to Sexual Abuse of Children.* University of Stirling: Institute for the Study of Violence.

Finkelhor, D. (ed) (1986) *A Sourcebook on Child Sexual Abuse.* London: Sage.

Foucault, M. (1977) *Discipline and Punish.* Translated by Alan Sheridan. London: Allen Lane.

Gordon, L. and O'Keefe, P. (1988) 'Incest as a form of family violence: Evidence from historical case records'. *Journal of Marriage and the Family 46*, 27–34.

Gordon, M. (1989) 'The family environment of sexual abuse: A comparison of natal and stepfather abuse'. *Child Abuse and Neglect 13*, 121–130.

Hall, L. and Lloyd, S. (1989) *Surviving Child Sexual Abuse.* London: Falmer.

Haugard, J.J. and Emery, R.E. (1989) 'Methodological issues in child sexual abuse research'. *Child Abuse and Neglect 13*, 89–100.

Herman, J. (1981) *Father-Daughter Incest.* Cambridge MA: Harvard University Press.

Horton, A.L., Johnson, B.L., Roundy, L.M. and Williams, D. (eds) (1990) *The Incest Perpetrator: A Family Member No One Wants to Treat.* London: Sage.

Kelly, L. (1988) *Surviving Sexual Violence.* Cambridge: Polity Press.

Kelly, L, Regan, L. and Burton, (1991) *An Explanatory Study of the Prevalence of Sexual Abuse in a Sample of 16–21 Year Olds.* The Polytechnic of North London, Child Abuse Studies Unit.

Lamb, S. (1991) 'Acts without agents: An analysis of linguistic avoidance in journal articles on men who batter women'. *American Journal of Orthopsychiatry 61(2)*, 250–257.

MacLeod, M. and Saraga, E. (1987) 'Abuse of trust'. *Journal of Social Work Practice, November*, 71–79.

MacLeod, M. and Saraga, E. (1988) 'Challenging orthodoxy: Towards a feminist theory and practice'. *Feminist Review 28, spring*, 16–55.

Mrazek, P.J., Lynch, M.A. and Bentovim, A. (1983) 'Sexual abuse of children in the Unted Kingdom'. *Child Abuse and Neglect 7*, 147–153.

Nelson, S. (1987) *Incest – Fact and Myth.* Edinburgh: Stramullion.

Rabinow, P. (ed) (1984) *The Foucault Reader.* Harmondsworth: Penguin.

Roberts, J., Dempster, H, Taylor, C. and McMillan, B. (1991) 'A study of the frequency of reported child sexual abuse in one Scottish region'. *Child Abuse Review 7(1)*, 3–6.

Russell, D.E.H. (1984) 'The prevalence and seriousness of incestuous abuse: stepfathers vs. biological fathers'. *Child Abuse and Neglect 8*, 15–22.

Russell, D.E.H. (1986) *The Secret Trauma: Incest in the Lives of Girls and Women.* New York: Basic Books.

Schlesinger, B. (1982) 'An inventory of findings', in Schlesinger, B. (ed), *Sexual Abuse of Children. A Resource Guide and Annotated Biography.* London: University of Toronto Press.

Schlesinger, B. (1986) 'The Badgley report on sexual offenses against children', in Schlesinger, B. (ed), *Sexual Abuse of Children in the 1980s.* London: University of Toronto Press.

Scully, D. (1990) *Understanding Sexual Violence: A Study of Convicted Rapists.* Boston: Unwin Hyman.

Showers, J., Farber, E.D., Joseph, J.A., Oshins, L. and Johnson, C.F. (1983) 'The sexual victimisation of boys: A three year survey'. *Health Values 7*, 15–18.

Tamarack. L.I. (1986) 'Fifty myths and facts about sexual abuse', in Schlesinger, B. (ed), *Sexual Abuse of Children in the 1980s.* London: University of Toronto Press, 3–15.

Waterhouse, L. and Pitcairn, T. (1991) *The Effect of Social Worker/Family Relationships on Child Abuse Case Outcome.* ESRC Report R000231436, November.

Williams, L.M. and Finkelhor, D. (1990) 'The characteristics of incestuous fathers', in Marshall, W.L., Laws, D.R. and Barbaree, H.E. (eds), *Handbook of Sexual Assault: Issues, Theories and Treatment of the Offender.* New York: Plenum.

Wyatt, G. (1985) 'The sexual abuse of Afro-American and White-American women in childhood'. *Child Abuse and Neglect 9*, 507–519.

Part II

Responding to child abuse

Chapter 7

Working Together in Child Protection

Christine Hallett

The child protection system in the UK is characterised by the emphasis placed in practice as well as rhetorically on a multidisciplinary approach. The need for interagency collaboration in child protection is also widely accepted elsewhere; but by comparison with many other European countries, the multiagency involvement evident in the British system is more firmly entrenched and securely established at all levels. It can be seen in daily practice at field level in case conferences, meetings, core groups and joint interviews; at policymaking levels in the Area Child Protection Committees established in each locality or region; and, also, at the level of central government, which has issued a stream of detailed circulars of guidance over the last twenty years or so, despite some criticism that central government in England and Wales lacks the requisite interdepartmental coordinating committee to ensure 'proper planning and cooperation in measures to tackle child abuse' (HC 570–1 1990–91 p.xi.)

There are three main theoretical perspectives which offer explanations as to why agencies would collaborate with each other in child abuse or any other field. The first, the exchange perspective associated with the work of Levine and White (1961) emphasises voluntary collaboration (the exchange of goods or services) which is freely entered into and perceived to be of mutual benefit to all concerned. The second, a power dependence approach associated with the work of Aldrich (1976) and the early work of Benson (1975), is one in which agencies can persuade or coerce others into collaboration (because others may need their referrals, resources, expertise, legitimacy and so on). The third, mandated coordination, is where a superordinate agency, often a higher level of government, instructs subordinate organisations to work together (see Hallett and Birchall 1992 for a fuller discussion).

In the UK in child protection there is a system of mandated coordination, in which local agencies are required by central government to work together although, to date, this has been an administrative requirement imposed by circular and government guidance, rather than by statute. A problem with mandated coordination is that people and agencies will not necessarily collaborate just because someone tells them to work together. Different professionals and agencies in the child protection network(s) may have differing degrees of acceptance of or commitment to the injunction to cooperate and differing capacities to resist. The motivations to work together may be different; the skills, capacities and competence to do so may vary, as does the degree to which they can, in fact, be directed to do so.

The professional practice literature in the period of rediscovery of child abuse in the 1960s accepted, almost universally and often uncritically, the need for a multidisciplinary approach, and this has largely continued to the present day. The mandate to coordinate was powerfully shaped by received ideas and reflected in clinical practice, especially the multidisciplinary emphasis on the management of child abuse associated with the work of Henry Kempe (Kempe and Helfer 1972) and his colleagues in the United States of America. This practice wisdom influenced the government guidance in the United Kingdom which for the last 20 years or so has reinforced multiagency collaboration (Home Office 1991, Scottish Office 1989). Data from our research into coordination policies and practices in child protection[1] suggests that this orthodoxy is also widely shared amongst professionals from varied disciplines at field and senior management levels. While Blyth and Milner (1990) suggest that 'given the choice, most professionals would probably work better alone' (p.195) rather than engage in multidisciplinary work, this view does not seem to be shared, in respect of child abuse, by the vast majority of participants in our research.

Nonetheless, there is a paradox. Working together is required by central government guidance and local procedures and is accepted in principle and generally regarded as necessary and desirable in practice by many of those involved, yet, at the same time, it is often characterised as problematic. In part, this stems from the powerful impact of a succession of over 40 widely pub-

---

1   The research into coordination policies and practices in child protection carried out by Elizabeth Birchall and Christine Hallett was funded by the Department of Health in England. Phase one of the research comprised a review of the literature on coordination and child protection, published in 1992 under the title *Coordination and Child Protection: A Review of the Literature* (HMSO). Phase two was a questionnaire survey of some 350 professionals (doctors, health visitors, social workers, teachers and police officers) exploring their views and experiences of interagency work in child protection and their responses to brief and extended vignettes concerning potential incidents of child abuse. Phase three comprised an in-depth case study of coordination policies and practices through analysis of case records and interviews with the varied professionals involved in two local authorities in the north of England.

licised inquiries into cases of child abuse, mainly in England, and of a larger number of internal case reviews conducted more quietly, but perhaps no less effectively, by Area Child Protection Committees or similar mechanisms throughout the United Kingdom.

A dominant theme of the inquiries, beginning with the Maria Colwell case which was so important in forming the government response in the early 1970s, (DHSS 1974) has been of continuing and repeated failures in interagency communication, of a major and minor nature (DHSS 1982, DH 1991). The Jasmine Beckford Report (London Borough of Brent 1985) was perhaps an exception for, although it revealed shortcomings in interagency work, the main thrust of the panel's (or was it Louis Blom-Cooper's?) criticism was reserved for what was seen as the dominant mode of social work in child abuse: insufficient attention to the child's needs, interests and protection. More recently, and with equally, if not more, profound consequences for the response to child abuse in the United Kingdom, the Cleveland Report (1987) returned to the theme of grave weaknesses in interagency collaboration arguing:

> 'No single agency has the pre-eminent responsibility in the assessment of child abuse and child sexual abuse specifically. Each agency has a prime responsibility for a particular aspect of the problem. Neither children's nor parents' needs and rights can be adequately met or protected unless agencies agree a framework for their interaction.'

This helped to recast working together as not only working together with other professionals but as working together with parents and with children.

The impact of the inquiries has been profound, affecting popular and professional consciousness, conceptions of the problem and the policy responses deemed appropriate. The overwhelming impression is of serious deficiencies in the capacity of professionals to work together effectively to protect children, despite the fact that the cases are a tiny minority of the many thousands dealt with each year and probably, by definition, are atypical.

The public inquiries cannot take all the blame, however, for working together is also portrayed as intrinsically difficult in the professional practice literature, not only in the United Kingdom but in other countries (e.g. Sweden) which have not been rocked by a succession of public inquiries. Different professionals and agencies have different knowledge bases, different techniques of intervention, different operational priorities in respect of abused children, differing degrees of professional freedom or bureaucratic control, and different timescales, in the face of which they must collaborate. To illustrate the last point – on timescales – my colleague Elizabeth Birchall tells of a conversation between herself as the (then) Area Director of a Social Services Department in southern England and the Commanding Officer of the local army base in her patch; it included the following: 'Ms Birchall, I can equip an entire division in Hong Kong in 72 hours. Why can't your social workers get this man's marriage sorted by Friday'.

Besides these differences, those concerned need to work across the status divisions in the interprofessional arena of gender, ethnicity and occupational prestige. The network is complex, large and diverse posing severe logistical and resource difficulties in getting it to function.

The nature of child abuse

One of the points of difficulty which might be expected centres on differing professional perceptions of what constitutes child abuse; what is sufficiently serious to warrant professional concern and intervention and what should be done in consequence. Child abuse is the label attached to a selected and varied set of outcomes considered abusive to children. Not all harms to children are considered, by governments anyway, to be child abuse.

Gil's (1975) definition that child abuse is: 'inflicted deficits between circumstances of living which would facilitate the optimal development of children, to which they should be entitled, and their actual circumstances' (p.347) is rejected by successive British and by many overseas governments.

There has been a widening of the term child abuse from the 'battered babies' of the 1960s through emotional abuse and neglect to sexual abuse and organised and ritualistic abuse. Yet, as the behaviour and harms associated with the term child abuse expand, we have to ask: is such a wide catch-all term helpful in understanding causation, consequences for the child, possible interventions and preventive strategies, and do professionals dealing with child abuse share understandings on these matters? The changing term child abuse seems ripe for disaggregation. It is not a syndrome or a disease. It is a 'label' given to certain behaviours or situations in which parenting falls short, sometimes very seriously so, of accepted standards at any given time. It is, thus, a political (small 'p') or moral (but not necessarily moralistic) judgement.

Ideas of what constitutes abuse are not fixed and immutable, they change over time. Some cases are relatively clear at the stage of identification – others, much less so. Complex judgements, of a multidisciplinary kind, are required, therefore, which take into account the context in which certain events have occurred. For example, O'Toole, Turbett and Nalepka (1983) used an experimental design to study the influence of socioeconomic status, ethnicity and level of injury on physicians' and nurses' recognition and reporting of child abuse in the United States of America. In a vignette involving a child with a serious injury, 70 per cent of physicians judged abuse to be present when the parent was of low socioeconomic status compared with 51 per cent when the parents' socioeconomic status was high. In another vignette involving a child with a minor injury, 43 per cent of physicians recognised abuse when the parent was black, compared with 23 per cent when the parent was white. A similar study by Hampton and Newberger (1988) examined the variables associated with the initial diagnosis of child abuse by hospital personnel and with the proportion of cases subsequently reported to child protection agencies in the United States of America. This study concluded that, in the hospital sample, social class and race are the most important perpetrator characteristics that distinguish reported from unreported cases of abuse.

Robert Dingwall *et al.* (1983) studied these processes at work in three local authorities in England. They found that casualty officers' suspicions of child abuse were based on social assessments of the family rather than the specific nature of the child's injuries. They describe these as essentially moral judgements concerned with the nature of child protection in a liberal democracy. These studies clearly demonstrate, as Dingwall *et al.* state, that 'abuse and neglect are the products of complex processes of identification, confirmation and disposal rather than inherent in the child's presenting condition and, at least in some sense, self-evident' (p.31).

So at the referral, investigation and assessment stages, subjective judgements are made about whether certain behaviours or outcomes constitute child abuse. They are affected by many factors, including the social class and ethnicity of the children and families, workers' frames of reference and personal values, local levels of awareness and local operational procedures. The latter help to account for the wide variations between authorities across England in levels of identified and registered child abuse – which do not appear to be easily explicable in terms of more objective criteria (HC 570–1 1990–91 p.v). Data from the study of a sample of registered cases in our research suggests that, in practice, there is little evidence of significant interprofessional differences on these matters, at least concerning cases perceived as serious enough to have entered the system. There is fairly widespread agreement amongst the professionals that, in general, cases referred to or identified by the relevant agencies as child protection cases are appropriate and that the thresholds of intervention being applied in practice are broadly acceptable. If anything, it appears that cases which should be dealt with may be being excluded through pressure of work or shortage of resources. There is certainly no criticism of the key agencies, principally social workers, for acting too precipitately, too intrusively or too coercively, or for intervening without justification in family life.

Among professionals then, there does not seem to be confirmation of the trend emerging in the United States of America of a reporting system said to be discredited through high numbers of unsubstantiated cases, which have risen as a proportion of referred cases from 35 per cent in 1975 to 65 per cent in the late 1980s (Besharov 1987). This is not to suggest that in the UK the professionals' views about the nature of the cases in the system and the thresholds of intervention would necessarily be shared by the public at large, or by the children and families concerned. Indeed there are examples in our research of some families and alleged perpetrators minimising the events and construing them differently from the professionals. One mother, for example, informed by the police that her daughter had been sexually abused and asked to go to collect her, is reported by the social worker as being extremely distressed and saying that she had feared rape or violent assault and had not imagined that it would 'simply involve inappropriate touching'. The child herself seemed unconcerned and is recorded as having remarked 'all this fuss because I sat on [a family friend's] knee'.

Several studies of the perspectives of children and their families on their involvement with the child protection system are in progress or have recently been completed (e.g. Cleaver and Freeman (forthcoming); Corby 1987; Dempster 1991; Waterhouse and Pitcairn 1991; Sharland, Jones and Aldgate (forthcoming); Shemmings and Thoburn 1990; Hooper 1991). However, in the UK we lack studies of the views and attitudes of members of the community or public at large, unconnected with the child protection system, comparable with those undertaken in the United States of America by Giovannoni and Becerra (1979) and by Van Wersch (1991) in Holland which would enable a comparison of lay with professional views about what constitutes child abuse and what is sufficiently 'serious' to warrant state intervention.

The role of the police and the criminal justice system in child protection

While a multidisciplinary approach in child protection is widely accepted in many countries, Britain is, perhaps, unusual in the extent of involvement of the police. This has not always been a feature of the British scene and, as Parton (1991) notes, a significant trend in recent years has been a greater prominence accorded to the police, evident both in official guidance and in practice.

In the early 1970s, for example, there were discussions and some disputes about the wisdom or necessity of police involvement in child abuse and of the value of prosecution in relation to physical injury. Some leading activists argued that child abuse was principally a manifestation of family dysfunction rather than of criminality. The preferred response was therapy, not prosecution. This is reflected in the important DHSS Circular, issued in 1974 following the case of Maria Colwell, which included the police in the list of 'others who may be invited' to case conferences, not those who should always attend (DHSS 1974).

There were articles in the professional journals and discussions about the difficulties caused for some, for example, doctors, by police attendance at conferences, resulting in a Circular issued by the Home Office and the DHSS in 1976 (DHSS 1976) emphasising the need for closer cooperation between the police and other agencies, and recommending that Area Review Committees (as they were then called) should work towards a police presence at all case conferences. This guidance was 'low key', emphasising the police role in supplying information on criminal records, where relevant, and on their previous dealings with the family. More significantly, the circular stresses that, not just in prosecution but also in investigation, the police should be guided although not bound by the decisions of an early case conference (Hallett and Stevenson 1980). The circular stated

> 'In considering the need for an investigation, the Departments hope that where a case conference has been held chief officers of police (whilst retaining the capacity to take independent action) will take into account any views expressed by the conference about the effect of an investigation on the welfare of the child.' (DHSS 1976 p.3)

There has been a profound shift since then, partly caused by the rise of child sexual abuse as a significant social problem and fuelled by the crisis in Cleveland. The police were identified in the 1986 draft of Working Together (DHSS 1986) as one of the three key investigating agencies alongside the NSPCC and the social services department and the reality in practice now is of extensive police involvement and close collaboration between police and the social services or social work department at the referral and initial investigation stage, with special joint police/social work assessment teams in some areas.

This has led to a situation where British child protection services with their close involvement of the police and potentially the criminal justice system are characterised by some of our European colleagues as punitive, coercive, unhelpful and anti-therapeutic. This was an important theme of the ISPCAN European Conference held in Prague in 1991. This critique of the British system emphasises both its tendency to deter children, families and abusers from seeking help for fear of the consequences in the criminal justice system and the inadequacies of the treatment accorded to abusers if they are prosecuted and sentenced. Although practice can vary widely within as well as between countries, there is a trend in some European countries to a de facto decriminalisation of the problem of child abuse – for example, in Belgium, Germany and Holland, with child abuse conceived as a failure of family functioning requiring a therapeutic, non-punitive response which largely excludes the criminal justice system (see, for example, Levold and Bergstein 1991; Marneffe 1991; and Wolff 1991). Marneffe suggests that the accessible, affordable, high quality service offered by her centre in Brussels, combined with a guarantee of anonymity and the absence of judicial intervention, has increased the proportion of those voluntarily seeking help from 3 per cent to 30 per cent.

Others, however, are wary of the extension of the therapeutic writ, seeing it, inter alia, as a challenge to the civil liberties of citizens. Giovannoni and Becerra (1979) contrast the value systems employed by legal/criminal justice personnel on the one hand and therapeutic personnel on the other, suggesting that 'the former would rather risk false negatives and set high standards of proof before stigmatising people and imposing treatment whereas the latter would prefer false positives and offer overtreatment rather than neglect' (Hallett and Birchall 1992, p.212).

In such circumstances, some suggest that 'the child welfare crypto-justice structure makes decisions about guilt and innocence, punishment and reform and the sanctions to be applied long before...formal adjudication...' (Wakefield and Underwager 1988, p.151), thus confusing treatment and punishment for all members of the family in ways which damage both justice and therapy.

The debates rest on different assumptions about the nature and causes of child abuse: in essence, whether it is a sickness or a crime requiring treatment or punishment and on which approach or combination of approaches most effectively controls abusive behaviour and helps those involved. There are sharp differences of view. Some argue for the positive therapeutic value of the involvement of the police. From the viewpoint of the survivors and non-abusing parents some support and validation may be derived from the demonstration which police involvement provides that the actions perpetrated constitute a violation of the law and are a legitimate matter of public concern, as well as of private pain or sorrow. This helps some, including those who have been abused, to place the responsibility where it clearly belongs, on the adult abusers and, in the field of child sexual abuse, principally upon men and youths. The involvement of the police is also reported to be helpful in particular circumstances, such as in cautioning or prosecution for child physical abuse, in demonstrating the unacceptability of certain actions and acting as a deterrent against repetition.

Whatever the potential or actual therapeutic value, there is a strong argument that for so long as crimes such as neglect, physical injury and sexual abuse remain on the statute book they should be enforced, lest messages are given that, although technically illegal, such actions have a degree of public sanction and acceptance (as used to be the case with domestic violence to women). The public interest, especially the future protection of children, as yet unharmed, may best be served through prosecution, although this will not necessarily serve the interests or accord with the wishes of each individual abused child. There is a danger in policy developments which would remove such legal protection as there is from children at risk of or subject to child abuse.

Somewhat surprisingly, in Britain at present there are, it appears, no available national data about the outcomes of police involvement in the child protection system. Creighton and Noyes (1989) report prosecutions in 9 per cent of physical abuse cases and 28 per cent of sexual abuse cases in their study of children on NSPCC Registers which cover 9 to 10 per cent of the child population in England and Wales. Data from one police authority in England reveal that of all allegations of abuse reaching the force in 1989 and 1990, the outcomes were as in the following table:

Table 7.1. Outcomes in cases of abuse investigation by police in an English Authority

	1990	1989
No Further Action (which included investigation in an undisclosed no. of cases)	60%	(approx. 75%)
Caution	approx. 6%	(approx. 6%)
Court appearance	approx. 6%	(approx. 14%)
O/standing at end of year	approx. 25%	(approx. 7%)

One should be cautious about extrapolating too readily from a local set of figures. Nonetheless they are of interest and response to them is shaped by individual views and prejudices. Some might argue that a prosecution rate of between 6 per cent and 14 per cent is small reward for the survivors of abuse who will have experienced police or joint police/social services investigation often an unwelcome experience, no matter how sensitively it is handled.

In the research cases in our study, the other professionals concerned, including social workers, doctors, teachers and health visitors, reported general satisfaction with the police role in child protection and the way in which they exercised their discretion. There were some difficulties: the pressure of work in the police special units and different operational priorities, leading to delay in investigations; problems resulting from the varied levels of experience of investigation between specialist police and generic social workers; and an occasional atrocity story about, for example, an inappropriately administered caution. There were also reported to be therapeutic difficulties in working with alleged abusers and their families where they perceived or chose to present the fact that the police had investigated but taken no further action as evidence of their innocence.

The major problem, however – not of interagency difficulty for it was also shared by the police – was a resigned sadness and disappointment, and sometimes anger, about the difficulties of securing evidence watertight enough, especially in cases of child sexual abuse, to lead to prosecution and conviction in circumstances where those who had interviewed the children and others were convinced that abuse had occurred. Given this difficulty, some question the wisdom of routine police involvement. In our study, however, the extensive role of the police in child protection was not fundamentally questioned in principle, despite some difficulties in practice. This is a significant transformation since the 1970s: and one which, although reinforced by Cleveland and the apparent rise of child sexual abuse, has, perhaps, arisen by stealth.

Costs and compliance in multiagency work

One striking feature about the British multiagency system in child protection is that it is largely uncosted, at least at the point of service delivery. Within social services and social work departments, this is somewhat surprising given the parallel developments in community care which emphasise tight financial controls. Social services departments have been designated by the government as the lead agency, both in community care and in child protection. In community care, developments are characterised by case management, including delegated budgets to team or individual case level, in the context of the further development of a mixed economy of welfare, with packages of care comprising costed options. As yet, child protection case conferences are not faced with a specified budget for the protection of individual children, nor are decision-makers required to choose between costed options – weekly social work visiting as against a day nursery place, for example. As I have argued elsewhere (Hallett 1991), the two systems reflect the different traditions in British social services: the more professionalised child care service and the welfare departments, more concerned with the allocation of resources. It is unclear for how long the two parallel but in some ways very different assessment and resource allocation systems in community care and in child protection will be able to co-exist.

Beyond the social services, there are now signs that in the interagency system the question of costs and trading across market boundaries are becoming salient issues. One of the most difficult concerns the costs of running the Area Child Protection Committees. These committees, established in the 1970s, have occupied an equivocal and uncertain position. They are vital to the child protection system in each locality with key responsibilities in establishing, maintaining and reviewing local procedural guidelines; in undertaking case reviews; in promoting and reviewing interagency training and interagency liaison; and in theory, although less well developed in practice, in reviewing work on the prevention of child abuse. They work, however, on the basis of goodwill and within severe resource constraints. The government advice to establish a budget for each Area Child Protection Committee has led to heated discussion (and wide variations) in many of the committees about the feasibility of so doing and the basis for the division of costs between the agencies involved.

At field level too, there are examples of an increasing concern about who should bear the costs of child protection. In health care, this is complicated by developments in internal markets with fund-holding GPs and hospital trusts. One paediatrician remarked recently in the course of our research that 'child abuse is like justice, the taxpayer pays'. But there are important questions about whether fund-holding GPs, for example, will be keen to refer cases of child abuse and incur the costs of paediatric assessment, paediatric monitoring and possibly extended use of child psychiatric services. There are also concerns about whether the full range of paediatric services, including child protection, plays a significant part in district health authorities' purchasing plans, or in providers' service specifications. There are also debates, for example, about the apportionment of the costs incurred by police surgeons in medical examinations. A police surgeon in our research indicated that the police authority paid for medical examinations which they had requested, but those done at the request of the social services department (whether or not the patients were on the practice list) were as she put it, 'on the house' – in effect, a subsidy from independent contractors to the child protection system.

Difficulties are also reported to be emerging in respect of local management of schools. A senior education officer in one authority contrasted the previous position of a centralised training budget for child protection in which training was provided to teachers effectively free at the point of consumption with the current position whereby head teachers with budgetary responsibility weighed up the relative advantages of 'repairing the broken window' as against releasing classroom staff for child protection training.

These are worrying trends. One of the reasons for a more elaborate system of interagency collaboration in child protection in the United Kingdom than in some other countries (for example, Switzerland and the USA) stems from the degree of centralisation and relative uniformity in the social welfare system established in the 1940s and developed since, including a comprehensive National Health Service, a comprehensive state education system and a relatively uniform pattern of social services provision. Some countries with fragmented service delivery systems spanning the voluntary, private and statutory sectors and with much greater local variation and unevenness of provision have looked with envy on the British system, in which a degree of coordination and systemisation was possible and had been achieved. One of the advantages was that there was a strong core of state run services and there were possibilities for trying to ensure that there was a fair degree of compliance with the central government mandate to work together. It is not, perhaps, a coincidence the most problematic group in interagency collaboration is the general practitioners who retained their status as independent contractors in 1948 with problems for the planning of services and their wholehearted integration ever since.

It would be ironic, and a source of regret, if policy initiatives of recent years such as local management of schools, NHS Trust hospitals, and GP fund-holding practices were to undermine the willingness and the capacity of the different professions and agencies to work together in the interests of children. From a policy perspective, fragmentation, delegation to local control and a market-driven system make coordination and planning much more difficult as is evident in the United States of America and elsewhere. Is this the best way forward?

In concluding, it is important to note the danger of transforming coordination from a means to an end in itself, with the focus on how well agencies can work together, rather than on the consequences for the protection of children, their families and abusers. Coordination or working together is widely portrayed in the literature as desirable and appears to be widely accepted in practice, in principle at least, at many levels. Given a choice, few of us would prefer to be uncoordinated. There is a danger, however, that 'working together' may be used merely rhetorically. The vagueness of the term can lead to its invocation as the policy solution of choice for all sorts of problems (from child abuse to salmonella in eggs) whose origins and solutions may lie elsewhere. As Weiss puts it, 'coordination cannot guarantee new resources, cannot devise new treatment methods, cannot solve problems of alienation or mistrust, cannot transmute ineffective systems into effective ones' (Weiss 1981, p.43).

Working together can certainly perform important functions in child protection:

- in aggregating and deploying different skills and resources in investigation, assessment and intervention and, although much less developed in the UK, in prevention
- in achieving greater efficiency through the avoidance of duplication and muddle for the families and children and of gaps in services allowing children to fall through the net
- in providing mutual support and challenge in difficult work
- in enhancing the capacity to deliver comprehensive holistic services.

Yet, a concern for the process of working together should not divert attention from the outcomes and general trends in the child protection system, whether viewed by consumers, professionals or policymakers. The task is to ensure the protection of children and appropriate responses to children, families and abusers. Multi-agency work has an important part to play – but it is only a part.

References

Aldrich, H.E. (1976) 'Resource dependence and interorganisational relations'. *Administration and Society 7*, 419–454.

Benson, J.K. (1975) 'The interorganisational network as a political economy'. *Administrative Science Quarterly 20*, 229–249.

Besharov, D. (1987) 'Contending with overblown expectations'. *Public Welfare, winter*, 7–11.

Blyth, E. and Milner, J. (1990) 'The process of interagency work', in Violence against Children Study Group (ed) *Taking Child Abuse Seriously*. London: Unwin Hyman.

Cleaver, H. and Freeman, P. (forthcoming) *Parental perspectives of suspected child abuse and its aftermath*. Research in progress, University of Bristol.

Cleveland Report (1987) *Report of the Inquiry into Child Abuse in Cleveland*. London: HMSO.

Corby, B. (1987) *Working with Child Abuse: Social Work Practice and the Child Abuse System*. Milton Keynes: Open University Press.

Creighton, S. and Noyes, P. (1989) *Child Abuse Trends in England and Wales 1983–1987*. London: NSPCC.

Dempster, H. (1991) 'A woman-centred approach to child sexual abuse: understanding the reactions of women to the sexual abuse of their children' (unpublished paper) International Federation of Social Workers, 10th European Seminar, Glasgow, September.

Department of Health and Social Security (1974) Non-accidental injury to children, Letter *LASSL(74)13*.

Department of Health and Social Security (1982) *Child Abuse: A Study of Inquiry Reports 1973–1981*. London: HMSO.

Department of Health and Social Security (1986) *Child Abuse – Working Together*. London: HMSO.

Department of Health (1991) *Child Abuse: A Study of Inquiry Reports 1980–1989*. London: HMSO.

Department of Health and Social Security and Home Office (1976) Non-accidental injury to children: the Police and Case Conferences, Letter, *LASSL(76)26*.

Dingwall, R., Eekelaar, J. and Murray, T. (1983) *The Protection of Children*. Oxford: Basil Blackwell.

Gil, D. (1975) 'Unravelling child abuse'. *American Journal of Orthopsychiatry 45*, 346–354.

Giovannoni, J. and Becerra, R. (1979) *Defining Child Abuse*. New York: Free Press.

Hallett, C. (1991) 'The Children Act 1989 and community care: comparisons and contrasts'. *Policy and Politics 19 (4)*, 283–291.

Hallett, C. and Birchall, E. (1992) *Coordination and Child Protection: a Review of the Literature*. Edinburgh: HMSO.

Hallett, C. and Stevenson, O. (1980) *Child Abuse: Aspects of Interprofessional Cooperation*. London: George Allen & Unwin.

Hampton, M.R. and Newberger, E. (1988) 'Child abuse incidence and reporting by hospitals: significance of severity, class and race', in Hotaling, G., Finkelhor, D., Kirkpatrick, J. and Straus, M. (eds), *Coping with Family Violence*. Newbury Park: Sage Publications.

HC 570–1 (1990–91) *Public Expenditure on Personal Social Services: Child Protection Services*. London: HMSO.

Home Office (1991) *Working Together*. London: HMSO.

Hooper, C. (1991) 'Child sexual abuse, child protection and the politics of motherhood'. Social Policy Association Conference, University of Nottingham, July 1991, unpublished.

Kempe, C.H. and Helfer, R.E. (eds)(1972) *Helping the Battered Child and His Family*. Philadelphia: Lippincott & Co.

Levine, S. and White, P.E. (1961) 'Exchange as a framework for the study of interorganisational relationships'. *Administrative Science Quarterly 5*, 583–601.

Levold, T. and Bergstein, V. (1991) 'Family therapy as an approach to child protection work'. 3rd European Conference on Child Abuse and Neglect, Prague, Czechoslovakia, June 1991, unpublished.

London Borough of Brent (1985) *A Child in Trust: Report of the Panel of Inquiry into the Circumstances Surrounding the Death of Jasmine Beckford*. London Borough of Brent.

Marneffe, C. (1991) 'Family intervention or intrusion: what happened to the therapeutic view?' 3rd European Conference on Child Abuse and Neglect, Prague, Czechoslovakia, June 1991, unpublished.

O'Toole, R., Turbett, P. and Nalepka, C. (1983) 'Theories, professional knowledge and diagnosis of child abuse', in Finkelhor, D., Gelles, R.J. Hotaling, G. and Straus, M. (eds) *The Dark Side of Families*. Beverly Hills: Sage Publications.

Parton, N. (1991) *Governing the Family*. London: Macmillan.

Scottish Office (1989) *Effective Intervention*.

Sharland, E., Jones, D. and Aldgate, J. (forthcoming) *Professional interventions in child sexual abuse*. Research in progress, the Park Hospital, Oxford.

Shemmings, D. and Thorburn, J. (1990) *Parental Participation in Child Protection Conferences*. Norwich: University of East Anglia.

Van Wersch, S. (1991) 'Parents' conceptions of child abuse and neglect: A comparative study among ethnic groups'. First National Congress on the Prevention of Child Abuse and Neglect, Leicester, September 1991, unpublished.

Wakefield, H. and Underwager, R. (1988) *Accusations of Child Sexual Abuse*. Springfield, Illinois: Chas C. Thomas.

Waterhouse, L. and Pitcairn, T. (1991) 'Child protection viewpoint'. First National Congress on the Prevention of Child Abuse and Neglect, Leicester, September 1991, unpublished.

Weiss, J. (1981) 'Substance is symbol in administrative reform: the case of human service coordination', *Policy Analysis 7 (1)*, 21–45.

Wolff, R. (1991) 'Who protects whom? Crisis in child protection systems'. 3rd European Conference on Child Abuse and Neglect, Prague, Czechoslovakia, June 1991, unpublished.

Chapter 8

The Children Act 1989 and Child Protection
European Comparisons

James Christopherson

The Children Act 1989 represents a major change in child care law for practice and policy. In some cases the assumptions which underlie the philosophy of the Children Act have been axiomatic elsewhere for many years. In other countries the debate between advocates of voluntary and compulsory measures of intervention in child protection is as active, and perhaps as acrimonious, as it can be in this country. This chapter seeks to identify similarities and differences between British child protection legislation and approaches accepted elsewhere, and to show how these comparisons reflect the changing views of the rights of the child, the responsibilities of parents and the duty of the state to protect vulnerable children and facilitate their development. Five changes introduced by the Children Act 1989 with important consequences for child protection are discussed. These include: first, partnership between parents and local authority; second, the duty of the local authority to provide services to children in need in general, rather than just to do what will be necessary to prevent them coming into care; third, the role of the courts and their share in the planning of intervention; fourth, the concept of 'significant harm'; and fifth, the right of the child to have his or her wishes and feelings taken into consideration, and even to have direct access to the courts.

Partnership between parents and the local authority
English child care legislation has been characterised by changes which either stress the importance of the rights of the parent, arising out of a belief in the family as the best setting in which to bring up children, or uphold a belief that

children have the right to be protected from abusive or otherwise morally blameworthy parents (Parton 1985). The Children and Young Persons Acts of 1963 and 1969 sought increased provision for giving help to families, while the Children's Act 1975, responding to the moral panic created by the Maria Colwell Inquiry (DHSS 1974) and government belief in such notions as 'the cycle of deprivation', led to increases in the power of the State. The 1980s, similarly, have seen a succession of inquiries into the deaths of children whom the local authorities had apparently failed to protect, but also one, perhaps more celebrated than all the others, where the child protection agencies had moved to protect children from abuse which the public could not believe had taken place (Cleveland 1988).

Continental child care systems have similarly been influenced by public concerns prevailing at a given time, and sometimes by particular *causes célébres*. In Sweden, for example, the scandal surrounding the removal of Alexander Aminoff from his home in 1979 could be seen as having led to legislative changes requiring local welfare departments to seek to work voluntarily with parents before taking statutory action (Brown 1984). Up until then Swedish child care was governed by the Child Youth and Welfare Act 1960, section 26 of which gave powers of removal when a child's development was endangered by a parent or guardian's 'unsuitability' or 'inability' to bring up the child properly. This led to very high numbers of children in compulsory care. Alexander was alleged to have been removed crying and struggling from school and placed in a psychiatric clinic for six weeks without contact with his mother, because of her 'flamboyance, aggression and eccentricity'. The campaign, which had claimed that the reason for Alexander's removal had been the fact that his mother came from an aristocratic family, was successful despite, or because of, conflicting information about subsequent events. Two new Acts, covering voluntary and compulsory admission of children into care, came on to the Swedish statute book. These made it clear that compulsory admission to care was only to be used where parents refused to cooperate with social work intervention. The Acts were the Social Services Act and Care of Young Persons Act both of 1983.

In Alexander's case, as was the case with the English children removed from their homes for reasons of alleged sexual abuse (Cleveland Report 1988), the real truth of what happened, if it is ever known, may be less important than the media version of events in influencing public opinion and legislative changes. In Sweden, parents' rights had been made stronger. In the Children Act 1989, parents' rights, now expressed as 'responsibilities' become considerably stronger. Not only is parental responsibility still shared by parents and the local authority after a care order has been made, but even where parents are shown to have inflicted 'significant harm', the court must still be satisfied, in the light of the plans presented to it, that making the order will be better for the child than making no order at all. Just as was the case in Sweden, where the social work establishment bitterly opposed the changes in legislation, so some writers in England, such as Staines (1991), have seen the Act as a manifestation of the extreme Right in aiming to go back to an idealised version of the Victorian family as if then harm to children will be eradicated, supported in 'unholy alliance' by the Hard Left, who see child abuse intervention as an unwarranted intrusion and a distraction from what should be the main task of social work, the alleviation of poverty.

British practice up to the present (Dale *et al.* 1986; Moore 1985) has averred that statutory intervention to protect the child is essential, even if parents are apparently cooperative. Writers like Staines (1991) see the idea of partnership as fanciful, arguing that clients are inherently disadvantaged and ill-equipped to enter into collaborative agreements by virtue of the very reasons which bring them into contact with social services and social work departments. Some continental writers (see, for example, Aucante and Verdier 1990) see this viewpoint not only as brutal to the child, but as ineffective, believing that the identification of problems in family relationships can stimulate motivation for change within the individual and that motivation for change is more likely on a voluntary rather than than compulsory basis (Koers 1981). Professionals in some other countries have sought, therefore, to minimise statutory involvement and to work with parents in partnership as much as possible. In the Netherlands, for example, the child protection system is coordinated not by the statutory Child Protection Boards, but by the 'confidential doctors' who coordinate the provision of services to families where abuse is suspected, and may work with the families to ensure that the abuse is not repeated. Only when the family prove uncooperative is statutory protection sought through the Child Protection Board and the Juvenile Judge, and this occurs in less than 10 per cent of cases (Dean 1989). The Children Act 1989 seems likely to bring British principles for deciding when state intervention in family life is justified nearer to the European model. The Department of Health Guidance and Regulations make clear that care proceedings are inherently traumatic, and are only to be used 'in the absence of adequate parenting and cooperation' thereby stressing partnership first (Department of Health 1991a).

The duty of local authorities to provide services to children in need

The Act imposes on local authorities a general duty to promote the welfare of 'children in need', and to promote the upbringing of such children by their families. 'Children in need' are defined more broadly than was the case under the old preventive section of the Child Care Act 1980 (S1), which required risk of actual admission to care. Now only the ensuring of a 'reasonable standard' of health and development is required to justify the use of resources. Furthermore, all children with disabilities are entitled to service. Services provided to children in need can include day care of various kinds, advice and counselling, befriending, or ultimately the provision of accommodation. This shift towards greater eligibility for child care services may pave the way in Britain, as is the case in some other European countries, for an increased emphasis in child care policy and practice on prevention rather than cure.

In France, for example, the Department of Protection of Mothers and Children (PMI) provides health care facilities to all children under five, and also supervises foster families and day-care provision (Girodet 1989). Another French agency (l'Aide Sociale d'Enfance) provides support for families in the home as well as day care and voluntary residential care. Italy has gone further and made a conscious choice to concentrate resources on preventing abuse by providing comprehensive service to under fives, rather than having a sophisticated system for intervening after child abuse has been identified (Caffo 1983).

The role of the courts and their share in the planning of intervention

Under former British legislation the role of the court in planning and supervising intervention in child protection varied according to the legal procedure under which the child had initially been brought into care. For those brought before the juvenile court under the terms of the Children and Young Persons Act 1969, the court only decided whether to make an order, or in the case of a supervision order, whether to impose a limited number of possible conditions. The court then played no further part until a request for a revocation was brought. On the other hand, children brought before the High Court under wardship provisions needed to be brought back before the court every time significant decisions were to be made about their lives, even to the extent of giving consent for medical examinations in cases of alleged subsequent abuse. The new Act (1989) seeks to restrict the use of wardship, while giving the higher courts power to hear care proceedings in exceptional circumstances. Although cases will not routinely have to be referred back to the court, in some circumstances the continued involvement of the court in decision-making will still be required, for example, where it is proposed that a child should be placed in secure accommodation or outside England and Wales.

Most child protection cases will be heard in the Family Proceedings section of the magistrates court. The court will need to be satisfied that making an order will be better for the child than making no order, and local authorities, therefore, will need to include in the application clear plans for how they intend to help the child if the order is made. The British system for managing child abuse up until now may have concentrated on short term assessment at the expense of long term follow up and treatment, thereby failing to make maximum use of professional effort and any parental resolve to avoid future incidents. The need to satisfy the court that the child will benefit from any legal order may encourage local authorities to establish clear plans for helping children beyond the stage of initial investigation and identification of abuse. Deciding a course of action in individual cases of child abuse for judicial purposes may force local authorities to confront from the outset questions of parental motivation for change, resources available to provide a service and the consequences for the child if nothing is done. This, at the very least, is likely to set before the court a realistic appraisal of the potential outcomes of different decisions for the children, their parents and care-givers and for practitioners. The requirement for clarity in the Act may help to avoid misunderstandings for those involved and to focus attention and effort on the future rather than the past.

The Children Act 1989 is moving away from most European jurisdictions, where the judge maintains an interest in all, not a minority of children who are compulsorily living away from their families. In France and Germany the coordinating role of the judge is central. On the other hand, the reduction in the power of the courts implied by the Act still leaves the courts more powerful than is the case in Denmark and Norway, where decisions about removing children from home are taken by elected members of the local social services committees with appeal referred to the Ministry of Social Affairs (Merrick 1989).

The concept of 'significant harm'

The Act markedly alters the way in which local authorities, and subsequently the courts, decide which children should be made the subject of care proceedings and which should not. In some ways, the criteria for defining which children are suffering 'significant harm' are expanded, for it will be possible to bring proceedings on the basis of the harm that is likely to be suffered in the future. Furthermore, under Section 31(9) there no longer has to be evidence that any physical or emotional damage has so far been caused.

In other ways, however, the criteria may be tighter. First, what has happened in the child's past care is only relevant in so far as it sheds light on the likelihood of abuse in the future. If the court were satisfied that there was no such likelihood, a court order is inapplicable even where abuse is known to have happened previously. Second, even where the court is satisfied that significant harm has been caused to the child the court has, furthermore, to be satisfied that it will be better for the child to make an order than not. Finally, the harm must be 'significant', which the Guidance Notes for the Act suggest will be a matter for the court to decide in any particular case. Indeed, section 47 lays down that the local authority may decide not to refer a case to the court either because the harm involved is not 'significant' or it does not feel an order would be in the child's interests.

European countries for a long time have relied legislatively less on the specifics of the alleged abusive acts and more on the implications of past events for the future care of the child. In part this is a function of the greater importance given to working with families on a voluntary basis, and a legal framework in which civil proceedings may be couched in more general terms. The German system, for example, imposes a duty on the wardship judge to alleviate any danger to the physical, mental or psychological interests of the child brought about by parental care or neglect, or guiltless failure on the part of the parents. By contrast, the Children Act 1989 says that the significant harm must result from:

> 'the care given to the child, or likely to be given to him if the order were not made, not being what it would be reasonable to expect a parent to give to him.' (Children Act 1989 S31(1)(b))

So if parents act reasonably, and yet significant harm is caused to the child, then no action will be taken, in contrast to the German system, where the child can be protected even from parents to whom no blame attaches. Only caselaw will resolve whether any behaviour which causes significant harm to a child can be regarded as 'reasonable'. Identifying what risks are 'reasonable' to take will play a central part in establishing grounds for child care intervention in the future. Minor but still painful injuries to children who play rugby are commonplace, for example, and very serious injuries do occur from time to time. It is unlikely however that parents who allow their children to play rugby would be regarded as acting 'unreasonably'. In this context the definition of 'reasonable' appears to have a moral element to it. Behaviour seen as morally acceptable is unlikely to be regarded as unreasonable. Yet, deciding moral limits in disciplining or punishing children or in determining when children are of an age to consent to sexual relations may be less than straightforward in the absense of a moral consensus within or between countries.

In France the moral basis of the assessment of parental care is much more explicit. Article L166 of the French Code of Public Health states that 'if the health of the child is compromised by the absence of suitable care, by ill treatment or bad example' (my translation) (Ministère des Affairs Sociales et de la Solidarité Nationale 1987) then the criteria for unreasonable behaviour or influence will be seen to be met. This has a parallel under the earlier British child care legislation in the concept of 'moral danger', which came to acquire a particular meaning in relation to the 'promiscuity' of teenage young women, and few surely will lament its absence from the Act of 1989.

Finally it is important to note that the concept of reasonable care may relate not only to parental behaviour, but to the capacity to parent. Indeed, the Guidance and Regulations for the Act (1989) make clear that if parents are doing their best then grounds for intervention may not be fulfilled. The Guidance Notes (Department of Health 1991a) make clear that the standard only has to be reasonable, so that it is not sufficient to show, for example, that parental care may fall short of that offered by foster parents or other care givers.

The right of the child to have his or her feelings taken into consideration

Under previous legislation local authorities were required to 'have regard for the wishes and feelings of the child' although in practice little store was often set by them. This may have been especially unfortunate in cases of child abuse where children may have been too frightened or confused to express their points of view and may have come to see themselves as 'objects of concern' or that little interest was being taken in them. The new Act strengthens the position of children in three ways which may be seen as innovative in a European context.

1. Children of all ages will have the right to have their wishes and feelings taken into account when decisions are made about them. It is part of the skills which professionals who work with children must have to enable even very young children to communicate about their feelings and expectations for the future (Department of Health 1991b). Courts in Britain must decide in each individual case whether the child 'is of an age and understanding etc', and courts regularly interview children as young as six years. In France, by contrast, children only have access to the court when they become 13 years of age. Before this age they have to make their opinions heard through the medium of the Social Inquiry Report (Aucante

and Verdier 1990). As Girodet points out, children are entitled to legal advice in the French system, but professionals are under no obligation to advise them of that right (Girodet 1989). In the Netherlands too children under 12 years do not have the right to be heard by the court, nor can those over 12 years appeal against decisions made about them (Childright 1988). Section 41 of the Children Act 1989 sets out the conditions under which the court may appoint a solicitor to represent the child.

2. The Act restores to children the right to 'take refuge'. Furthermore, the managers of refuges can, if necessary, take an Emergency Protection Order on a child who is in the statutory care of a local authority. The provision of refuges has a long and chequered history on the Continent, some having spontaneously started up following the student revolutionary movements of the 1960s in the face of active opposition by the police, while others, particularly in Germany, were thought to have close links with terrorist groups. Many refuges were perfectly reputable, but also faced police opposition because they seemed to encourage children to run away. Gradually these more reputable establishments, such as the Zeezecht in Amsterdam, won the respect of the police. Similar establishments, called Points Jeunes, were set up in Lille and Paris (though the latter did not survive for financial reasons) (Aucante and Verdier 1990) and finally by the Children's Society in London. Interestingly, the new Act gives the responsibility of liaison with the refuges on a case-by-case basis to the police, although licensing them remains the responsibility of the local authority.

In Denmark, there is a long tradition of boarding provision for teenagers. Adolescents often seek to be sent to such establishments and notional admission to care is a way of paying for it (Grinde 1987).

3. The Act requires local authorities to establish formalised complaints procedures for children who are being looked after by them. It espouses the need to ensure access to complaints procedures, not only for children who are being accommodated by the local authority, but for all users of child care services including their parents, all foster parents, children designated as 'in need', their parents and any other person who either has parental responsibility for the child, or any other interest in the child that the authority deems relevant (Department of Health 1991b). An independent person must be involved in the resolution of these complaints, and proper procedures followed. Local authorities must take active steps

to ensure that children are made aware of their right to make representations or complaints (Department of Health 1991c). Lately a number of authorities, such as Leicestershire and Durham, have devoted considerable resources to ensuring that children in care were made aware of their rights. For abused children the significance of this legislative change is especially important when it is known that a small proportion go on to experience abuse within the institution employed to protect them.

European countries vary in the amount of resources devoted to the maintenance of children's rights. In France, children's access to the courts is limited. In the Netherlands, on the other hand, a special voluntary agency exists specifically to give advice to children in conflict with the Child Protection Boards. These Boards are responsible for dealing with statutory intervention in child abuse cases together with the management of juvenile offenders and children who are the subject of matrimonial disputes. Finally, another voluntary agency runs a chain of shops which give legal advice to children (Childright 1988).

Discussion

Debate in Europe is likely to continue to focus on the balance struck between the rights of the family and the rights of the child, often described in ways which make these rights seem mutually exclusive. Yet, discussion of the Children Act 1989 and the assumptions on which it is based may inevitably take place primarily in the context of an English legal and child care perspective with less attention given to comparable systems in other European counterparts despite the similarity of concerns posed by the legal requirement to protect children. The Act aims to increase the rights of the child, and make the role of parents more central, and as such it may be seen as reducing the power of the state, and making it more accountable in law. The stress which the Act lays on partnership between individual parents, or between the parents and the local authority, may need careful handling in referrals of child abuse if the child's perspective is not to be lost. Partnership, while highly desirable, is a means to an end, not an end in itself.

Debate in Europe has a different origin. The aftermath of Nazism has ingrained deep suspicion about the power of the state to interfere in people's lives. Germany keeps no registers of abusing parents, because of fear of how they might be used if an equally malevolent government were returned to power. For the same reason agencies are bound by very strict rules of confidentiality and as a result interprofessional cooperation is constrained.

In France there has long been a belief that institutional care, especially if provided compulsorily by the state, is likely to be deeply damaging to children. For example, Masson is very critical of the effect the system has on children. The child is 'set apart' and this in itself constitutes an abuse, encroaching on the child's self esteem and individuality (Masson 1980).

This criticism is echoed by René Clément, who is a psychologist working for a Direction Départmentale des Affaires Sanitaires et Sociales, the French equivalent of a Social Services Department. He argues that the act of splitting parents and children is an act of violence carried out by an organisation whose brief is to cure. It is made more distressing by the fact that such violence is sometimes inevitable in the absence of a clear alternative treatment (Clément 1981).

While, periodically, inquiries into institutional damage to children reach the headlines in England, for example the Curtis Committee (1946), the Court Lees Inquiry (1967) and more recently the 'pin-down' Inquiry (Staffordshire 1991), in England these events seem to remain peripheral to discussing the morality of how allegedly abusing parents or those entrusted with the care of children are treated, the consequences for the children, and the capacity of the state, as personified by the social worker, to police them. The stress on partnership in the Children Act 1989 and the requirement to present plans to the court that will justify the making of an order will certainly reduce the numbers of children who are compulsorily removed from home. This should release resources to increase provision to 'children in need'. If the services provided are more attractive to parents and children, both of whom now have greater rights to seek them, then the number of children who receive help should increase. Sometimes this help will take the form of provision of accommodation by the local authority. Even though the total number of children living away from their parents may not fall, a smaller proportion are likely to be subject to a care order, thereby increasing the chances for voluntary cooperation between the local authority and families.

The success of the Act in improving the public and private circumstances of children subject to child abuse and in need of child protection will depend, in part, on the resources made available. If additional resources are not provided, then the increased safeguards of parents' rights when, for example, Emergency Protection Orders are sought, may lead to more children suffering fatal or very serious abuse. Local authorities may also be forced to divert more resources to those parents and children who have exercised their increased rights under complaints procedures or ultimately in the courts. So also the success of the Act will depend on a change in professional attitudes. It is essential that social workers embrace the notion of partnership, working with parents and giving children their say, so that they as professionals will come to be seen as allies, rather than as enemies. Without this alignment child protection work may become even more difficult with increases in the number of litigations and a growing reliance on adversarial methods of conflict resolution. Fully resourced and implemented, the Children Act 1989 should ensure a better level of service to more abused children, paving the way for local authorities to assist parents in caring for and protecting their own children.

References

Aucante, M. and Verdier, P. (1990) *On ne m'a demande mon avis.* Paris: Editions Robert Laffont.

Brown, A. (1984) 'Swedish motherhood'. *The Spectator,* 2 June.

Caffo, E. (1983) 'The importance of early intervention for the prevention of child abuse', in Leavitt, J. (ed), *Child Abuse and Neglect: Research and Innovation.* The Hague: NATO AS1 Series, Martinus Nijhoff Publishers.

Childright (1988) *Shopping for Rights 47,* 18–19.

Clément, R. (1981) 'Objects de soin et de mesures..ou personnes en devenir', in Dolto, F., Rapoport, R. and Thuis, B. *Enfance en Souffrance.* Paris: Stock/Laurence Pernoud.

Cleveland Report (1988) *Report of the Inquiry into Child Abuse in Cleveland 1987.* Right Hon. Lord Justice Butler-Sloss (Chairman). London: HMSO.

Court Lees Approved School – Administration of Punishment (1967). Home Office: Cmnd 3397.

Curtis, Lady (1946) *Care of Children Committee.* Home Office: Cmnd 6922.

Dale, P. *et al.* (1986) *Dangerous Families: Assessment and Treatment of Child Abuse.* London: Tavistock.

Dean, M. (1989) 'The Dutch dilemma'. *The Guardian,* 15 May.

Department of Health (1991a) Guidance and Regulations vol 1 Court Orders, para 3(12) 22.

Department of Health (1991b) Guidance and Regulations vol 3. London: HMSO para 5.35.

Department of Health (1991c) Guidance and Regulations vol 4. London: HMSO chapter 5.

DHSS (1974) *Report of the Committee of Inquiry into the Care and Supervision Provided in Relation to Maria Colwell.* London: HMSO.

Girodet, D. (1989) 'Prevention and protection in France', in Davies, M. and Sale, A. (eds) *Child Protection in Europe.* London: NSPCC.

Grinde, T.V. (1987) 'Child welfare in the Nordic countries'. *Child Abuse Review 1(17),* 14–20.

Koers (1981) *Kindermishandeling.* Rotterdam: A.D. Donker.

Masson, A. (1980) *Mainmise sur l'Enfance: Genèse de la Normatique.* Paris: Payout.

Merrick, J. (1989) 'Prevention and protection in Europe', in Davies, M. and Sale, A. (eds) *Child Protection in Europe.* London: NSPCC.

Ministère des Affaires Sociales et de la Solidarité Sociales (1987) *50000 Enfants sont Maltraités.* Paris: Comité Français d'Éducation pour la Santé.

Moore, J. (1985) *An ABC of Child Abuse Work.* Aldershot: Gower Publishing.

Parton, N. (1985) *The Politics of Child Abuse.* London: Macmillan.

Staffordshire (1991) *The Pin Down Experience and the Protection of Children – the Report of the Staffordshire Child Care Inquiry.* Staffordshire Libraries.

Staines, D. (1991) 'The dawning of a new era'. *Community Care 26*, September.

Chapter 9

Children's Hearings – A Legal Perspective After Orkney

Joe Thomson

Introduction

Since its inception over 20 years ago, the Scottish system of child care law has been considered by many as a model of an enlightened approach to both the treatment of juvenile offenders and children in need of care. Based on the recommendations of the Kilbrandon Report,[1] the system was instituted by the Social Work (Scotland) Act 1968. The Act set up children's hearings where lay people with knowledge and experience of children determine how children in need of care are to receive the help they require. Crucial to the system is the reporter whose task is to decide whether a child requires compulsory measures of care and who takes the case before the children's hearing. However, the system attempts to recognise the importance of family autonomy by insisting that a children's hearing cannot proceed to the disposal of a case unless the parents and child accept that one or more grounds exist which are indicative that the child is in need of compulsory measures of care (a ground of referral). When the parents or child do not accept the ground of referral, if there are to be further proceedings the reporter must take the case before the sheriff: only at this stage do the traditional courts play a part in the system. If the ground of referral is established by evidence, the case is then remitted by the sheriff to the children's hearing for disposal.

The whole ethos of the system is to enable children who are in need of care as a result of family problems to receive the help they require. It is undoubtedly a 'welfare' based system. Yet the Social Work (Scotland) Act 1968 provides a system of procedural checks designed to balance the legitimate interests of the

---

1   Cmnd 2306.

State in ensuring that children receive the care which they require and the legitimate interests of parents to bring up their children and of children to be with their parents. The events in Orkney have given some cause for concern whether the 'balance' achieved by the Social Work (Scotland) Act 1968 is satisfactory. The purpose of this paper is to consider whether this concern is justified. But before doing so, it is essential to give an outline of the children's hearing system and the grounds of referral.

The children's hearing system

If a child is thought by, for example, a social worker or police officer, to be in need of care, the case is passed to the reporter. The reporter, while an officer of a local authority, acts independently of it. The reporter may have a legal background but this is not essential. It is the reporter's duty to investigate the case. Once this initial investigation has taken place, several courses of action are open to the reporter. First, the reporter could take the view that no further action is required. Secondly, the reporter may consider that the family is able to cope with social work support, i.e. that the child will be able to receive the care he or she requires on a voluntary basis. If, however, the reporter thinks that the child requires compulsory measures of care, he/she must arrange a children's hearing to consider the case.[2] The reporter can also call upon the local authority social services department to provide a social background report.

In every local authority there is a children's panel made up of persons with a knowledge of or interest in social work and child care.[3] It cannot be emphasised enough that members of the panel are lay people, reflecting the views of society in general as to the nature of child care.[4] The children's hearing consists of three members of the panel, one of whom acts as a chairman:[5] both a man and a woman must be among the members.[6]

A children's hearing is not a court, nor are its proceedings intended to be formal. Instead, the proceedings are deliberately informal and conducted in private. The child and the parents are present and are not usually legally represented. The reporter will also be present and there can be representatives

---

2   Social Work (Scotland) Act 1968, S39(3). (References are to the 1968 Act unless otherwise stated).

3   Persons are appointed to the panel by the Secretary of State after a stringent selection process and training: S33(1).

4   But difficulty has been experienced in obtaining the services of persons in social groups (d) and (e).

5   The chairman may but does not require to have a legal background.

6   S34(1) and (2).

from the social work department. The rationale of the system is to enable the hearing to reach the decision which is best for the child. While this informality is probably desirable at the disposal stage, i.e. when the hearing considers what steps should be taken to help the child and his/her family, the advantages of procedural informality are less obvious at the earlier stages of the process.

Grounds of referral

Before a child[7] can be considered to be in need of compulsory measures of care, the reporter must take the view that one or more of the following 'grounds of referral' are applicable. These are listed in S32(2) of the 1968 Act viz:

(a) the child is beyond the control of his or her parents; or

(b) the child is falling into bad associations or is exposed to moral danger; or

(c) lack of parental care is likely to cause the child unnecessary suffering or seriously to impair the child's health or development; or

(d) the child is a victim of a Schedule 1 offence[8] or the child is a member of the same household as a child who has been a victim of a Schedule 1 offence; or

(e) the child is, or is likely to become, a member of the same household as a person who has committed a Schedule 1 offence; or

(f) in the case of a female child, she is a member of the same household as a female who has been the victim of the crime of incest which was committed by a member of the same household; or

(g) the child has failed to attend school regularly without reasonable excuse; or

(h) the child has committed an offence; or

(i) the child has misused a volatile substance; or

---

7   Child is usually a person under the age of 16: S30(1)(a).
8   i.e. an offence listed in Schedule 1 to the Criminal Procedure (Scotland) Act 1975.

(j) the child has absconded from a place of safety or the control of a person under whom he has been placed by a supervision requirement;[9] or

(k) the child is already in the care of a local authority and his behaviour is such that special measures are required for his adequate care and control.

Several points should be noticed. First, the Social Work (Scotland) Act 1968 proceeds on the basis that if a child has committed a criminal offence this is symptomatic of the child's failure to develop social skills: this failure will often be the result of difficulties in the child's family. The child who commits an offence is therefore in need of measures of care, not punishment. This welfare-based approach to the problem of juvenile crime is an axiomatic tenet of the system. Accordingly, the juvenile offender is treated in exactly the same way as any other child in need of care. This ground of referral was probably the most controversial aspect of the Social Work (Scotland) Act 1968.[10] For many years it was the ground upon which most referrals were brought.

Cases of abuse

This position is now changing. More and more cases are concerned with children who have been physically and sexually abused. In this situation, several grounds of referral are open to the reporter. In the case of neglect, the relevant ground is (c) above: the test whether lack of parental care is likely to cause a child unnecessary suffering or seriously impair a child's health or development is objective, i.e. whether a reasonable person would draw such an inference from the nature and extent of the parental care.[11] When there has been a physical or sexual assault on the child, the relevant ground is (d) above.[12] Schedule 1 offences include those concerned with physical and sexual abuse of a child. But it is important to note that the ground is applicable if, as a matter

---

9   On supervision requirements, see *infra* pp.171.

10   See, for example, Martin, F.M. and Murray, K. (1982) *The Scottish Juvenile Justice System.* Edinburgh: Scottish Academic Press; Asquith, S. (1983) *Children and Justice.* Edinburgh: Edinburgh University Press.

11   *M v. McGregor* 1982 *Scots Law Times* (SLT) 41; see also *Finlayson (Applicant)* 1989 SCLR 601 where the ground was established even although the parents' refusal to allow conventional medical treatment on their haemophilic child was the result of concern that the child might thereby contract AIDS.

12   It will also be noted that grounds exist when the child concerned has not been assaulted but lives in the same household as another child who has been assaulted or a person who has been convicted of a Schedule 1 offence.

of fact, the child has been a victim of an offence: there is no need to identify, let alone convict, an alleged perpetrator. Thus the scope of the ground is wide.

Another possibility is ground (a) above: moral danger is established if the child's parents or friends are prostitutes, drug addicts, alcoholics, homosexuals or members of occult organisations.[13]

If the parents and child accept that the ground of referral exists, the hearing will consider how best to dispose of the case. But if the parent or child does not accept the ground of referral, unless it is prepared to discharge the referral there and then, the hearing must direct the reporter to make an application to the sheriff for a finding whether the grounds of referral are established.[14] An application must also be made to the sheriff if the child is too young to understand what is involved and cannot therefore accept the ground.[15]

The application is heard by the sheriff within 28 days of being lodged. The child must be present[16] and the child and the parents can be legally represented. These are legal proceedings. If the sheriff decides that none of the grounds of referral has been established, he will dismiss the application and discharge the referral: if the sheriff is satisfied that any of the grounds of referral has been established, he will remit the case to the reporter to make arrangements for the children's hearing to consider and determine the case. The ground must be established by evidence. When the ground is that the child has committed an offence, the sheriff must apply the standard of proof required in criminal procedure, i.e. he must be satisfied beyond reasonable doubt that the child committed the offence and corroboration is necessary. But in relation to the other grounds, it is sufficient that the sheriff is satisfied on the balance of probabilities that the ground exists and corroboration is not required.[17]

This is particularly important when the alleged ground is that the child has been a victim of a Schedule 1 offence. In Harris v. F,[18] the Inner House of the Court of Session held that the ground was established on the balance of probabilities even where the alleged perpetrator was identified: the fact that the alleged perpetrator might subsequently be acquitted in criminal proceed-

---

13   See, for example, *B v. Kennedy* 1987 *SLT* 765.
14   S42(2)(c).
15   S42(7): but if the ground is accepted by the child's parents, the sheriff may dispose with the hearing of evidence if satisfied that in all the circumstances it would be reasonable to do so.
16   S42(3).
17   S1(1) of the Civil Evidence (Scotland) Act 1988.
18   1991 *SLT* 242.

ings because it cannot be proved beyond reasonable doubt that he committed the offence is irrelevant: 'Protection of the child is, in my opinion, a justification for applying the lower standard of proof...and it still is a justification even if the person concerned is ultimately acquitted of the offence in the criminal courts'.[19] Moreover, the sheriff can proceed to make a determination, even if criminal proceedings are pending against the alleged perpetrator of the offence.[20]

It will, therefore, be clear that the need to protect the child – which is the whole purpose of the legislation – overrides the civil liberties of the alleged perpetrator of a Schedule 1 offence. And, it must also be remembered, that the ground can be established even if the perpetrator of the offence is unknown and unlikely to be discovered.

If the parents and child have accepted the grounds of referral or the grounds of referral have been established in proceedings before the sheriff, the children's hearing can then dispose of the case. The hearing will have social background reports and other information. The hearing will endeavour to provide the course of action which is in the best interests of the child. The hearings have a wide range of powers including the right to make a supervision requirement requiring the child to submit to supervision by a social worker or to reside in a residential establishment or with foster parents. The hearing can also attach detailed conditions to the requirement, for example, as to access by the parents to the child when he/she is in local authority care. The supervision requirement is subject to review by the children's hearing. Moreover an appeal is competent to the sheriff not only in relation to the making of the supervision requirement itself but also any conditions laid down in it. If the sheriff is satisfied that the decision of the children's hearing is not justified, he will remit the case to the children's hearing with his reasons but he cannot give the hearing directions on the steps they should take when reconsidering the case.[21]

Two further procedural matters fall to be considered. First, the Act provides emergency procedures which enable a child to be taken to a place of safety. By S37(2) a police constable or any person authorised by a court or justice of the peace, may take a child to a place of safety *inter alia* on the ground that the child has been or is believed to have been a victim of a Schedule 1 offence. While a child can be detained in a place of safety for up to seven days, it is the duty of

---

19   *Ibid per* Lord Justice Clerk (Ross) at 246.

20   *Ferguson v. P* 1989 *SLT* 681.

21   *Kennedy v. A* 1986 *SLT* 358.

the reporter as soon as he/she has been informed to arrange a children's hearing to sit not later than the first lawful day after the commencement of the child's detention. If the children's hearing is unable to dispose of the case, the hearing can issue a warrant requiring the child to be detained in a place of safety for up to 21 days.[22] This warrant can be renewed only once. There is an appeal to the sheriff from the decision of the children's hearing to issue such a warrant.[23] It was envisaged that place of safety orders would be used only in emergency situations where steps had to be taken quickly in order to protect a child who is in danger: and because the effect of the order is drastic, the child's case must be taken to a children's hearing as soon as possible.

Second, it is an important feature of the system that the parents and child are present at every stage of the proceedings. This is to protect the interests of both the parents and the child. However, S40(2) provides that where a children's hearing is satisfied that it would be detrimental to the child to be present when the case is being heard, the case can be considered in the child's absence. Once again it was envisaged that this would be used only in exceptional cases when, for example, the child had been seriously assaulted by a parent and would be terrified to be present in the same room.

This section of the paper has attempted to give an outline of the legal framework in which children's hearings operate. While based on the welfare of the child, the Social Work (Scotland) Act 1968 appeared to provide a system of procedural checks and balances whereby the State's – legitimate – power to intervene to protect children was regulated in the interests of family autonomy. This was largely achieved by the carefully structured interplay between children, parents, reporters, children's hearings and courts laid down in the 1968 Act. The system appeared to work well, at least in so far as it was not thought that the statutory powers enjoyed by child care agencies under the Act constituted a serious threat to parental and children's rights. How far has the confidence placed in the system been undermined by the events in Orkney?

Sloan v. B[24] – the Orkney case

In this section, it is intended to discuss the legal issues raised by the Orkney case. It is hoped that such a discussion may demonstrate how far – if at all – the children's hearing system outlined above fails to hold an acceptable balance

---

22   S37(4).
23   S49.
24   1991 *SLT* 530.

between the State's powers and family autonomy. This is, of course, only considered from a legal perspective.

Before the legal issues can be addressed, it is necessary to give an outline of the facts of the case. Children were removed from their families in South Ronaldsay and taken to the mainland under place of safety warrants granted by a sheriff in Orkney. When a children's hearing was convened, they decided to exercise their discretion and hear the case in the absence of the children.[25] The hearing then issued a warrant for the further detention of the children in a place of safety. The parents refused to accept the grounds of referral which involved allegations of Schedule 1 offences and, accordingly, the hearing directed the reporter to make an application to a sheriff for a finding as to whether the grounds of referral were established. On appeal, it was held that the children's hearing had grounds for issuing the warrant and that the decision to proceed in the absence of the children was justified.[26] After 21 days, the place of safety warrants were renewed by the hearing and again an appeal was unsuccessful. Finally, the proceedings began before Sheriff Kelbie in respect of whether or not the grounds were established: after hearing legal argument, but without hearing the evidence, the sheriff dismissed the application on the ground that the proceedings were incompetent. In his view, the applications were 'fundamentally flawed' as the children's hearing had directed the reporter to make the application without the children having had an opportunity to accept or dispute the ground of referral. An appeal was then made to the Inner House of the Court of Session.

The Lord President (Hope) held that the sheriff had no power to dismiss the proceedings on the ground of procedural irregularities without having first heard the evidence which was to be led. In other words, the sheriff must determine whether, in the light of the evidence, the ground of referral has been established: only then can an issue of competency be raised. The purpose of care proceedings is to help the child: a child prima facie requires measures of care if a ground of referral is established. Complex legal technicalities such as issues of competency must not be allowed to prevent a child from receiving the care which he needs. Once again, concern for the welfare of the child underpins the statutory procedures.

The Lord President (Hope) then went on to consider whether or not the proceedings were 'fundamentally flawed' because the children had never been

---

25   i.e. by virtue of their powers under S40(2), discussed *supra*.

26   An application was then made to the Inner House of the Court of Session to allow the children to give evidence before the sheriff on the mainland, rather than in Orkney.

given the opportunity to accept or reject the grounds of referral before the children's hearing. As we have seen, it is axiomatic that a children's hearing cannot proceed with a case unless the grounds of referral are accepted by the parents and the child: if either the parent or the child does not accept the ground of referral, Section 42 provides that the reporter must take the case to the sheriff for a finding whether or not the ground of referral is established. Only if the ground is established can the children's hearing make a disposal. Thus it would appear that the children should have had the opportunity to accept or reject the ground of referral. But this is to ignore S40(2) which gives the children's hearing discretion to dispense with the presence of the children at the hearing when it is in the children's best interests to do so. However, it is expressly stated in the Act that S40(2) is subject to S42(1), which provides that at the outset the chairman of the hearing should explain the ground of referral to the parent and the child, thus presupposing that the child is present. But the Lord President (Hope) held that the children's hearing could dispense with the children's presence in spite of S42(1), provided the purpose of S42(1) was not undermined. The purpose of S42(1) was to protect the child by providing an opportunity to both the parents and the child to dispute the ground of referral: if the ground were not accepted by either the parent or the child, proceedings would then have to be brought for a finding by the sheriff. But that purpose would still be achieved in the absence of the child, provided the parents disputed the ground. In these circumstances, proceedings would still have to take place before the sheriff, even although the children had not been given the opportunity to accept or reject the ground of referral: the child's acceptance or refusal 'could add nothing to what had occurred already to make it necessary for there to be a direction to the reporter to make an application [to the sheriff]...'.[27] Consequently, provided the parents dispute the ground of referral, the child still obtains the protection given by S42: the child's rights would only be prejudiced if the parents accepted the ground of referral. If the parents did so, the proceedings would have to be postponed until the children were given the opportunity to be heard. In the Orkney case, the parents had, of course, disputed the ground of referral and the case had been referred to a sheriff for a finding: accordingly, the children had not been prejudiced by the decision that they should not be present at the hearing, a decision which had been taken in their best interests.

---

27   *Sloan v. B* 1991 SLT 530 *per* Lord President (Hope) at 548.

It is the present writer's view that the approach taken by the Inner House was entirely justified.[28] In the usual case, the children and the parents would be present at the hearing: but if the S40(2) direction was properly exercised and it would be against the children's interests to be present, for example, if the children were terrified of their parents, it would defeat the purpose of S40(2) if the presence of the children was mandatory when the ground of referral was presented to the parents. Lord Hope solves the problem by arguing that the children need not be present provided the parents refuse to accept the ground of referral, thus triggering the proceedings before the sheriff which are required under the Act for the protection of the rights of the parents and the child.

The decision of the Inner House in Sloan v. B[29] is again an example of the courts attempting to further the welfare of the child which underlies the 1968 Act. It is the role of the judiciary under the British constitution to interpret the language of a statute so as to further the evident purpose of the legislation. This was what was done in the Orkney case. However, the Scottish system of child care depends ultimately on the professionalism of reporters and social workers and the sensitivity and common sense of members of the children's panels to determine what course of action furthers the welfare of a child in a particular case. It is for the inquiry under the chairmanship of Lord Clyde to discover whether these were lacking in the Orkney case.

In so far as the legal issues which were raised are concerned, few would argue that a children's hearing should not have discretion to consider a case in the absence of the child. This is a valuable power provided the discretion is exercised properly. As the Lord President (Hope) emphasised, the S40(2) discretion is intended to be used for the benefit of the child. The 1968 Act does not expressly provide a mechanism for review of the children's hearing's decision to dispense with the children's attendance at the hearing. Generally, we must therefore trust the bona fides of the members of the hearing that it is in fact in the child's best interests to do so. In a case of blatant abuse of the children's hearing's power, it would be possible to seek judicial review of the decision. But, as we have seen in the Orkney case, the children were not prejudiced by not being present at the hearing, as their parents had disputed the ground of referral.

While not an issue in the appeal to the Inner House, one important matter calls for comment. The children in this case were taken into care by virtue of

---

28   For full discussion, see Thomson, J.M. *'Sloan v. B* – the Legal Issues' 1991 *SLT* (News) 421.

29   1991 *SLT* 530.

place of safety orders. The statutory procedures were followed and the place of safety warrants were duly issued by the children's hearing. The parents exercised their rights to appeal from these decisions and the appeals were lost. While the procedural safeguards were followed, there remains concern among some sections of the public that parents can lose the custody of their children in this way. In the present writer's view, it is difficult to see what further legal procedures could prevent injustice arising. A place of safety order cannot lawfully be made unless the grounds exist and the children's hearing must be convinced that it is in the child's best interests that detention continue. This would appear to have been the hearing's view in this case and, on appeal, it was held that they had grounds for taking this view. Again, one must inevitably trust the bona fides of the reporter, panel members and the judiciary. However, some fears could perhaps be allayed if, in deciding whether to issue a warrant for the continued detention of a child, it was a mandatory requirement that the children's hearing should see the child, when the child had sufficient maturity to understand the nature of the proceedings.

Conclusion

The Orkney case raised important legal issues. The decision of the Inner House confirmed that the system was not structurally flawed. The case also illustrates the limits of the law in the child care system. While procedural checks and balances attempt to reconcile the interests of the State in intervention and the civil rights of parents and children, inevitably these procedural safeguards are limited.

In the Scottish system, the major protection of the civil rights of parents and children is the requirement that they must accept the ground of referral: if not, then the case cannot proceed unless the ground of referral is established in a court of law. Because of the sheriff's approach to the competency issue, this was not done in the Orkney case; though if, after the appeal, the reporter had wished to continue with the proceedings, the ground of referral would have to have been established. The disquiet in the case largely stemmed from the use of emergency procedures viz the place of safety warrants, and the decision to dispense with the presence of the children at the hearing. Unless we are to argue that these powers should not exist, inevitably we must trust the professionalism of the reporters and social workers and the common sense of panel members to exercise the powers properly. The legal safeguards – for example, an appeal from the children's hearing's decision to issue warrants for the detention of the child – only operate to prevent blatant abuse, i.e. when the decision to do so is one which no reasonable children's hearing could lawfully reach. The appeal court cannot simply review the merits of the decision. Given the emergency nature of these provisions and the fact that the parents and children retain their rights to dispute the ground of referral, is a risk of occasional injustice one society should accept given the need in emergencies to prevent serious harm to children? If the situation in Orkney was not such an emergency and the procedures should not have been used, only time and the Clyde inquiry will tell.

A final comment. Some of the children in the Orkney case were mature minors. It is a serious criticism that their views were not heard at any stage in the process. They could, in my view, have exercised a right to be heard by seeking access to their parents under S3 of the Law Reform (Parent and Child)(Scotland) Act 1986, since, in spite of the place of safety warrants, the children retained their prima facie rights to see their parents. As I have suggested, if a child is sufficiently mature, whatever the technical legal position, it is surely incumbent on the children's hearing to see a child and seek his/her views: if this had been done, much of the trauma surrounding the Orkney case could, perhaps, have been avoided.

It is thought that the basic premises upon which the children's hearing system in Scotland is built remain valid in spite of the events in Orkney. Indeed, compared to the difficulties experienced south of the border, the strengths of the Scottish system appear to be vindicated. No system is perfect and some – relatively modest – changes to the Scottish system have been suggested in this paper. Indeed, the criticism remains that the grounds of referral may still appear to be largely reactive – inhibiting prevention of abuse in the first place. On the other hand, family autonomy remains an ideal in our society and the grounds of referral reflect this concern. The major lesson of the Orkney case is that the whole system ultimately turns on the professionalism and integrity of those involved, social workers, reporters, judiciary and panel members. The case illustrates the limits of legal regulation of the exercise by them of the discretionary powers which are inevitable in any system of child care law. But the room for abuse, such as it is, would be even further diminished if the views of the children at the centre of the case were always taken into account when the children are sufficiently mature to understand the nature and purpose of the proceedings.

Chapter 10

Discrimination in Child Protection Services
The Need for Change

Robin Clark

In August 1990 a two-year-old boy died in Victoria, Australia, within a few weeks of his case having been referred to Child Protection Services. He died as a result of severe abdominal trauma allegedly inflicted by the partner of the mother. The partner was subsequently charged with manslaughter.

The family was well known at the local medical clinic and the mother had been attending a local counsellor regularly for help with her own personal problems. In the two months before his death as many as eight professionals were involved.

For those acquainted with the circumstances of the young boy's death there was a sense of disbelief. This was not an isolated family unknown to health and welfare services. Statutory Protective Services were responsible for investigating family circumstances and for assessing the child's well-being. Yet, the child died. Accountability was laid at the door of state services for their apparent failure to protect him. The public noted the substantial increases in funding for child protection services. A sophisticated electronic children-at-risk register, a 24-hour crisis service and a protective service workforce greatly strengthened in numbers and offered considerable training, apparently failed to provide the answer. Although in this case the main investigators were police officers, the history is similar to many where social workers have been involved.

This chapter seeks to analyse critically the Victoria Child Protection Program in Australia. The tendency of child protective services to unfavourably single out poor families in child abuse decision making is argued. This criticism is not unique to Australian social services. The Victorian service is modelled on a system which has become the standard answer of many governments to child abuse and neglect. At the heart of the system are child protection workers, who are charged with responsibility to make judgements and to act on behalf of the community to protect children. In 1990 police officers and social workers in the Victorian State Community Services Department were authorised to investigate and respond to referrals of child abuse. In this context it seems appropriate to highlight expectations placed on professionals in child protection; to examine how reasonable these expectations are; and, to debate their fairness and suitability when so many of the beneficiaries of child protection services face major social adversity.

Victoria child protection data

Victoria, a southern Australian state, has a population of approximately four million and a child population (birth to 17 years) of about one million. Despite popular descriptions of Australia as 'the lucky country', in Victoria in 1990 some 8 per cent of children were from families living in poverty. Similar to other urbanised societies, a growing number of adolescents were living on the streets without hope of a better future. Many of these children and young people were in public care.

Although Victoria was late in developing a coherent child protection policy, over the last decade ground has been gained and a protective service similar to those in Britain and the United States of America firmly established. Reporting of child abuse and neglect is not mandatory as in the United States, rather, any individual 'may' report in good faith a suspected case of abuse or neglect. Education programmes designed to encourage reporting have increased referrals to the Victoria service by a factor of eight in the past six years. The number of referrals to the service in 1990 was approximately 1 per cent of the child population. Although 9165 children were referred, only 25 per cent of cases were substantiated leading to the child's registration on the At Risk register. Roycroft (1987) reports that English authorities investigate four times as many cases as are registered, and Besharov (1986) has raised concern at the large number of unsubstantiated cases which flood the system in the United States, potentially distracting attention from those children most in need.

Of all cases registered in Victoria in 1990 only 3.9 per cent of children were defined by protective workers as severely at risk; 27.9 per cent as significantly at risk; and 68.2 per cent moderately at risk. While professionals use a standard classification guide the risk level registered is the subjective judgement of the protective worker.

Protective services initially were set up to respond to endangered children. Referral patterns and information on registrations in Victoria suggest a divergence from this original objective. There is now mounting evidence that the present direction of protective services in many parts of the world is seriously flawed for three reasons. These include confusion about the target population; interpretation of register statistics; and assumptions about the nature of the problem itself.

The target population

The private nature of the problem of child abuse makes it difficult to accurately establish its extent. Statistics show a significant increase in the number of children reported to child protection authorities (Birchall 1989). This rise is variously interpreted as a rise in domestic violence generally, a change in society's tolerance of violence towards children or of more sophisticated case finding procedures. It may also suggest, however, a more fundamental problem: a redefinition of family problems as child abuse.

An examination of the Victoria data shows that approximately 50 per cent of all registrations are for emotional abuse and neglect. Despite attempts to tighten definitions, these categories, particularly emotional abuse, appear to be indiscriminately used. It could be argued that child protection workers, by virtue of their training and professional orientation, find it difficult to walk away from what seems less than satisfactory child rearing. When there is no way of predicting whether a particular parent's behaviour will result in severe harm to the child practitioners may opt for caution and register. It seems in a number of cases it is not the severity of abuse which prompts registration, but professional anxiety.

Young and Brooks (1989) analysed case reports of all children reported in New South Wales in 1987 and concluded that only a small proportion of children registered suffered severe maltreatment. A further Australian study by Monnone, Craig, Barry and Young (1989) of a random sample of registered cases of emotional abuse revealed general patterns of poor child care but in only half the cases actual abuse of the child was cited as of concern. The authors conclude that many cases are registered because parents are experiencing difficulties rather than independent evidence of abusive behaviour toward or of harm suffered by the child. Monnone *et al.* recommend that such families should be offered services without having to undergo a formal notification and consequent investigation with the possible loss of good faith these procedures may evoke.

These findings are not peculiar to Australia. Besharov (1987) and Pitcairn, Waterhouse *et al.* (1993) have commented on similar trends in the USA and Scotland respectively. The domain of child welfare appears to be growing as a consequence of changing definitions of abuse. The tendency for child protection registration to become the main response to general concerns about parent–child relations is problematic. Not only does this tendency fail to distinguish families urgently in need of help where child safety is threatened, but may also serve to heighten anxiety and conflict amongst parents, children and professionals.

Referral rates or 'recycling'?

Register statistics frequently confuse incidence (number of new reports), and prevalence (number of children affected) (Burgdoff and Edmonds 1980). Knudsen (1989) studied 8000 reports over 19 years in a county in Indiana, USA, and found in any calendar year at least 40 per cent of all reports concerned children already known to child protective services, and of these multiple reports, 10–15 per cent involved a child reported earlier in the same year. While this level of re-reporting raises questions about the adequacy of earlier intervention, Claburn, Magura and Cheziak (1977) in their retrospective study of families under the supervision of the State Department in the USA found that prior experience with the child welfare system was the strongest single predictor for re-opening a case. This repeated recycling of children through the child welfare system suggests that families already known to social work services may be subject to a level of continuing surveillance and suspicion which goes beyond the personal to a political dimension whereby control may be excerised unnevenly by the state over families. Are there some families whose social credit has run out?

Understanding the nature of child abuse

Causation

Child protection services on the one hand seem elaborate and sophisticated, while on the other costly and potentially discriminatory and not discriminating enough. Despite organisational systems for managing child abuse the cause of the problem is poorly understood. There are studies which emphasise the individual psychological pathology of parents (Kempe and Helfer 1972). A further common explanation is the theory that abusing parents were themselves abused. A review of the literature, however, casts serious doubt on the validity of the evidence (Jayaratne 1977; Kadushin 1974; Benjamin 1980; Kauf-

man and Zigler 1987) and calls into question much of the research which
purports to establish this transmission theory. Kaufman and Zigler (1987)
criticise Steele and Pollack's (1968) widely reported study for their lack of
specificity about the history of abuse, and they conclude that the apparent
effects of childhood abuse upon subsequent parenting cannot be separated
from the effects of poverty, stress and social isolation. Gil's (1970) research
found an over concentration of physical abuse among the poor and socially
isolated minorities suggesting that social and economic conditions may be
contributory factors both directly and indirectly in the public processes of
identification.

Prediction

In the medical sciences the usual response to a new disease follows a path of
isolating the cause. This model has proved seductive to social scientists and
frequently in child abuse practitioners and policy makers call for predictive
studies.

In the USA and to a lesser extent the United Kingdom efforts have been
made to identify populations most at risk of harming their children. Caplan,
Walters, White, Parry and Bates (1984) investigated similarities and differences
in families whose children had been abused. Their findings, not different from
those in other studies (Cichatti, Tarddson and Egeland 1978; Jason and Andereck 1983), noted that abusing parents are not a homogeneous group. Poverty
and unemployment as general conditions fail to predict which poor or unemployed families are vulnerable. Cohn and Garbarino (1982) are of the view that
in developing prevention strategies it is not feasible to offer sources of support
only to high risk groups because who they are remains unclear.

Given the difficulties of defining child abuse and of determining its extent,
it is not surprising that the reliance on a quasi scientific approach to determining
the causes of child abuse has been problematic. The sophisticated methods for
isolating single elements to determine causation in the physical sciences can
rarely be applied in the social sciences, with the result that questions of
causation are usually answered by reference to association between variables.
Simpkins (1984) conceptualised the different variables potentially relevant to
child abuse and concluded that positive associations were found between all
the variables in all the categories. It is this aspect of the problem which has led
Cohn and Garbarino (1982) to observe that who abuses and neglects is clearer
than why. Parton (1985) adds that even when abuse is known to have occurred,
the frequency and implications for the children remain unclear.

Child protection services and poor families

Research (Besharov 1987; Edgar 1988; Whittaker and Garbarino 1983) questions whether there is a major risk of child protective services becoming a universal response to poverty and all the misfortunes which usually accompany it. Some practitioners have argued that child abuse crosses class boundaries. This assertion is difficult to support when widespread public awareness campaigns have increased the number of reported cases and yet, the distribution between socio-economic classes has not altered (Pelton 1981). In Victoria, Australia (Statistics Department of Community Services, Victoria 1989) 56 per cent of all children registered were from families on a social security pension or benefit and a further 17.5 per cent were on the lowest income level. Almost 75 per cent, then, of all children registered in Victoria in 1990 could be classified as coming from poor families.

Information gathered in New South Wales presents a similar profile. A study by Young, Baker and Monnone (1989) revealed that reports of child abuse and neglect were nearly six times higher in poor areas. The authors conclude that while children in all socio-economic levels are at risk of abuse, the risk is appreciably higher for children from families living in poverty. Is this the case or is it that the poor are more likely to be reported?

In the United Kingdom, Dingwall, Eekelaar and Murray (1983) tracked decision making processes for a large number of clients referred to local authority social service and social work departments because of child abuse. They argue that while poorer families as a group are proportionately more vulnerable to state intervention, there are additional factors operating which result in only certain families being singled out for compulsory state surveillance of their child rearing practices. Dingwall described these families as those whose 'social credit' with local health and welfare agencies had run out; families who were seen either to have exhausted normal avenues of support or to have exhausted professionals responsible for finding solutions to personal and social problems.

Batten (1988), in examining a sample of child protection cases found that those families more likely to be taken to court were single female headed households where the sole income was a social security pension and where housing also constituted a problem. There is an increasing amount of data (Clark 1989; Monnone *et al.* 1989) supporting Batten's conclusion. Furthermore Creighton (1984) and Greenland (1987) provide evidence from their British studies that families who are socio-economically disadvantaged make up the bulk of registered cases. Additional biases also may be operating in case finding. As Dingwall, Eeklaar and Murray (1983) point out, this is not surprising in an area of work where practitioners must search for some corroboration between the incident, the explanation offered and the demeanor of the adult.

The need for change

As a member of the panel established to inquire into the circumstances of the young boy's untimely death reported at the outset of this chapter, I took part in the interviews of those who had been involved in the case. The inquiry report (Confidential Report of the Ministerial Panel of Inquiry into the death of D.V. 1991) highlights the way in which the investigators, including local medical practitioners, were distracted by the question of blood tests and uncertainty as to whether the child's bruises were the result of a blood disorder. This was an important and relevant question. What was notable, however, was the way the investigators 'marked time', while they waited for what they apparently hoped would be conclusive medical evidence. Dingwall, Eekelaar and Murray (1983) have reported extensively on the tendency for other professionals to defer to doctors in cases of physical abuse. Significant, here, was the failure to provide adequate surveillance of the child while investigation proceeded.

Recent reports of inquiries into the fatal non-accidental injury of children suggest a substantial repetition in the findings and recommendations. The irony is twofold. Governments continue to spend large sums of money on a short term investigative service focused on abuse which is not the main problem for most of the families referred. At the same time, such protective services are limited in their ability to protect the truly endangered child because of the serious difficulties in predicting the likelihood of abuse in individual cases. Why, despite growing calls for change in the approach to service delivery in child protection (Besharov 1987) has so much of the system remained the same?

The role of the media

Kempe's packaging of the problem as 'the battered child syndrome' (Kempe, Silverman, Steele, Drocgemueller and Silver 1962) was masterly in terms of the enduring interest it captured. Presenting the phenomenon of child abuse in these graphic terms enables individuals to distance themselves from such extreme behaviour, while at the same time fuelling public interest in personal tragedies. Those who control the media may recognise that public interest will be lost if the phenomenon of child abuse is portrayed as a social issue with economic and political implications (Nelson 1984; Parton 1985).

The search for a scientific approach

Child abuse and neglect continues to be viewed as a problem of individual children and their families. Socio-economic and political factors when referred to have been used to support this individualism. Since poverty and social isolation are often to be found in association with reported cases of abuse, these factors are sometimes taken as having predictive potential for the single case instead of being judged in terms of how well they explain the phenomenon of abuse and neglect.

Elaborate reporting systems, registers and electronic data bases have given Child Protection Services an illusion of action and control. This apparent science may comfort managers and politicians, leading them to place more faith in the social workers' predictive tools than is justified empirically. A mismatch between the expectation which child protection workers have of themselves and which the public and other professionals have of them and the skills they can reasonably be expected to acquire may result.

Those involved in developing and implementing child protection programmes seek to revise procedures and practice standards, supposedly searching for the error proof instrument of assessment and prediction. While striving for improved practice is essential, the problems should not be minimised. An inquiry into a child's death in New South Wales pointed to 90 points in the management of the case where different judgements might have been made (Lawrence 1982). This finding sits uneasily with a recommendation from a recent major English inquiry (Blom-Cooper 1985), where professionals, especially social workers, are urged to refine techniques for predicting accurately those children who will continue to be at risk of abuse.

Dingwall (1989) warns against the search for the predictive check list because it undermines the place of professional judgment. There may in any given case be enough certainty for action but not enough certainty to make the required course of action absolutely clear. Downie and Loudfoot (1978) also sound a note of caution arguing that the need for practical judgement is inescapable, radically limiting the possibility of expertise. In spite of all this, no other child welfare programme affords the opportunity for storing such detailed information, enabling cross tabulations of family characteristics by all forms of abuse.

Rising public expectations may lead practitioners to gather increasing amounts of information about each family lest they miss some vital clue to an underlying pathology. They are expected to spot the child who is referred today for relatively minor abuse but may be seriously abused tomorrow. More and more families may be added to the register with insufficient attention paid to the outcomes of these decisions for children, parents and professionals.

Child protection workers

A small exploratory study of child protection workers' decision making (Clark 1989) sheds some light on the dilemmas faced by social work practitioners in statutory child protection. Eleven child protection workers randomly selected were interviewed on three separate occasions through the life of a case. While no claim can be made for the general applicability of the study given the small sample, difficulties in prediction and the use of statutory authority clearly emerged.

The child protection workers presented a cross section in terms of age, background and experience. They were clear about the mandate given them by legislation in the child welfare sector, although accounts of their interventions suggested that they were unclear about how this mandate should be translated into practice. In any case, legislative definition is broad and provides only a limited guide. Some workers, then, used the legislative mandate to impose their interpretation of events and force a course of action; others, uncomfortable with their own coercive function sought to re-interpret situations into ones in which the client had voluntarily entered.

While the law provides child protection workers with the authority to take the matter to court, the mandate does not of itself endow workers with a greater capacity to predict risk, nor provide them with the skills needed to reduce the likelihood of risk to the child. There is no body of research to guide their decision-making, with the result that child protection workers found themselves making moral rather than technical or scientific judgements. Given that a large proportion (up to 65%) of cases are referred not because court intervention is necessary, but because of poverty, poor parenting and turbulent relationships, it becomes apparent that families require creative intensive help and support, possibly over long periods. The public, and even child welfare services, however, may expect, once a child is referred for child abuse, that the child's on-going protection is assured and that the processes and procedures associated with child protection referrals will be relevant to the social needs of the child and parents. In this context, given the nature of the task, the physical danger and the high personal, professional and political cost of error, it is not surprising that practitioners went about their task in such a way as to reduce anxiety and uncertainty.

Finally, it was evident that some workers behaved in a way which Campbell (1987) described as 'bureaupathic'. In their efforts to impose some coherence on a situation which they found difficult to understand or control, some workers forced their case practice with families into a highly bureaucratic form. Given the difficulty which child protection workers encounter in reconciling the rights of children with those of their parents, an emphasis on 'due process' is understandable. Such an approach may provide a kind of false bureaucratic security, may diminish the risk and burden of 'moral' interpretation, yet may ultimately prohibit change in a system found wanting.

Implications for policy and practice

Has the recent expansion of child protection services resulted in more effective interventions or, instead, the unfair labelling of certain groups of families as abusive or neglectful of their children? Have child protection services merely extended the arm of the state? Has the introduction of child abuse programmes enabled governments to avoid addressing the complex social factors which underpin a whole range of conditions which families, especially poorer families encounter? How might a new approach to the social problem of child abuse be cast?

Any new approach must be underpinned by a change in public attitudes to violence generally in the community and a greater consensus about when state intervention is truly necessary. The focus of services needs to move away from the individual child and family and onto the development of more durable support systems. Improved social security measures, together with more accessible health services, family supports and education are required. The role of prevention needs to be carefully addressed so that it becomes part of an integrated strategy of support for children and parents.

In the present economic climate the way ahead for achieving change is difficult but not impossible. To wait for large scale social reform is no solution. Some steps, however, might be taken now to begin a process of reform which may improve public understanding of child abuse and may ensure that child protection services cease to be used as a means of dealing with the many social ills which afflict children and parents.

1. The problem of child abuse and neglect needs to be set squarely in the context of economic and social policies – while continuing to respond to individuals in distress.

2. The extent of serious harm to children needs to be better understood professionally and reported more accurately by the media.

3. Recognition needs to be given to some of the elements of effective child protection policy which already exist in those universal and universally accepted programmes. These include maternal and child health centres; health visitors; neighbourhood houses; day nurseries; youth drop-in and so on.

4. Child protection services should not be used as a gateway to other services for families who suffer adversities in health, education and wealth, but who do not abuse their children. This serves only to misrepresent the problem and stigmatise families.

5. Finally, professionals must change their way of thinking and working, recognising that those certainties which seem available in the natural and medical sciences are not available, to the same degree in responding to child abuse. While continuing to strive for more effective practice with individual children and families there is a need to concentrate more on the way in which the welfare of all children could be enhanced in the hope that endangered children too will receive the help they need.

References

Batten, R. (1988) *Searching for the Difference: An Exploratory Study of Decision Making.* Unpublished thesis. Melbourne University.

Benjamin, M. (1980) 'Abused as a child abused as a parent – practitioners beware', in Volpe, R., Bretton, M. and Milton, J. *The Maltreatment of School Aged Children.* Lexington, U.K.

Besharov, D. (1986) 'Unfounded allegations – a new child abuse problem'. *The Public Interest, Spring (82),* 23.

Besharaov, D. (1987) 'The future of child protection services'. *Public Welfare,* Winter.

Birchall, E. (1989) 'The frequency of child abuse – what do we really know', in Stevenson, O. (ed) *Child Abuse.* Hemel Hempstead: Harvester Wheatsheaf, 1–27.

Blom-Cooper, L. (1985) *A Child in Trust.* London Borough of Brent.

Burgdoff, K. and Edmonds, J. (1980) 'Sample design and estimation procedure', in National Study of the Incidence and Severity of Child Abuse and Neglect.

Rockville, M.D. cited in *Child Abuse and Neglect 13,* 41–43.

Campbell, L. (1987) *Case Planning in Child and Family Welfare.* Unpublished thesis, Melbourne University.

Caplan, P., Walters, T., White, G., Parry, R. and Bates, R. (1984) 'Toronto multiagency child abuse research project: the abused and the abuser'. *Child Abuse and Neglect 8,* 343–351.

Cichatti, D., Tarddson, B. and Egeland, B. (1978) 'Perspectives in treatment and understanding of child abuse', in Goldstein, A. (ed) *Prescription for Child Mental Health and Education.* New York: Pergamon.

Claburn, E., Magura, S. and Cheziak, S. (1977) 'Case re-opening: an emerging issue in child welfare services'. *Child Welfare LVI* (10).

Clark, R. (1989) *Reflecting on Decision Making in Child Protection Practice.* Unpublished thesis. Melbourne University.

Cohn, A.H. and Garbarino, J. (1982) 'Toward a required approach to preventing child abuse', cited in Giovannoni, J. 'Prevention of child abuse and neglect'. *Social Work Research and Abstracts, Spring,* 27.

Creighton, S. (1984) *Trends in Child Abuse.* London: NSPCC.

Dingwall, R., Eekelaar, J. and Murray, T. (1983) *The Protection of Children: State Intervention and Family Life.* Oxford: Basil Blackwell.

Dingwall, R. (1989) 'Some problems about predicting child abuse and neglect', in Stevenson, O. *Child Abuse.* Hemel Hempstead: Harvester Wheatsheaf, 28–53.

Downie, R. and Loudfoot, E. (1978) 'Aim skill and role in social work', in Timms, N. and Watson, D. (eds) *Philosophy and Social Work.* London: Routledge and Kegan Paul, 122.

Edgar, D. (1988) Child Abuse: Social Forces and Prevention. Paper presented at Conference Prevention of Child Abuse, Adelaide.

Gil, D. (1970) *Violence Against Children.* Cambridge, Mass.: Harvard University Press.

Greenland, C. (1987) *Preventing CAN Deaths.* London: Tavistock.

Jason, J. and Andereck, N. (1983) 'Fatal child abuse in Georgia: The epidemiology of severe physical abuse'. *Journal of Child Abuse and Neglect 7(1),* 1–9.

Jayaratne, S. (1977) 'Child abuse as parents and children: a review'. *Social Work,* January.

Kadushin, A. (1974) *Child Welfare Services.* London: Macmillan.

Kaufman, J. and Zigler, E. (1987) 'Do abused children become abusive parents?' *American Journal of Orthopsychiatry,* April.

Kempe, C.H., Silverman, F., Steele, B., Drocgemueller, W. and Silver, H. (1962) 'The battered child syndrome'. *Journal of the American Medical Association (1),* 17–24.

Kempe, C.H. and Helfer, R. (1972) *Helping the Battered Child and his Family.* Philadelphia: J.M. Lippincott.

Knudsen, D. (1989) 'Duplicate reports of child maltreatment'. *Child Abuse and Neglect 13.*

Lawrence, Prof. R. (1982) *Responsibilities for Service in Child Abuse and Protection.* Report on the Death of Paul Mont Calm. University of N.S.W.

Ministerial Panel of Inquiry into the Death of D.V. Confidential Report to the Minister for Community Services, July 1991.

Monnone, T., Craig, E., Barry, D. and Young, L. (1989) 'An investigation into the nature of registered emotional abuse', in *Child Abuse and Neglect in N.S.W.* Child Protection Council.

Nelson, B.J. (1984) *Making an Issue of Child Abuse – Political Agenda Setting for Social Problems.* Chicago: University of Chicago.

Parton, N. (1985) *The Politics of Child Abuse.* London: Macmillan.

Pelton, L.H. (1981) *The Social Context of Child Abuse and Neglect.* N.Y.: Human Sciences Press.

Pitcairn, T., Waterhouse, L., McGhee, J., Secker, J. and Sullivan, C. 'Evaluating parenting in child physical abuse'. Chapter 4 in this book.

Roycroft, B. (1987) Statement of the President of the Association of Directors of Social Services (To the Cleveland Inquiry). Newcastle on Tyne: ADSS.

Simpkins, L.G. (1984) 'Child abuse and neglect in families: an analysis of family focused projects', cited in Stein, J. and Rzepnicki, T. *Decision Making in Child Welfare.* Massachusetts: Hingham.

Statistics Department of Community Services, Victoria, 1989.

Steele, B. and Pollock, C. (1968) 'A psychiatric study of parents who abuse infants and small children', in Helfer, R. and Kempe, C.H. *The Battered Child Syndrome.* Chicago: University of Chicago Press.

Whittaker, J. and Garbarino, J. (1983) *Social Support Networks: Information Helping in the Human Services.* New York: Aldine.

Young, L., Baker, J. and Monnone, T. (1989) 'Poverty and child abuse in the Sydney metropolitan area'. *Child Abuse and Neglect in N.S.W.* Sydney: Child Protection Council.

Young, L. and Brooks, R. (1989) 'The profile of child abuse and neglect in N.S.W'. *Child Abuse and Neglect in N.S.W.* Sydney: Child Protection Council.

Chapter 11

Facing the Facts
Self-Help as a Response to Childhood Sexual Abuse

Siobhan Lloyd

The concept of self-help as a powerful tool in the process of recovery from childhood sexual abuse has gained strength in recent years (Herman and Schatzow 1984; Deighton and McPeek 1985; Agosta and Laing, 1988; Hall and Lloyd 1990). Data on the efficacy or outcome of self-help initiatives is not easily identified, but the literature abounds with accounts of self-help for male and female survivors, their partners and children who have recently been in abusive situations.

This chapter examines the role of self-help as a key part in the healing process. It acknowledges the potential of self-help to empower survivors of abuse and help them in coming to terms with their past. It draws together the available evidence on self-help from working with adult survivors, adolescents and children who have experienced childhood sexual abuse. It also briefly presents the evidence from working with perpetrators of sexual abuse and refers to the literature on self-help for helpers themselves who work in this area. Finally it examines the implications for service providers of a self-help model which truly empowers those who are part of the process.

Self-help and empowerment: a context for change
A starting point for the discussion is presented by an exploration of the relationship between self-help and empowerment. Adams (1990) presents a useful historical perspective on the self-help movement in its broadest terms. He points out that during the mid-Victorian era self-help was seen as an expression of individualism, whereby individuals and groups were expected

to deal with their own problems. The role of the professional 'helper' was restricted to 'telling people to pull themselves up by the boot straps' (Adams 1990). A rather different perspective is presented by Kropotkin (1902) who argues that mutual aid is a sign of a healthy community, and it leads to the fulfilment of the individual. More recently, Katz and Bender (1976) have suggested that self-help encourages group formation for the pursuance of mutual aid. Here, the important role played by groups is developed. They argue that self-help is usually pursued by groups of peers who come together to support each other in coming to terms with a common issue or to effect change on an issue of personal or social concern.

Moeller (1983) identifies six features of a self-help model. These are: all members are equal in status; each member makes decisions for themselves; each group is responsible for their own decisions; members join because of their own problems; the proceedings are confidential; participation is free. This model implies that self-help occurs primarily in a group setting.

Pancoast, Parker and Froland (1983) locate self-help initiatives alongside and complementary to 'formally provided services'. The implication here is of a mutually beneficial relationship, but one which is without conflict or ambiguity. This view ignores the potentially powerful 'gingering' role of self-help as gaps in formal service provision are identified and alternative models of practice explored. They argue that the core values of self-help-self-management, co-operation, shared experience and, most importantly, empowerment, may create a paradox for professionals who support the idea. Empowerment, they suggest is much more than an enabling process: it implies the handover of management from professional to client, a process which in turn can lead to liberation from professionals (Lieberman and Bond 1978; Adams and Lindenfield 1989).

Empowerment also implies the reconceptualising of power itself so that it is not understood as power 'over' but as an egalitarian and enabling means of problem-solving. Amad (1990), writing about anti-racist social work practice, provides a checklist which would set the agenda for empowerment in all areas of social work practice. She identifies two areas where workers should address their own values and assumptions. These are: first, developing interpersonal skills and promoting trust and rapport, and second, acknowledging the power of institutional values and rules, and professional norms and values. Her checklist acknowledges the concept of empowerment as core to a social work ethos in the way it facilitates access to resources and acknowledges clients as citizens with equal rights. It also sees empowerment as a social work resource and service by sharing the organisational power invested in workers by working in partnership with clients. Furthermore, empowerment is seen as a model of social work practice itself, through the explicit goal of clients gaining power and control through open communication, information, knowledge of services and resources and networking. As such, it is a form of practice which does not blame individuals and it credits change to clients themselves.

A final point here relates to the possibility of discriminatory practice by a helper for reasons of race, gender, sexuality, disability, age or creed. If practice is to be truly empowering then helpers will need to address these issues in training and supervision.

The relevance of this for self-help in the area of sexual abuse is clear. It confirms that the voice of survivors of abuse is heard and listened to, that helpers acknowledge at the outset that the 'expert' view is that of the survivor, that survivors have power and control over the pace and depth of the work and that helpers are enablers and facilitators rather than benefactors who 'help victims'.

Self-help, empowerment and sexual abuse: the contribution of feminism

The women's movement has made a significant contribution to placing the issue of sexual abuse on the public and professional agenda (MacLeod and Saraga 1988). It has also provided an important strand in the evolution of self-help as part of the process of recovery from sexual abuse. Its roots lie in the development of modern feminism. The growth of consciousness-raising groups enabled women to come to their own personal understanding of the way in which society's structures, attitudes and actions controlled and disempowered them (Ernst and Goodison 1981). Feminist therapy, one of the areas of mental health work which has challenged prevailing ideologies of female psychology, has relocated what has commonly been seen as the 'personal' emotional failure of individual women into a shared experience exploring the degree to which this apparent weakness is socially determined (Dominelli 1989). The feminist slogan 'the personal is political' is a public manifestation of this process, suggesting that personal problems are recognised as having historical and cultural roots and dimensions. It also suggests that if we change ourselves we change the world (Phillipson 1992).

In relation to sexual abuse, the feminist stance examines the kind of society we live in. It sees child sexual abuse as part of the spectrum of male dominance over women and children, especially girls. A feminist analysis also holds male power responsible for maintaining the silence on sexual abuse since the complaints of mothers and children can too easily be dismissed as untrue or unreasonable so long as the status of men, women and children remains unequal.

Combining these twin themes of consciousness-raising through sharing experiences in groups and an analysis based on power and gender has enabled the voice of survivors themselves to be heard. Women's Aid groups, Rape Crisis and survivors' groups have brought the issue of male violence against women into the public domain. The aims of feminist practice in relation to childhood sexual abuse are fourfold and they relate clearly to the process of empowerment and self-help. They include: enabling survivors to have their voices heard; reversing the victim-blaming practices of the past; influencing policy-making by campaigning for more resources for survivors and influencing practice within statutory and voluntary agencies (Hall and Lloyd 1990).

Self-help and empowerment: the voice of survivors

The last ten years have witnessed an important development in the literature on sexual abuse. The voice of survivors themselves, in prose, poetry, song, letters and novels has provided a courageous testimony of painful childhood experiences. These communications have also provided the basis for greater understanding of the reality of childhood sexual abuse. The existence, in published and unpublished form, of survivors' writing has had a number of consequences. First, it has broken the silence surrounding childhood sexual abuse in a very graphic and open way. Second, it has provided a vehicle to encourage other survivors to disclose details of their experiences. In doing so it has acknowledged and validated issues which are common to all survivors of childhood sexual abuse. This, in turn, has led to a greater professional and societal understanding of the effects of abuse. Third, it has forced helpers to evaluate the assumptions on which their work is based and the therapeutic methods which they use. This is a dynamic process of challenge and change, two important effects of which have been to empower survivors themselves and to call into question the potential misuse of professional authority and power.

Writing about one's experience can also be interpreted as a process of self-help, albeit from an individual perspective. There are now a large number of useful collections of personal accounts of childhood sexual abuse. These originated in North America during the late 1970s and early 1980s (Armstrong 1978; McNaron and Morgan 1982; Bass and Thornton 1983; Ward 1984). Longer autographical accounts detail the impact of sexual abuse on adult life. Some of these focus on the way in which the child coped with the abuse when it was happening (Brady 1979; Allen 1980; Angelou 1984; Danica 1988). These accounts are very useful for adults to set alongside their own experiences and in so doing to identify with the experiences of others.

Other personal accounts go further. Some provide a graphic insight into the ways in which childhood memories have been suppressed, only to emerge in later life (Matthews 1986; Fraser 1987; Driver and Droisen 1989). There are also a number of helpful and courageous books written by survivors describing the process of recovery from sexual abuse. Sometimes this has happened with the help of professionals, volunteers or other survivors; sometimes the survivor gives an account of work which she has undertaken alone (Evert and Bijkerk 1987; Spring 1987). A final group of autobiographical accounts have been co-authored by survivors and their therapists or helpers (Sisk and Hoffman 1987; Utain and Oliver 1989). These give valuable insight into the process of giving and receiving help, and are empowering in the sense that responsibility for the work and the writing itself is shared between the survivor and her helper. This is the model favoured by feminist therapists.

There are also a number of novels which deal with the subject of childhood sexual abuse (Hart 1979; Morris 1982; Murphy 1987; Gaitskill 1991) and accounts of abuse told in the form of letters (Walker 1983). These books are helpful in reaching a readership which might not otherwise have confronted the issue.

Most of the literature referred to above relates to women who have been abused by a trusted adult, usually male. In the last few years a number of books written by and for male survivors have begun to appear (Quinn 1984; Bolton, Morris and MacEachron 1989; Lew 1990). These books follow a similar pattern to those written by women. They cover a number of themes relating to the survivors' childhood experience and adult lives. The main themes are interwoven with short personal accounts from survivors themselves.

Self-help handbooks: a vehicle for recovery and empowerment

A development from the personal accounts of survivors has been the publication of self-help handbooks and manuals aimed at individuals and groups. These were first written with and for women in abusive adult relationships with men (NiCarthy, Merriman and Coffman 1984). They have now become a fulcrum around which other literature turns. A key feature of these books is their attempt to empower survivors by stressing their strengths and their potential for recovery by actively engaging with the meaning and consequences of the abuse for themselves. The books have come directly from the experience of survivors and their helpers in groups and one-to-one counselling. They include a mixture of personal accounts, identification of the long-term effects of sexual abuse, themes in the recovery process and exercises to help this recovery. At their best they are written in an accessible and straightforward style which directly addresses the survivor and their helper and in so doing have the added effect of demystifying the helping process (Donman and Lenton 1984; Baer and Dinock 1988; Bass and Davis 1988; White 1988; Finney 1990; Hall and Lloyd 1990; Kunzman 1990; Parks 1990; Parrish 1990; Dinsmore 1991).

Most of these books have been written by and for female survivors. There are, however, a number of handbooks which have been written for men (Quinn 1984; Lew 1990) and younger survivors (Bain and Saunders 1990). There are also handbooks which focus on specific topics including sexuality (Maltz and Holman 1987; Woititz 1989; Maltz 1991) and Christianity (Hancock and Mains 1987; Wilson 1986). Recent additions to the literature include self-help books for partners (Davis 1991; Graber 1991) and mothers of children who have been abused (Byerly 1985). Bass and Davis (1988) for example, is written primarily for female survivors of abuse. Many of the issues it covers, however, apply equally well to male survivors. The underlying themes of the book are: acknowledgment of the abuse, recognising the long-term effects, building an inner strength and moving towards a process of healing. The text is punctuated with accounts from survivors of their experience, emphasising not only their pain, but their resourcefulness and strengths. An accompanying text (Davis 1990) provides a workbook which again can be used by both survivors and their helpers. It is structured to allow the reader to use a range of writing exercises, art projects and activities as tools in the recovery process. The tools and techniques presented in the book can be easily used on a self-help basis, working one-to-one or in a group with other survivors. The process of using the workbook helps to transfer the individual's position of subordination or subjugation to one where a growing sense of self control and self esteem is found.

Self-help and adult survivors

Women who have experienced childhood sexual abuse have, for at least the last ten years, been meeting in groups with other survivors. The growth of survivors' groups originated with Women's Aid and the Rape Crisis movement (Hall and Lloyd 1990). The most important aspect of self-help groups for survivors is described by one writer who points out that being in a group allows a survivor to identify with others the same sense of anger, shame, fear, needs and hopes (Levy 1978; Gordy 1983; London Rape Crisis Centre 1984; Yassen and Glass 1984; Goodman and Nowak–Schibelli 1985).

There are three common models for survivors' groups. First, there are self-help groups which have been formed by survivors themselves, usually without the help or support of professional workers or volunteers. They tend to operate without a formal leader. The main issue for these groups is their difficulty in maintaining continuity. The second type of groups are mutual support groups, which come together under the auspices of an organisation such as Women's Aid or Rape Crisis. They usually have one or two facilitators who may or may not have been sexually abused. Facilitators can be very helpful in maintaining continuity, especially during periods when energy levels are low within the group. The third type of groups are professionally led and these are usually found within a residential or hospital setting. These groups may have a tighter structure with members screened or assessed before joining.

The benefits of group membership for female survivors are outlined by a number of writers (Tsai and Wagner 1978; Herman and Schatzow 1984; Blake-White and Kline 1985; Bergart 1986; Davenport and Sheldon 1987; Sgroi 1989; Hall and Lloyd 1990). They include the identification with and support from others who have had similar experiences and the opportunity to give and receive challenges to well-entrenched distortions of reality. They can also enable survivors to test out new-found feelings and emotions and wishes, and to make requests of others. Groups can also encourage survivors to experience giving and receiving help and affection from other women. Finally they can encourage the testing out of boundaries in relationships.

There is a healthy debate on the relative merits of open or closed groups. Closed groups enable trust, a core issue for survivors, to be established more easily. They also make planning the group sessions easier (Sgroi 1989). Open groups, on the other hand, encourage easy access to a source of help when a woman decides to seek help. They do, however, increase the risk of breaches of confidentiality as members constantly join and leave. They also pose problems for more established members who may not want to repeatedly share information about themselves as new members join the group (Hall and Lloyd 1990).

A further consideration in relation to survivors' groups is the contact which individual members have with therapists or helpers outwith the group setting. Sgroi (1989) suggests that group members should plan to be seen individually at least once per month during a group cycle. This, she suggests, will secure time for working through issues specific to the individual which have arisen in the group.

Sgroi (1989) also raises a number of additional issues. These include the need to consider co-facilitation of the group. She suggests that facilitators should take responsibility for maintaining both the format and structure of the group. The gender of facilitators should also be addressed and the relative advantages and disadvantages for a group of working with a facilitator who has experienced sexual abuse. She suggests that the number of group sessions in a cycle is ten to fourteen weeks so that three cycles per year can take place. This allows a four or five week interval between cycles to plan for the next group and allows time to process and follow up what has occurred in a completed cycle.

Several writers detail themes which might be usefully addressed in a survivors' group (Gil 1983; Deighton and McPeek 1985; Hall and Lloyd 1990). These include dealing with fear; coping with pain, anger, loss; feelings towards the abuser; feelings towards adult care takers, sexuality and acknowledging personal achievements.

Self-help or therapeutic groups for male survivors are less common. Lew (1990) offers guidelines for the establishment of these groups. He notes that many of the issues raised in groups for men are similar to those which arise in groups for female survivors. There are, however, additional areas where work can be undertaken, particularly in relation to male sexuality and power.

Self-help and younger survivors

Reports of self-help groups for younger survivors have concentrated on the experience of older children, especially adolescents (Furniss, Bingley-Miller and Van Elburg 1988; Nelki and Watters 1989). Most of the published material relates to the way in which groups might be set up and run and the methods for addressing specific issues. Groupwork is usually described in the context of 'group therapy' rather than with a focus on self-help. The element of self-help arises as part of the group process. Corder, Haizlip and de Boer (1990) suggest that group therapy provides a 'peer forum, essential for full recovery'. They argue that it allows children to understand their 'sense of differentness and to deal with the negative sense of self which they might have as a result of the abusive experience' (p.244). They report that children in groups become more verbal and more comfortable with discussing aspects of all areas of their lives with their mothers.

The general picture to emerge is of therapeutic, professionally-led groups which encourage self-help among members as part of the process of the work (Berliner and Ernst 1984; Berliner and MacQuivey 1984; Mowbray 1988). We also learn that groups which aim to increase self-awareness and improve self-esteem are the norm. The methods employed by facilitators tend to be directive and they include role play, videos and specially constructed games in addition to talking. A cycle of between eight and twelve weekly group meetings appears to be the norm, although some groups have as many as twenty sessions over a five month period (Corder *et al.* 1990).

Some group programmes include a parallel group for non-abusing care givers (Damon and Waterman 1986). In these groups information is given about work undertaken in the children's group and similar topics are explored. These include safe touching, telling someone about abuse, anger, punishment, guilt and responsibility. In some examples a final joint session is arranged between caregivers, the children and their therapists.

Accounts of these groups present some outcome data on the work under-taken. Assessment is usually by questionnaire administered to the caregiver before the group starts and some time after it has finished. The questionnaire asks for behavioural symptoms shown by the children prior to the group and again eight weeks after the group has finished. The evaluation reports a statistically significant reduction of behavioural problems reported by caregivers. Overall, these groups aim to facilitate an understanding of what has happened in the past and, through group membership, to enhance self-esteem (Stewart and Greer 1984).

Self-help and non-abusing parents

It is increasingly recognised that non-abusing parents, especially mothers, can play a pivotal role in the recovery of their children from childhood sexual abuse (Caplan 1985; Dempster 1989; Reid 1989). Too often the only support offered is in the context of 'treatment' for the family as a whole. The limitations of the family therapy model, particularly in the early post-investigative stage, is well documented (MacLeod and Saraga 1988). Its main shortcoming is the way in which it defines family dysfunction as the cause of sexual abuse rather than a consequence of the problem.

There is still a lack of outcome research on the effectiveness of parents' groups. An exception is described by Winton (1990). Here, a thirteen week open group was established with the support of a male and female therapist. The group had educational and therapeutic aims and encouraged a supportive environment for participants to share their concerns and resolve identified problems. Evaluation of effectiveness was measured against three outcome criteria: a decrease in children's dysfunctional behaviour, a decrease in parental stress levels and a positive assessment of the support group as helpful to them.

The research reports significant improvement in the areas of fear, inhibition, neurotic behaviour, psychotic behaviour and sexual behaviour. Parental stress levels, however, were not significantly reduced after attending the group and this was attributed to a range of internal and external factors including employment, adult relationships and uncertainty about the future. Finally, a high positive rating was given to the group as a helpful and supportive environment. In particular parents valued the opportunity to express their feelings about the abuse, the support of the therapist and the fact of discovering that they were not alone.

Groups for mothers, in which they can find support from other women, are increasing in number (Hildebrand and Forbes 1987; Sgroi and Dana 1987). In these groups mothers are encouraged to value themselves and their children. The groups generally appear to have three sets of aims: to report any significant changes in the behaviour of their children, to reduce their own parental stress levels and to recognise their own needs. Similar groups are known to exist for foster parents and residential and day care staff but there is an absense of literature in this area.

Self-assessment questionnaires administered after the groups have finished report that the mothers' stress levels were still high, even when their children were showing signs of recovery. Positive assessment ratings were given to meeting others in a similar situation at group meetings, an acknowledgement from professionals that their needs were valid and an opportunity to express their feelings about the abuse. A separate but related issue is the extent to which education on parenting should be included in such self-help or therapeutic groups. Winton (1990) helpfully notes that non-abusing parents can be and feel victimised too and they often need a forum to deal with issues affecting themselves and their children as a result of the abuse. Dempster (1989) makes a similar point when she powerfully argues that the feelings and reactions of mothers mirror those experienced by children who have been sexually abused. Using Finkelhor and Browne's model she clearly illustrates a mother's stigmtisation, powerlessness, sense of betrayal and traumatic sexualisation in the post-disclosure period (Finkelhor and Browne 1985). A self-help resource, which brings a mother into contact with other women with similar feelings could go a long way towards her own recovery from the trauma of a child's disclosure of sexual abuse.

Self-help and perpetrators of child sexual abuse

The concept of self-help as a response to perpetrators of child sexual abuse may seem like a contradiction in terms. Accepting that abusive behaviour originates from an abuse of power and trust implies that work with abusers should confront issues of denial, premeditation, responsibility and harm (Cowburn 1990). There will be little room for the aims of mutual support and trust. Instead, groups for perpetrators focus on confronting abusive behaviour, effecting change in behaviour to prevent or reduce the likelihood of further offending and increasing social skills. The element of self-help would appear to be possible only when denial, minimalisation and resistance to change have been challenged (Morrison, Bentley, Clark and Shearer 1989).

There are a number of accounts of groupwork with male perpetrators of child sexual abuse (Salter 1988; Cowburn 1991; Erooga, Clark and Bentley 1991). They all note four phases of change for perpetrators as a consequence of the work. The first is one of guilt and false motivation which is characterised by a presentation of remorse, self-pity and guilt. Phase two, awareness and resistance, is characterised by a cognitive awareness of the issues, especially when work is done to confront abusers with the perspective of the child who has been sexually abused. The third phase, awareness and internalisation, is where perpetrators' evaluations of their behaviour are honestly believed rather than repeated as correct (Erooga *et al.* 1991). The last phase is about maintaining the changes in attitudes and behaviour and preventing relapse. At the time of writing, the authors were conscious that none of the men had reached this stage, so the group's success could not be evaluated.

Other authors have stressed the emphasis which should be given in working with perpetrators to mandated treatment, setting treatment goals, an explicit value stance from the professional, setting limits and limiting confidentiality. There is also a core acceptance that work cannot be carried out without confrontation (Finkelhor 1986; Salter 1988).

Another account of groupwork with sex offenders against children is given in Bennett, Corder and Jehn (1991). In this account the perpetrators were all female. The group meetings followed a similar pattern to those described above and the evaluation of the group by group members acknowledged its informative, supportive and helpful functions. It also reported an increased awareness of the effects of abuse and acknowledgement of responsibility for the abusive behaviour. Finally, participants reported an increase in their self-confidence and ability to express and assert themselves. The crucial measure of outcome, however, is whether group members of either gender commit further sexual offences against children.

Self-help and the helpers: workers' support groups

Child sexual abuse is not an easy area in which to work. The issues with which workers are confronted on a daily basis constantly challenge their professional practice and personal values. There can still be personal and professional pressure to turn away from the possibility of sexual abuse, to pretend that it is not happening or to express concerns in private but do little in public for fear of making things worse or handling a situation badly. It is also important to acknowledge that among the large numbers of adults who were sexually abused as children there are people in a helping role. Their personal experiences may make them more alert to the possibility and consequences of abuse but they may find themselves under additional pressure because of their personal experience.

Another, related factor is at work here. Helpers, irrespective of their past, often experience similar emotions to the child victim or adult survivor with whom they are working. If these emotions are not explored, the consequences for the client are potentially harmful. They can lead to lack of empathy, punitive responses or burnout (Alpert and Schechter 1979). Distancing, for example, can lead to a denial of the helpers' own vulnerability and can increase the potential for victim-blaming and labelling. Alpert and Schechter (1979) have provided a useful framework which illustrates some of the areas of congruence between a helper and survivor of sexual abuse, together with the techniques for dealing with those feelings.

Meeting others with similar worries and concerns is equally important. Many workers are now meeting in groups for information-sharing and as an informal means of developing trust between agencies, for training purposes and, importantly, for the purpose of self-help for themselves.

The final word in this respect rests with Susan Sgroi:

> 'What about the requirements for magic? The magic approach will doubt-less be inexpensive, easily learned and effortlessly applied. The reality is that there is no-one just over the horizon to come and rescue the clients or the professionals who are committed and paid to serve them.' (Sgroi 1989 p.185)

Conclusions

The general review of the literature given above reflects the increasingly important role of self-help for survivors of child sexual abuse, for their non-abusing caregivers and perhaps for abusers too. The development of self-help initiatives also poses a number of important questions for professional services and support.

First, there is the question of the degree of involvement of professional workers or volunteers in self-help initiatives. Certainly with groups for younger survivors there will need to be some sort of input to maintain continuity and momentum. The same could be said for self-help groups of adult survivors. Here the issues are of building trust, the expression of difficult feelings and maintaining boundaries. Groups for non-abusing caretakers will also have the same need for professional involvement if we accept the argument that their reactions to the abuse sometimes mirror those of abused children. With groups of perpetrators the need for facilitators is paramount so that group members can be consistently challenged on their abusive behaviour and its consequences.

Second, there is the question of membership of self-help groups. The arguments for and against open and closed groups appear to apply to all survivors' groups. The balance here does tilt in favour of closed groups, chiefly for reasons of building trust and maintaining confidentiality.

A third issue relates to resources for self-help. Grants to survivors' groups and caregivers' groups should be generously awarded and the development of specialist projects in this area encouraged. Making premises available and offering the use of agency resources for publicity, mailing and other communications would be helpful as a first step. To date, survivors have provided most of the written resources themselves. Health and welfare agencies might usefully respond by acknowledging the vital role of self-help in breaking a last barrier of silence surrounding sexual abuse.

Finally there is the important question of evaluation. If we accept that self-help and, ultimately, empowerment are the goals, then survivor-evaluation must play a central part in the evaluation process. Without acknowledging and hearing the voice of survivors, the silence of previous generations is destined to continue.

References

Adams, R. (1990) *Social Work and Empowerment*. London: Macmillan.

Adams, R. and Lindenfield, G. (1985) *Self-help and Mental Health*. Ilkley: Self-help Associates.

Agosta, C. and Loring, M. (1988) 'Understanding and treating the adult retrospective victim of child sexual abuse', in Sgroi, S., *Vulnerable Populations. Evaluation and Treatment of Sexually Abused Children and Adult Survivors*. Toronto, Mass: Lexington Books.

Allen, C.V. (1980) *Daddy's Girl*. New York: Berkeley Books.

Alpert, M. and Schechter, S. (1979) 'Sensitising workers to the needs of victims: common worker and victim responses'. *Victimology 4(4)*, 385–389.

Amad, B. (1990) *Black Perspectives in Social Work.* London: Venture Press.

Angelou, M. (1984) *I Know Why the Caged Bird Sings.* London: Virago.

Armstrong, C. (1978) *Kiss Daddy Goodnight.* New York: Pocket Books.

Baer, E. with Dinock, P. (1988) *Adults Molested as Children: A Survivor's Manual for Women and Men.* Orwell VT Safer Society Press.

Bain, O. and Saunders, M. (1990) *Out in the Open. A Guide for Young People who have been Sexually Abused.* London: Virago.

Barnett, S., Corder, F. and Jehu, D. (1990) 'Group treatment for women sex offenders against children'. *Groupwork 3(2),* 191–203.

Bass, E. and Davis, L. (1988) *The Courage to Heal: A Guide for Women Survivors of Child Sexual Abuse.* New York: Harper and Row.

Bass, E. and Thornton, L. (eds) (1983) *I Never Told Anyone. Writings by Women survivors of Child Sexual Abuse.* New York: Harper and Row.

Bennett, S., Corder, F. and Jehu, D. (1990) 'Group treatment for women sex offenders against children'. *Groupwork 3(2),* 191–203.

Bergart, A.M. (1986) 'Isolation to intimacy: incest Survivors in group therapy'. *Social Casework 67,* 266–275.

Berliner, L. and Ernst, E. (1984) 'Groupwork with pre-adolescent sexual assault victims', in Stuart, I.R. and Greer, J.G. (eds), *Victims of Sexual Aggression. Treatment of Women, Children and Men.* New York: Van Nostrand Reinhold. 105–126.

Berliner, L. and MacQuivey, K. (1984) 'A therapy group for female adolescent victims of sexual abuse', in Rosenbaum, E. (ed), *Varieties of Short-Term Therapy Groups.* New York: MacGraw Hill.

Blake-White, J. and Kline, G.M. (1985) 'Treating the dissociative process in adult victims of childhood incest'. *Social Casework 66,* 394–402.

Bolton, F.G., Morris, L.A., MacEachron, A.E. (1989) *Males at Risk: The Other Side of Child Abuse.* Newbury Park: Sage.

Brady, K. (1979) *Father's Days: A True Story of Incest.* New York: Dell.

Byerly, C.M. *The Mother's Book.* Iowa: Kendall/Hunty Publishing Company.

Caplan, P. (1985) 'The scapegoating of mothers: a call for change'. *American Journal of Orthopsychiatry 56,* 610–613.

Corder, B., Haizlip, T. and de Boer, P. (1990) 'A pilot study for a structured time-limited therapy group for sexually abused pre-adolescent children'. *Child Abuse and Neglect 14(2),* 243–253.

Cowburn, M. (1990) 'Work with sex offenders in groups'. *Groupwork 3(2),* 157–171.

Damon, L. and Waterman, J. (1986) 'Parallel group treatment of children and their mothers', in MacFarland, K. and Waterman, J. (eds), *Sexual Abuse of Young Children: Evaluation and Treatment.* London: Holt, Reinhart and Winston, 244–298.

Danica, E. (1988) *Don't: A Woman's Word.* Charlottetown: Gynergy Books.

Davenport, S. and Sheldon, H. (1987) 'From victim to survivor'. *Changes 5,* 379–382.

Davis, L. (1990) *The Courage to Heal Workbook. For Women and Men Survivors of Child Sexual Abuse.* New York: Harper and Row.

Davis, L. (1991) *Allies in Helping.* New York: Harper Collins.

Deighton, J. and McPeek, P. (1985) 'Group treatment: adult victims of sexual abuse'. *Social Casework 66,* 403–410.

Dempster, H.L. (1989) *The Reactions and Responses of Women to the Sexual Abuse of their Children: A Feminist View and Analysis.* Unpublished MSc thesis, University of Stirling.

Dinsmore, C. (1991) *From Surviving to thriving: Incest, Feminisim and Recovery.* Albany: State University of New York Press.

Dominelli, L. (1989) *Feminist Social Work.* London: Macmillan.

Donman, L. and Lenton, S. (1984) *Helping Ourselves: A Handbook for Women Starting Groups.* Toronto: Women's Press.

Driver, E. and Droisen, A. (1989) *Child Sexual Abuse. Feminist Perspectives.* London: Macmillan.

Ernst, S. and Goodison, L. (1981) *In Our Hands: A Woman's Book of Self-Help Therapy.* London: Women's Press.

Erooga, M., Clark, P. and Bentley, M. (1990) 'Protection, control, treatment, groupwork and sexual abuse perpetrators'. *Groupwork 3(2),* 172–190.

Evert, K. and Bijkerk, I. (1987) *When You're Ready: A Woman's Healing from Childhood Physical and Sexual Abuse by her Mother.* Walnut Creek: Launch Press.

Finkelhor, D. (1986) *A Sourcebook on Child Sexual Abuse.* Beverley Hills, LA: Sage.

Finkelhor, D. and Browne, A. (1985) 'Initial and long term effects: a conceptual framework', in Finkelhor, D., *A Sourcebook on Child Sexual Abuse.* Beverley Hills: Sage.

Finney, L.D. (1990) *Reach for the Rainbow.* Park City: Changes Publishing.

Fraser, S. (1987) *My Father's House. A Memoir of Incest and Healing.* London: Virago.

Furniss, T., Bingley-Miller, L. and Van Elburg, A. (1988) 'Goal-oriented group treatment for sexually abused adolescent girls'. *British Journal of Psychiatry 152,* 97–106.

Gaitskill, M. (1991) *Two Girls: Fat and Thin.* London: Chatto and Windus.

Gil, E. (1983) *Outgrowing the Pain. A Book For and About Adults Abused as Children.* San Francisco: Launch Press.

Goodman, B. and Nowak-Schibelli, D. (1985) 'Group treatment for women incestuously abused as children'. *International Journal of Group Psychotherapy 35,* 605–616.

Gordy, P.L. (1983) 'Groupwork that supports adult victims of childhood incest'. *Social Casework 64,* 300–307.

Graber, K. (1991) *Ghosts in the Bedroom.* Florida: Health Communications Ltd.

Hall, L. and Lloyd, S. (1990) *Surviving Child Sexual Abuse. A Handbook for Helping Women Challenge their Past.* Basingstoke: Falmer Press.

Hancock, M. and Mains, K.B. (1987) *Child Sexual Abuse: A Hope for Healing.* Crowborough: Highland Books.

Hart, T. (1979) *Don't Tell Your Mother.* London: Quartet Books.

Herman, J. and Schatzow, E. (1984) 'Time-limited group therapy for women with a history of incest'. *International Journal of Group Psychotherapy 34*, 605–616.

Hildebrand, J. and Forbes, C. (1987) 'Groupwork with mothers whose children have been sexually abused'. *British Journal of Social Work 17*, 285–304.

Katz, L. and Bender, B. (1976) *The Strength in Us. Self Help Groups in the Modern World.* New York: Franklin Watt.

Kropotkin, P. (1902) *Mutual Aid – A Factor in Evolution.* Boston: Porter Sargeant.

Kunzman, K.A. (1990) *The Healing Way: Adult Recovery from Childhood Sexual Abuse.* Center City: Hazelden Foundation.

Levy, L.H. (1978) 'Self-help groups viewed by mental health professionals: a survey and comments'. *American Journal of Community Psychology 6(4)*, 305–313.

Lew, M. (1990) *Victims no Longer.* New York: Harper and Row.

Lieberman, M.A. and Bond, G.R. (1978) 'Self-help: problems of measuring outcomes'. *Small Group Behaviour 9(2)*, 221–241.

London Rape Crisis Centre (1984) *Sexual Violence: The Reality for Women.* London: Women's Press.

MacLeod, M. and Saraga, E. (1988) 'Challenging the orthodoxy: towards a feminist theory and practice'. *Feminist Review 28*, 16–155.

MacLure, M.B. (1990) *Reclaiming the Heart: A Handbook of Help and Hope for Survivors of Incest.* New York: Warner Books.

McNaron, T. and Morgan, Y. (1982) (eds) *Voices in the Night.* Minneapolis: Cleis Press.

Maltz, W. (1991) *The Sexual Healing Journey: A Guide for Survivors of Sexual Abuse.* New York: Harper Collins.

Maltz, W. and Holman, B. (1987) *Incest and Sexuality. A Guide to Understanding and Healing.* Lexicon, Ma: Lexicon Books.

Matthews, C.A. (1986) *No Longer a Victim.* Canberra: Acorn Press.

Moeller, M. (1983) 'Self-help and the medical practitioner', in Hatch, S. and Kirkbusch, I. (eds), *Self-Help and Health in Europe. New Approaches in Health Care.* Copenhagen: World Health Organisation.

Morris, M. (1982) *If I Should Die before I Wake.* New York: Dell.

Morrison, T., Bentley, M., Clark, P. and Shearer, E. (1989) *Treating the Untreatable. Groupwork with Intra-Familial Sex Offenders.* London: NSPCC Occasional Papers.

Mowbray, C. (1988) 'Post-traumatic therapy for children who are victims of violence', in Burgess, N., Grotin, L., Holmstrom, L. and Sgroi, S. *Sexual Assault of Children and Adolescents.* Lexington: Health.

Nelki, J.S. and Watters, J. (1989) 'A group for sexually abused young children: unravelling the web'. *Child Abuse and Neglect 13(3)*, 369–377.

NiCarthy, G., Merriman, K. and Coffman, S. (1984) *Talking it Out. A Guide to Groups for Abused Women.* Seattle: Seattle Press.

Pancoast, D.L., Parker, P. and Froland, C. (1983) *Rediscovering Self-Help: Its Role in Social Care.* Beverley Hills: Sage.

Parks, P. (1990) *Rescuing the Inner Child: Therapy for Adults Sexually Abused as Children.* London: Souvenir Press.

Parrish, D.A. (1990) *Abused: A Guide to Recovery for Adult Survivors of Emotional/Physical Child Abuse.* New York: Station Hill Press.

Phillipson, J. (1992) *Practising Equality. Women, Men and Social Work.* London: Central Council for Education and Training in Social Work.

Quinn, P. (1984) *Cry Out.* Nashville: Pandora Press.

Reid, C. (1989) *Mothers of Sexually Abused Girls: A Feminist View of Theory and Practice.* Social Work Monograph. Norwich: University of East Anglia.

Salter, A.C. (1988) *Treating Child Sex Offenders and Victims: A Practical Guide.* London: NSPCC Occasional Paper.

Sisk, S. and Hoffman, C.F. (1987) *Inside Scars. Incest Recovery as Told by a Survivor and her Therapist.* Gainesville: Pandora Press.

Sgroi, S.M. (1989) 'Healing together. Peer group therapy for adult survivors of child sexual abuse', in Sgroi, S.M. *Vulnerable Populations,* Volume 2, New York: Lexington Books.

Sgroi, S.M. and Dana, N. (1987) 'Individual and group treatment of mothers of incest victims', in Sgroi, S. *Handbook of Clinical Intervention.* New York: Lexington Books.

Spring, J. (1987) *Cry Hard and Swim.* London: Virago.

Stewart, I. and Greer, J. (eds.) (1984) *Victims of Sexual Agression.* New York: Van Nostrand Reinhold.

Tsai, M. and Wagner, N.N. (1978) 'Therapy groups for women sexually abused as children'. *Archives of Sexual Behaviour 7,* 417–427.

Utain, M. and Oliver, B. (1989) *Scream Louder.* Florida: Health Communication.

Walker, A. (1983) *The Color Purple.* London: Women's Press.

Ward, E. (1984) *Father Daughter Rape.* London: Women's Press.

White, L. (1988) *The Obsidian Mirror: An Adult Healing from Incest.* Seattle: Seal Press.

Wilson, E.D. (1986) *A Silence to be Broken.* Leicester: Intervarsity Press.

Winton, M. (1990) 'An evaluation of a support group for parents who have a sexually abused child'. *Child Abuse and Neglect 14(3),* 397–405.

Woititz, J.T. (1989) *Healing Your Sexual Self.* Florida: Health Communications Inc.

Wood, E. and Hatton, L. (1988) *Triumph over Darkness.* New York: Echoes Network.

Yassen, J. and Glass, L. (1984) 'Sexual assault survivors' groups: A feminist practice perspective'. *Social Work 29,* 252–257.

Chapter 12

The Case For and Against Prevention

David Gough

Prevention is an ideal to which professionals aspire. By definition it is usually preferable to avoid unwanted events, though the degree to which this is considered necessary depends upon how unwanted or damaging the effects of these events might be.

In child abuse the costs are multiple. There are direct effects of abuse on the child, but there are also many secondary costs for other individuals, groups, or agencies. Not only are these secondary costs important in their own right, but they can feed back to create additional costs for the child who has been abused. The physical abuse of a child, for example, might result in the child being received into care and the dissolution of the family. Even if this is the best, or rather the least worst, outcome it is still a cost to the family and the child just as much as any agency intervention has financial costs however necessary or worthwhile that intervention. There are also broader costs to society which are greater than the sum of the psychological and material costs of individual cases. The high prevalence and political sensitivity of child abuse results in health and welfare services becoming preoccupied with investigation and reactive child protection rather than more positive supportive services to communities. The high prevalence of sexual abuse of children creates an atmosphere of fear and protection that lowers the quality of life for children, for families, and for everyone who has contact with children because of fears that anyone is a potential abuser.

The extent of abuse and the multiple costs that ensue make it an obvious candidate for prevention on economic grounds alone. The logic of this course of action depends, however, upon prevention being effective. Without clear evidence of the efficacy of prevention there will be scepticism about whether costs, particularly the financial costs, will be reduced. Some cases of child abuse may be prevented or ameliorated, but will this significantly reduce the social problems of abuse and will it result in more than marginal reductions to the costs of staffing and implementing reactive services?

Another factor working against investment in prevention is that the non financial costs of suffering in families are experienced by the family members and are hidden from view or can be safely ignored by other individuals not immediately affected. Health, welfare and the police and prosecution services are paid to contain these crises. To be cynical, the rest of the public need not be overly troubled. There may even be a political agenda arguing against providing preventive help lest it foster a culture of dependency and weaken the institution of the family. From this viewpoint, services should concentrate on intervening in the extreme pathological cases and leave good families (whatever that means) alone. Advocates of prevention counter this by publicising the extent of child abuse as a social problem rather than as an evil found in only certain families.

Definitions, explanations and cause

Prevention of child abuse is an even more complex issue because of the political dimension to the whole definition of the concept. Child abuse is an essentially social concept based upon the two dimensions of harm to a child and responsibility for that harm (Gough, Boddy, Dunning and Stone 1987). People do not agree about what are or are not appropriate experiences for children. Even if there is agreement about what is inappropriate or harmful, there may not be agreement about whether the circumstances that led to such harm should be considered child abuse. The events may be seen as accidental or there may be circumstances mitigating the responsibility for the behaviour that led to the negative outcome for the child. Definition is obviously more than the placement of children on child protection registers as such statistics are dependent upon agency responses to child abuse investigations (see, for example, Gough 1992).

Arguments about definition are not just academic because they determine what needs to be prevented by child abuse prevention programmes. Prevention is normally based upon an understanding of the cause. The strategy is to intervene in the causal chain to avoid the unwanted outcome. It is notoriously difficult to unravel the causal pathways of human social behaviour. This is even more complex when the behaviour in question is not open to simple behavioural definition and measurement.

There is no shortage of causal theories of child abuse. The problem is both the number of different theories and the variation in the levels of explanation involved. The levels of explanation range from biochemical, to individual, to family, to community, to societal and political explanations (Gough and Boddy 1986). Some writers have attempted to synthesise causal mechanisms into over-arching theoretical models (Gelles 1973), but these are difficult to test empirically and so tend towards being little more than lists of the mechanisms that they attempt to integrate.

Child abuse is probably multi-causal and in the absence of an over-arching causal theory many sub-theories each help to explain just part of the phenomena. The difficulty that this produces for child abuse prevention is choosing the causal pathway on which to intervene. The danger is that the one pathway may have only a weak overall effect. The intervention may be extremely potent on that specific pathway, but it may not have a significant effect at reducing the specific outcome of abuse (however defined). Alternatively, it may only have a significant effect on child abuse in specific circumstances when interacting in certain ways with other variables.

A sensible strategy might be to choose the most general explanation on the basis that this is likely to cover more specific explanations. Preventive interventions aimed at the community or society are therefore expected to have an influence at the family or individual level. The disadvantage of this approach is that it is so imprecise. If more narrowly focused interventions are only effective in certain conditions then there is no way of ensuring that these conditions are met by broadly based programmes. On the other hand, the macro programmes may be so good at promoting the positive care of children that there is a multiplier effect on to other areas of child and family functioning. As child abuse is but one possible negative outcome of a less than optimal child care environment, a broad-based form of prevention may also reduce the likelihood of other negative outcomes.

The macro approach to prevention is akin to the public health model in medicine, where improvements are made to the health of the environment in which people live or to their behaviour within these environments. Public health interventions have probably had more impact on the health of the population than the major advances in more micro and reactive medicine. A disadvantage with this strategy is that it is difficult to provide evidence in the short-term of the efficacy of broadly based programmes because of the number of other factors which may influence outcomes. A prevention strategy, then, at least in the short-term is really one of political commitment to change in societies' roles and responsibilities with respect to the care of children.

Models of prevention

The medical model underlies most approaches to intervention. The model distinguishes interventions aimed at the whole population (primary prevention), from interventions aimed at individuals or groups considered to be at risk (secondary prevention), from reactive interventions concerned to prevent unwanted events recurring (tertiary prevention). The main methods of prevention are to destroy the agent causing the illness, to reduce contact with the dangerous agent, or treatment to reduce the effects of unavoidable contact. In the prevention of malaria the protozoa causing the disease is destroyed by destroying the mosquitoes that carry them. Killing and controlling the mosquitoes also reduces contact with human beings as do repellent sprays and mosquito nets or simply avoiding living in or travelling to infected parts of the world. Drugs are used to mitigate the effects of any protozoa that do enter the blood stream (Gough 1988). In child abuse, the agent could be the perpetrator of the abuse. Health and welfare services might try to influence these individuals so that they did not behave in this way and so were less dangerous to the children. If this were not sufficiently effective they might try to reduce the contact between this agent and children, or to educate the children so that they were able to avoid either those who might be a danger to them or situations in which this danger might arise. Alternatively, they could be taught skills or coping responses that might help to mitigate the effects of abuse that did occur.

Parton (1985), in examining different models of child abuse, describes the medical model as one of medical deficit. The perpetrator is seen as deficient as a human being or, specifically, as a parent.

Parton distinguishes the medical model from legal and social welfare models. The social welfare model is similar to the medical model in that there is assumed to be some form of deficit. The difference with the social welfare model is the limiting of the explanation for the deficit in terms of social conditions and disadvantages. Parton argues that in the traditional form of this model intervention is based upon a rationale of compassion and rehabilitation. The more radical form of the social welfare model attempts to challenge the inequalities in society that produce such disadvantage. Under the legal model people are not considered to be deficient in abilities. Rather they choose whether to comply with the rules of society and thus they should be held responsible for any transgression of such rules. Prevention includes punishment which aim to deter both initial offending (primary and secondary prevention) and to persuade those caught breaking the rules not to repeat these offences (tertiary prevention).

Parton also distinguishes accounts of child abuse on the basis of whether the responsibility for the social problem is sought at the individual or collective level; whether the problem is seen as one of individuals or of society. Clearly, legal models stress the individual responsibility and the social welfare models stress the responsibility of society. The medical model is often concerned with individuals but can take a broader public health or societal view and promote positive public health (see, for example, Giovannoni 1982; Boddy 1986).

Hardiker, Exton and Barker (1991) provide an analysis that combines most of Parton's distinctions. They describe four models of welfare; residual, institutional, developmental and radical. The residual model emphasises values of individualism, freedom, and inequality. Every member of society is free to choose what is best for them and what they can achieve within the limits of their abilities and a basic framework of laws. Social and economic inequalities are necessary as a motivational force within this market system. Welfare intervention is an instrument of last resort when individuals, families and communities are unable or unwilling to ensure minimum standards are achieved. Within this model child abuse prevention would be concentrated on upholding the values of the family and community as carers and protectors of children. Intervention by state agencies would be as 'ambulance drivers' for the few residual, and by definition deviant, cases.

The institutional model espouses more liberal values of a shared consensus of social values within society. As with Parton's (1985) traditional social welfare model, the institutional model accepts that the state may have to intervene to mitigate some of the inequalities produced by market forces. The state therefore takes on the responsibility of intervening in a wider range of families. The state would also be sympathetic to arguments of prevention at the individual and family level – providing people with the educational or psychological resources to avoid social problems.

The developmental model is not prepared simply to mitigate the effects of social inequality within society, but argues that social change is required. Such change should occur through consensus and the formal political processes of democratic government: welfare services should be one of the mechanisms for change by promoting the interests of the disadvantaged sections of society. Intervention should, therefore, preferably be at the community and societal rather than the individual level. Welfare services are seen as potentially dangerous in hiding the worst aspects of social problems and reinforcing the inequalities that produced them.

The radical model is similar in arguing for structural change, but does not believe that this can be achieved by consensus through normal political channels. Rather it believes that conflict and radical opposition are necessary to achieve change.

Many of the theorists who argue for child abuse prevention could be described as working predominantly within an institutional model. They believe that the state should intervene to assist people disadvantaged by the social system and conceive of this intervention as being applied to individuals and families rather than to changing social structures. This does not imply that these authors are not concerned with structural inequality but that their skills and abilities are in the personal medical, psychological, social welfare or educational services and their work is directed towards that end. The remainder of this chapter considers some of the preventive programmes advocated or evaluated by these authors. The literature developed by authors more overtly aligned with the developmental model (see, for example, Gil 1979; Garbarino and Gillham 1980; Gelles and Cornell 1990; Violence Against Children Study Group 1990) is not considered except to inform criticism of some of the narrower child abuse prevention programmes. Authors advocating the radical model are less likely to use the term child abuse either because they consider the term itself to be based on an analysis that reinforces the social problems that they seek to change or simply because they are more concerned with macro rather than micro social change. An exception is feminist critiques of mainstream child abuse work that are considered to reinforce the gender inequalities that encourage sexual abuse (for example, MacLeod and Saraga 1991).

Educational strategies: children

In the last ten years there has been an explosion of programmes aimed at educating children so that they are better able to protect themselves from the dangers of sexual abuse. Most of these programmes have arisen in North America, but several have also been developed in other countries such as Australia and the United Kingdom (Gough 1991). The programmes are sometimes criticised for placing the responsibility for prevention on the victims of abuse rather than those who commit these offences or upon society for creating the context within which these assaults are so prevalent (Melton 1992). On the other hand, the reality is that dangers do exist and it may be just as unethical not to inform children of these dangers and to provide them with some advice as to how to avoid them.

Most of the programmes have the specific aims identified by Finkelhor (1986) of teaching children about the existence and nature of sexual abuse, increasing their awareness of who potential abusers may be, including people they know and like and members of their own family, and arming them with the knowledge and confidence to help them avoid abuse or seek assistance in response to abusive approaches. Much of the emphasis of early programmes was on teaching knowledge and concepts. Studies have shown that nearly all the programmes are effective in improving children's scores on knowledge tests, though a major exception is the formal evaluation of the Kidscape programme in Britain which showed that intervention and control groups improved equally from pre-test to post-test (Mayes, Gillies and Warden 1991). Despite the efficacy of most programmes the studies have shown that children, particularly young children, have more difficulty with abstract concepts such as what is an appropriate and inappropriate touch to your body or what is an appropriate secret (Berrick 1989; Conte and Fogarty 1989; Gilbert, Berrick, Le Prohn and Nyman 1989). Several studies also report a significant decay in children's knowledge gains over time (Finkelhor and Strapko 1991).

In comparative studies of different programmes Wurtele and colleagues (1986, 1989) have shown that behavioural training programmes are particularly effective at teaching even pre-school children appropriate responses to non appropriate approaches from others and argue that this is more effective and easier to teach than complex concepts of touch and secrets. This research team has also shown the generaliseability of their findings by testing children about hypothetical situations with a 'What if...' test rather than simply requiring children to repeat back the specifics that they have been taught. The problem with nearly all studies, however, is in knowing whether the programmes are able to protect children in real life. The exceptions are studies by researchers using confederates to test for the effectiveness of stranger abduction pro-grammes (Poche, Brouer and Swearington 1981; Fryer, Kraizer and Miyoshi 1987a, 1987b; Kraizer, Fryer and Miller 1988). The researchers arranged for a stranger to approach children individually whilst they were playing unsuper-vised to see if they should be lured to go with him. The studies raise ethical issues about subjecting children to such experiences, but both sets of researchers found that their interventions reduced the propensity of children to go with the stranger. The problem, though, is that children are probably at more risk from those known to them. In addition, research has found that perpetrators use a range of techniques to manipulate children into becoming victims (Budin and Johnson 1989; Conte, Wolf and Smith 1989) and the shift of the relationship to one of abuse is often gradual rather than simply abduction and assault (Berliner and Conte 1990).

There is little evidence that the educational programmes cause distress to the children, though little is known about any effects that there might be on their psycho-sexual development (Finkelhor and Strapko 1991). Similarly, little is known about the effects of the programmes on the children who are unfortunately still abused. In addition, perpetrators of abuse are often little older than children themselves (Bentovim and Vizard 1991) and all perpetrators were children once, so educational programmes could focus on preventing the development of abusive behaviour. It could be that current programmes have some effect in this regard, or it could be that they simply teach potential abusers the skills with which to become more sophisticated in their manipulative techniques.

Some argue that there is little that preventive educational programmes can do in terms of the social problem of sexual abuse (Melton 1991) and that it is dishonest and dangerous to suggest to children that they can be sufficiently empowered to resist abuse (Kitzinger 1991). Despite these deficiencies, the educational programmes have a powerful indirect effect at educating adults about sexual abuse and encouraging schools to develop proper policies for preventing and responding to sexual assault. Alternatively, it may be that the programmes, in often avoiding sensitive but basic subjects such as sex education and gender and power, end up reinforcing the value bases and assumptions that lead to children's rights being infringed.

Educational strategies for adults

Prevention of child abuse through the education of adults could include all forms of training for parenthood, antenatal classes and programmes concerned with relationships, conflict and violence, and sexuality. Taking a narrower focus, programmes developed specifically for child abuse include the following three categories. First, there are interventions to teach parents more productive ways of caring for their children so that they are less likely to become involved in a downward spiral of conflict. Second, there are strategies aimed at increasing general awareness about the nature and extent of child abuse and the services available to assist in such cases. Third, there are attempts to educate and/or involve local communities in child protection issues.

Attempts to teach parents more effective child care strategies are usually aimed at groups considered for some reason, whether justifiable or not, to require extra attention. For example, the National Committee for Child Abuse and Neglect in the United States funded 11 demonstration projects for child abuse prevention aimed at rural and minority populations (Gray 1983). Teaching was undertaken in a variety of ways including direct instruction, group discussions, educational films, and dramatic presentations.

Other educational prevention programmes of this type are targeted at groups with features considered indicative of risk of abuse or at those assessed individually as being high risk cases. The teaching is often in groups because this is more cost effective than individual instruction and because the group members can support each other and learn together (for example, Scaife and Frith 1988; Schinke, Schilling, Barth and Gilchrist 1986; Wolfe, Edwards, Manion and Koverola 1988). In general, these studies have shown that parents can be taught to change their child care behaviours (Gough, in preparation; Wekerle and Wolfe 1991).

Several of these programmes go beyond a purely educational model and are directed at psychological variables thought to mediate parental behaviour. For example, the ways in which parents cope with stressors. The programmes that include a high therapeutic component may have such a mix of education and therapy that they approximate to some of the approaches adopted in specialized child protection services.

The second educational strategy aimed at parents is education about the nature and extent of abuse. This is particularly developed in parts of North America and Australia compared to the United Kingdom. The National Committee for the Prevention of Child Abuse and Neglect in Chicago, for example, produce a range of materials for the public. These include car bumper stickers and television commercials advising parents to take time out and not to use violence at times of stress in the home. NCPA also distributed many million copies of a Spiderman comic with stories on sexual abuse. In Britain there has been an increase in pamphlets and other materials available for the general public, mostly produced by child care charities, but these materials are still relatively sparse and underdeveloped. A more important development in Britain has been the new Open University course on child abuse which is available to the public, although mostly used by professionals with some sort of involvement with child abuse cases.

Another source of general education about child abuse is the routine media of television and newspapers. Media coverage has typically followed from controversial child abuse cases which are thought (by some at least) to have been mismanaged. This results in a polarisation of issues and considerable adverse publicity for child protection agencies, and so it is unclear how educative this coverage is. The extent, however, of the attention to sensational cases has also led to some more detailed reporting on specific aspects of child protection, such as the complex problems surrounding child witnesses.

The need for general education resources on child abuse is unclear when there is so little information about the level of knowledge about the subject in the population. Most of the studies to date have examined variations in people's understanding of the definition of child abuse (Giovannoni and Becerra 1979; Stainton Rogers and Stainton Rogers 1989; Davenport, Browne and Palmer, submitted). The NCPA in Chicago, on the other hand, have undertaken annual surveys to examine views about the causes of child maltreatment, attitudes to the use of physical chastisement, and the extent of physical chastisement (Daro 1991). The surveys show a decrease in the use of physical chastisement from the higher levels reported by Gelles *et al.* (1990) in their telephone surveys. The NCPA survey also showed that there is an increased concern about the use of physical chastisement and this concern was particularly high amongst young, Black, non high school graduate respondents. Other commonly reported causes of child maltreatment were domestic violence between spouses and poverty. Younger respondents were most concerned about the use of physical chastisement in the home and at school, racism, and the use of the death penalty.

The third educational strategy concerns educating and/or including the local community in child protection issues. This may simply be a wish to inform the community that the child protection services exist and advise and encourage people to make appropriate use of them. Morreale (1986), for example, reports a programme aimed at promoting inter-professional relationships and team cohesion as well as good communication with the local community. Other authors put more stress on involving the community so that the child protection services can be more accountable to that community (Tipton 1986). If child abuse is a socially constructed concept about responsibility for inappropriate child care then it can be argued that the community should make a contribution to the development of such judgements. It has also been argued that the professionalising of help for families has been at the expense of civic help and participation in the welfare of the children in the community (Bush 1988). A greater community involvement in child protection services could help redress this balance.

Social support

Words like prevention and social support are attractive because they seem to encapsulate imprecise but useful broad concepts. Few would argue that prevention or social support should be encouraged, but the words are dangerous because they provide a false sense of precision and suggest that there is agreement as to what prevention or social support includes (Boddy 1986). Several authors have attempted to be more precise with the concept of social support by classifying differing dimensions or types of such support. Gottlieb

(1985), for example, distinguishes tangible aid, cognitive guidance, emotional support, socialising and companionship, and milieu reliability. The final dimension of milieu reliability refers to the support received by the belief that individual relationships or membership of a network of relationships would provide support if the need arose. The benefit arises from the belief in the potential support from these relationships rather than whether the assistance would in fact be forthcoming.

The dimensions of social support defined by Gottlieb would apply to many aspects of routine and specialised health and welfare services. Different types of social support are also major components of many child abuse prevention programmes, reactive child protection services, and therapeutic interventions. In child abuse prevention, however, there are several programmes where social support is the main focus or model. These programmes primarily involve the use of volunteer or para professional parent aides to support families in need. In some cases the intervention is highly task orientated. The focus of the work and any evaluation of progress is the accomplishment of tasks, normally tasks that have been first agreed as a priority both by parent and helper. By their nature, these programmes are usually time limited. Barth (1989), for example, reported a study where trained parenting consultants assisted mothers over a six month period to attain goals of parenting style, parenting skills, and accessing and making use of local resources.

Such time limited interventions may still involve a priority being given to the development of trust and confidence between the aides and the parents but this is bound to be a more restricted relationship than is possible in longer term supportive relationships. This restriction is sometimes intentional because of concerns that long term support might engender dependency and inhibit the parents from developing their own competencies (Miller, Fein, Howe, Gaudio and Bishop 1984, 1985). Others argue that longer term support, particularly from volunteers rather than professionals, enables parents to outgrow the need for help whilst short term professional interventions could reinforce the parents' sense of loss of control of their lives (Van der Eyken 1982). The importance of long-term relationships was also advocated by the nurturing re-parenting models of early child abuse centres (for example, Baher *et al.* 1976).

Prevention programmes that do concentrate on long term nurturing relationships are more likely to use trained supported volunteers than parent aides or other para professional paid staff. In Britain the Homestart and Newpin programmes have both developed sophisticated volunteer schemes.

The Homestart programme has over 140 schemes in operation around the world each with an average of one full time organiser, 27 volunteers, and 67 families. Volunteers have an initial training of one day per week for ten weeks followed by continued support and training whilst assisting families. Families receive an average of 14 months support.

Newpin has a more recent history but has already grown from its original base to form at least five schemes. Newpin puts a particular emphasis on the recruitment of volunteers from the same social background and circumstances as the families receiving support. Volunteers and clients are recruited in similar ways and clients often later become volunteers. The philosophy is of mutual support and growth, though the befriending volunteers may initially have less difficulties or problems in coping with difficult circumstances and will have also received training of one day per week for six months. Findings of a recent study (Cox, Puckering, Pound, Mills and Owen 1990) show that the clients of the scheme improved to a greater extent than wait list controls on measures of relationship with partner and maternal mental state. Also, those most actively involved with the scheme improved the most. Training and a continuing support group for the befrienders at the Newpin Centres also provide a place where parents can drop in and meet others and where befrienders and clients can meet outside their own homes. The idea is that all should feel members of the Newpin 'family' with all the support that a family implies.

A major issue raised by volunteer schemes is their similarity, difference, and relationship to services provided by statutory services. Gibbons and Thorpe (1989) compared a group of families receiving social work assistance with other families receiving support from Homestart volunteers. The families were similar in terms of social, economic, family, and personal difficulties, but received different types of service. The social work families received very few home visits compared to the Homestart families. Homestart families were involved in relatively more family support activities and reported a much higher rate of satisfaction with the service than social work families. Social work departments, however, have very different responsibilities to voluntary agencies and client satisfaction cannot be the only or sometimes even the main criteria for service evaluation. Client satisfaction may not be the best predictor of family change and in cases of child protection it is the well being of the child, however defined, that is paramount. Volunteer schemes can, therefore, not be a total substitute for statutory involvement. The issue is whether the volunteer schemes be separate, complementary, or an additional resource to social work provision (Gibbons and Thorpe 1989).

It is clear that there are many advantages of volunteers as a method of supporting families in need. One advantage is their low cost. The trouble is that service managers may see volunteers as a way of reducing service costs rather than meeting a service gap with limited resources or as the most coherent form of support for particular families with particular needs. Another advantage of volunteers is that they are appreciated by parents. They can also offer more time and be more supportive with their energies not being divided between many clients. Social workers have little time for visiting clients in their homes and this time is likely to decrease further as they develop their role as managers rather than direct providers of services to families. Volunteers are also not professionals and are not limited by professional responsibilities. Also, they are community based and so there is more opportunity for 'working with' rather than 'doing to' work with families. Finally, there is evidence that volunteer schemes are effective. This data comes not only from preventive services, but from the use of non professional supports in reactive services. It is difficult to show the effect of individual interventions in multi-component services, but in an analysis of a range of American demonstration child abuse programmes the use of non professional supports was one of the few factors to emerge as effective (Berkeley Planning Associates 1983; Daro 1987).

Neonatal services

Some intervention programmes have focused on the very beginnings of the parent child relationship in the neonatal period. Assistance to parents in the care of their infants has a long history and is the basis of early home visiting, including health visiting (Wasik, Bryant and Lyons 1990). Theorists disagree about whether early childhood experiences are reversible (Bowlby 1972; Rutter 1981; Clarke and Clarke 1984; Rutter and Quinton 1989), but most would agree that children thrive from warm consistent care from significant others to whom the child is securely attached (Crittenden and Ainsworth 1991). Poor parenting experiences as a child also seem to be a necessary, if not sufficient condition, for later serious parenting problems in the next generation (see Rutter 1989). To prevent difficulties in this early relationship is preferable to attempts to repair a relationship in difficulties.

Prevention programmes focused on the neonatal period have used education, social support, counselling, extra provision of routine services such as social work and health visiting, and direct therapy. Also popular is extra post partum contact between mother and child at birth in order to encourage and enable their early relationship together. Although such a strategy developed from theories of mother-infant bonding, many of the schemes were undertaken within rigid maternity schemes of mother-infant contact restricted to strict feeding time schedules. Many of these regimes would be considered unacceptable today and the extra post partum contact in the studies would now be routine.

Studies of neonatal prevention programmes vary in the groups at which they are directed. Some are directed at parents in general or parents with some minor indications of increased risk such as socio-economic group or first time mothers. These studies have reported only modest effects of the programmes compared to non intervention controls (for example, Siegal, Bauman, Schaefer, Saunders and Ingram 1980). Stevenson and Bailey (1988) did report a stronger positive effect from post-natal support groups to mothers in London, but this effect was only for attenders at the groups who had been experiencing some adversity in their lives. Attenders who were not experiencing such adversity had worse outcomes than controls. It seems, therefore, that the efficacy of the intervention depended upon the client group and it cannot be assumed that preventive interventions can be applied indiscriminately. The one research study that did demonstrate a marked positive effect on all participants (in the admittedly small sample) was an educational programme for first time fathers. The study showed that all the fathers could easily be taught to greatly improve their skills in caring for and interacting with their new born infants (Dachman, Alessi, Vraza, Fugua and Kerr 1986).

Many neonatal prevention programmes are targeted at 'at risk' groups, though there is variation in how such risk is defined. Often the risk is based upon membership of groups known to have a higher probability of experiencing stress or less resources to be able to cope with such stresses. Studies of these programmes have produced some limited positive results.

Larson (1980) reported that mothers offered a home visitor service achieved higher outcome scores than control group mothers on measures such as immunisation rates, care and interaction with the child, and the participation of father in child care. Mothers who were offered home visits that started pre-natally performed better than those who only received this assistance post natally. Positive findings of education and support have also been reported by Olds and colleagues (1986a,b, 1988) with the clearest evidence of programme effect being for single mothers on low incomes.

In another study, Barnard *et al.* (1988) and Booth *et al.* (1989) contrasted a traditional community nurse model of visitors offering support, advice, and assistance with accessing local resources with a more involved scheme where visitors used their personal relationships with the mothers to encourage the development of their interpersonal skills and problem solving abilities. On several outcome measures the group receiving a more involved visiting service performed best, but for many measures the outcomes depended upon the prior abilities of the mothers. So-called low ability mothers improved most in the involved group, but high ability mothers performed better subsequent to the more traditional model of home visitation. This differential degree of positive programmes' effect on different types of client supports the finding of Stevenson and Bailey (1988) on parent support groups. A more worrying finding reported by Affleck, Tennen, Rowe, Roscher and Walker (1989) is that extra supports offered to parents with children in special care units was associated with a decrease in scores of competence and control at post test. The authors suggest that the extra support to those who were already coping may have been disruptive rather than beneficial.

Barnard *et al.* (1988) and Booth *et al.* (1989) also reported that despite the improvement on many of the maternal scores of mental state, skills, interaction with their children, there was still evidence of continuing poor levels of attachment in the children. This is in line with results of other prevention programmes, such as the evaluation of the Newpin volunteer scheme (Cox *et al.* 1990), that there are greater improvements achieved by parents than by their children. These findings are also supported by research on maternal depression, which is associated with social and developmental problems for children (Cutrona and Troutman 1986; Murray 1992). Interventions shown to be effective for alleviating the maternal depression are not very effective at improving child functioning (Cooper, Murray and Stein 1991). The hope had been that improvements in the mothers would result in them being more available for their children and that the children would therefore benefit. The evidence is that children require assistance beyond the help given to their mothers.

Neonatal prevention programmes are also targeted at families identified individually as high risk rather than risk assessment being based on membership of a general risk group. Several authors have reported success with these programmes, but these results have not been confirmed by controlled experimental studies. The studies have, however, by the very lack of success of the interventions been able to confirm the initial prediction of a high rate of parenting problems in these families (Gray, Cutler, Dean and Kempe 1979; Lealman, Phillips, Stone and Ord-Smith 1983). In the study by Gray and colleagues (1979) there was some evidence of improvement: the children in the intervention group were subject to as many injuries as in the control group but the injuries were of a less serious nature.

Other special services

Beyond the educational, social support and neonatal programmes there are a range of other special preventive services that are modifications of routine provision or are additional forms of service. In reviewing support services for families, Goldberg and Sinclair (1986) listed the four categories of support to individual families, relevant day care, services for groups of families or family members, and multiple approaches. In the United States there is also a consid- erable number of special programmes for families, many of which are listed in 'National Resource' Center on Family Based Services (1986) and in Zigler, Wiess and Kagan (1986).

In Britain, the development of family centres has been one of the most evident new prevention resources of the last 15 years. As with the terms 'prevention' and 'social support', family centre means many different things to different people, which has led several researchers to chart and clarify the diversity of projects describing themselves as family centres (Phelan 1983; Holman 1988; Warren cited in Walker, H. 1991). The centres have been created by a range of agencies such as education and social service departments and voluntary agencies in order to fulfil different needs. It is therefore unsurprising that they should employ different methods and techniques. What is not clear is the extent that the aims and purposes are clearly articulated and, if so, whether they are likely to be achieved by the methods employed on a daily basis in the centres.

Walker (1991) lists some of the methods employed in family centres of psychotherapy, family therapy, group work, individual counselling, skills training/education, and parent toddler group play sessions. Walker also lists the different orientations of the centres ranging from a child health focus, to a child development focus, to supporting the parents' (usually the mother's) needs so that they are better able to care for their children. Some centres may adopt all these approaches. In family centres in child abuse special units, for example, there has often been a concern to nurture the parents and to teach them child care skills, yet to also ensure that the child is receiving appropriate care and stimulation and that they are healthy and achieving their develop- mental milestones. Other family centres may be less professionally directed and controlled without any one philosophy of service provision.

Holman (1988) lists three different models of family centre. The first is client focused with the clients being referred by statutory agencies as with a child abuse special unit. Even if parents are not obliged to attend there may be pressure on them to do so and the work of the centre is likely to be based on concepts of professional roles and tasks rather than by participation by the clients in decision making within the centre. The second, neighbourhood model has a broader range of activities and more open access to local families who are likely to be encouraged to participate in the centre and with staff roles being flexible to accommodate this. In the third model, community development, the emphasis is on the centre being a resource for local community action. The staff do not undertake professional casework on referrals. The management is under local community control allowing the centre to undertake local collective action. These distinctions by Holman mirror the models of welfare described by Hardiker, Exton and Barker (1991). The client focused family centre fits the residual model of services organised to provide therapy for the few families that do not achieve the basic minimum. The neighbourhood family centre is providing a local resource and thus fulfilling the institutional model's responsibility of meeting local needs. The community development family centre allows citizens to exert more control over resources and state systems and to achieve their rights as in the developmental model of welfare. In some cases this may operate within a radical/conflict view of society rather than the developmental/consensual model (Hardiker, Exton and Barker 1991). As with all prevention programmes different family centres will have different philosophies of purpose and hence different political perspectives about families and family roles (Walker, H. 1991). The contribution or efficacy of these programmes cannot be properly evaluated without these differences being made explicit.

In the United States writing on preventive services has in the last decade focused upon the prevention of children being taken into care because of concerns about child protection or because of the unacceptable behaviour of older children. These home based or family centred services are currently labelled family preservation services. Nelson, Landsman and Deutelbaum (1990) describe three types: crisis intervention; home based models; and, family treatment models. Crisis intervention is currently the main focus of interest particularly in relation to the Homebuilders programme (Whittaker, Kinney, Tracy and Booth 1990; Wells and Biegel 1991). To be accepted into the programme there must be a wish by at least one family member to keep the family together that is not opposed by any other key family member. Once in the programme attempts are made to resolve the crisis and to teach the family the skills they require in order to stay together. Services are crisis orientated and intense and offer counselling, advocacy, training, and material services with a 24 hour on call service. The emphasis is on promoting client independence and the service is short-term; preferably no more than 90 days and usually for only four weeks (Pecora, Fraser and Haapala 1991). The indications from early evaluation are that the programme does reduce the number of children who are not removed and increase the number who are quickly reunited with their families (Spaid and Fraser 1991; Wells and Biegel 1991). The issue for research, though, is in how to assess whether families should or should not be preserved and the criteria for deciding this. Although families can provide a supporting, caring environment for children, this is not always the case, and despite the risks of removing children it is equally dangerous to assume that family preservation should be the only criteria for success.

Conclusion

This brief review described a range of programmes within an institutional welfare model (Hardiker, Exton and Barker 1991) of child abuse prevention (for more detailed reviews see Wekerle and Wolfe 1991; Willis, Holden and Rosenberg 1992; Gough in preparation). The relevance of these programmes will depend on the perceived value of this model of welfare and the extent that the programmes may meet the requirements of other welfare models. If one accepts the general strategy of the programmes then there is the more narrow question of the cost benefit analysis of the value of individual programmes.

Several of the research studies were able to report significant benefits from the programmes. These studies are in their infancy but reports of positive results from well designed evaluations are not numerous. When they do occur, such as in the work of Olds and colleagues (1986a, 1986b, 1988), they are seized upon as justification of the whole enterprise of prevention. The issue is whether these results are sufficient to justify the investment in resources that the programmes require. If the benefits are not sufficiently great then either one should forego attempts at prevention as in the residual welfare model, decide upon more macro interventions as in the developmental or radical models, or search for more effective programmes within the institutional model.

One factor limiting the effectiveness of the programmes is their lack of specificity in tailoring the intervention to particular clients. Samples are defined on crude criteria with any greater specificity being reserved for matching intervention and control samples in experimental evaluations. One of the assumptions and attractions of prevention programmes has been that inaccuracy in risk assessment and client selection were not very problematic. If client selection included several false positives, then a few families may receive a programme that was not essential but still may be of benefit and would not be harmful. In addition there would not be the labelling associated with the reactive intervention of child protection. These assumptions may not be correct. Several of the studies reported differential effects of programmes on different types of clients and one study reported a detrimental effect on some individuals who were thought to have been managing quite well beforehand. Clearly the programmes have to be considerably more specific about whom they are intended for and the manner in which clients will benefit. A broad sweep strategy to psychological interventions are unlikely to produce the results sufficient to convince policy makers of further investment in these programmes.

We should not be surprised if our interventions do not create massive change in human behaviour. As Walker, J. (1991) remarks about social casework:

> 'individuals and families are particularly resistant to the attempts of outsiders to change the way they do things. This discovery should be reassuring, since the world would be a very unstable and capricious place if people were as easily influenced by the dispensation of casework of various kinds as its practitioners apparently believe.' (1991, p.168)

This does not mean that we should not offer services and provide assistance. Just as it is necessary to have reactive child protection services despite only limited evidence of benefits for the children (see for example the detailed follow up of child protection cases by Gibbons, Gallagher and Bell 1992), it is also necessary on humanitarian grounds to attempt to prevent both the direct and indirect suffering caused by child abuse. The main danger is that these efforts might be inappropriate or may mask some unmet needs. In reactive services, for example, it is clear that parents benefit from child day care (Gibbons 1992) and that child protection casework is focused on parents (Gough, Boddy, Dunning and Stone 1987; Gibbons, Gallagher and Bell 1992) though children are known to have poor social and developmental outcomes (Gibbons, Gallagher and Bell 1992) and yet benefit from therapeutic services aimed directly at them (Gough, in preparation). Greater vigilance and attention to the results of research, particularly by policy makers, should reduce the effects of some of these oversights.

The issue of prevention is clearly more complex than the assessment of the effectiveness of special programmes and routine services. It will be difficult, however, to address the more complex issues if we are unable to have a clearer perception of the aims of current services and whether these aims are or are not achieved.

References

Affleck, Tennen, H., Rowe, J., Roscher, B. and Walker, L. (1989) 'Effects of formal support on mothers' adaptation to the hospital to home transition of high risk infants; The benefits and costs of helping'. *Child Development 60*, 488–501.

Baher, E., Hyman, C., Jones, C., Jones, R., Kerr, A. and Mitchell, R. (1976) *At Risk: An Account of the Battered Child Research Department, NSPCC.* London: Routledge and Kegan Paul.

Barnard, K.E., Maguary, D., Sumner, G., Booth, C.C., Mitchel, S.K. and Spieker, S. (1988) 'Prevention of parenting alternations for women with low social support'. *Psychiatry 51*, 248–253.

Barth, R. (1989) 'Evaluation of a task centred child abuse prevention programme'. *Children and Youth Services Review 11*, 117–131.

Bentovim, A. and Vizard, E. (1991) *Children and Young People as Abusers.* London: National Children's Bureau.

Berkeley Planning Associates (1983) 'Evaluation of the clinical demonstration projects on child abuse and neglect'. Vols I-IX, prepared for National Center on Child Abuse and Neglect, June.

Berliner, L. and Conte, J.R. (1990) 'The process of victimisation: The victim's perspective'. *Journal of Child Abuse and Neglect 14(1)*, 29–40.

Berrick, J.D. (1989) 'Sexual abuse prevention education, is it appropriate for the preschool child?' *Children and Youth Services Review 11*, 145–158.

Boddy, F.A. (1986) 'Is child abuse preventable?' *Child Abuse Review 1(3)*, 17–21.

Booth, C.L., Mitchell, S.K., Barnard, K.E. and Spieker, S.J. (1989) 'Development of maternal social skills in multiproblem families: Effects on the mother-child relationship'. *Developmental Psychology 25(3)*, 403–412.

Bowlby, J. (1972) *Child Care and the Growth of Love.* Harmondsworth: Penguin.

Budin, L.E. and Johnson, C.F. (1989) 'Sex abuse prevention programs. Offenders' attitudes about their efficacy'. *Child Abuse and Neglect 13(1)*, 77–88.

Bush, M. (1988) *Families in Distress. Public, Private, and Civic Responses.* Berkeley: University of California Press.

Clarke, A.D.B. and Clarke, A.M. (1984) 'Constancy and chance in the growth of human characteristics'. *Journal of Child Psychology and Child Psychiatry 25(2)*, 191–210.

Conte, J.R. and Fogarty, L. (1989) 'Sexual abuse prevention programs for children'. Paper prepared for a special issue of *Education and Urban Society* (May).

Conte, J.R., Wolf, S. and Smith, T. (1989) 'What sexual offenders tell us about prevention strategies'. *Child Abuse and Neglect 13(2)*, 293–301.

Cooper, P.J., Murray, L. and Stein, A. (1991) *European Handbook of Psychiatry and Mental Health.* Barcelona: Prensas Universitarias de Zaragoza.

Cox, A.D., Puckering, C., Pound, A., Mills, M. and Owen, A.L. (1990) 'Newpin: The evaluation of a home visiting and befriending scheme in South London'. Report to Department of Health, London.

Crittenden, P.M. and Ainsworth, M.D.S. (1989) 'Child maltreatment and attachment theory', in Cichetti, D. and Carlson, V. (eds) *Child Maltreatment.* New York: Cambridge University Press.

Cutrona, C.E. and Troutman, B.R. (1986) 'Social support, infant temperament, and parenting self efficacy: a mediational model of post partum depression'. *Child Development 57,* 1507–1518.

Dachman, R.S., Alessi, G.J., Vraza, G.J., Fugua, R.W. and Kerr, R.H. (1986) 'Development and evaluation of an infant-care training program with first-time fathers'. *Journal of Applied Behaviour Analysis 19(3),* 221–230.

Daro, D. (1987) *Confronting Child Abuse, Research for Effective Program Design.* New York: The Free Press, Macmillan.

Daro, D. (1991) 'Public attitudes and behaviours with respect to child abuse prevention 1987–1991'. National Committee for Prevention of Child Abuse, Working Paper No. 840, Chicago, April.

Davenport, C., Browne, K. and Palmer, R. 'A vignette study of child sexual abuse: opinions on traumatic effects'. Paper submitted for publication, 1991.

Finkelhor, D. and Associates (1986) *A Source Book on Child Sexual Abuse.* Beverly Hills: Sage.

Finkelhor, D. and Strapko, N. (1991) 'Sexual abuse prevention education: A review of evaluation studies', in Wills, D.J., Holder, E.W. and Rosenberg, M. (eds) *Child Abuse Prevention.* New York: Wiley.

Fryer, G.E., Kraizer, S.K. and Miyoshi, T. (1987a) 'Measuring actual reduction of risk of child abuse: A new approach'. *Child Abuse and Neglect 11,* 173–179.

Fryer, G.E., Kraizer, S.K. and Miyoshi, R. (1987b) 'Measuring children's retention of skills to resist stranger abduction. Use of the Simulation Technique'. *Child Abuse and Neglect 11,* 181–185.

Garbarino, J. and Gillham, G. (1980) *Understanding Abusive Families.* Massachusetts: Lexington Books.

Gelles, R.J. (1973) 'Child abuse as psychopathology: A sociological critique and reformulation'. *American Journal of Orthopsychiatry, 43,* 611–621.

Gelles, R.J. and Cornell, C.P. (1990) *Intimate Violence in Families.* Second edition. Newbury Park: Sage.

Gibbons, J. (1991) 'Children in need and their families' outcomes of referral to social services'. *British Journal of Social Work 21,* 217–227.

Gibbons, J., Gallagher, B. and Bell, C. (1992) Report of the Family Health and Development Project. A Follow Up of Physically Abused Children. Draft report to the Department of Health, January.

Gibbons, J. and Thorpe, S. (1989) 'Can voluntary support projects help vulnerable families? The work of Home Start'. *British Journal of Social Work 19(3),* 189–201.

Gil, D. (1979) *Child Abuse and Violence.* New York: AMS Books.

Gilbert, N., Berrick, J.D., Le Prohn, N. and Nyman, N. (1989) *Protecting Young Children from Sexual Abuse. Does Preschool Training Work?* Massachusetts: Lexington Books.

Giovannoni, J.M. (1982) 'Prevention of child abuse and neglect: research and policy issues'. *Social Work Research and Abstracts 18(3)*, 23–31.

Giovannoni, J.A. and Becerra, R.M. (1979) *Defining Child Abuse.* New York: Free Press.

Goldberg, E.M. and Sinclair, I. (1986) *Family Support Exercise.* London: National Institute for Social Work Research Unit.

Gottlieb, B. (1985) 'Theory into practice: issues that surface in planning interventions which mobilise support', in Savason, I.G. and Savason, B.R. (eds) *Social Support: Theory Research and Applications.* Dordecht: Martinus Nijhoff.

Gough, D.A. 'Child abuse interventions: A review of the research literature'. In preparation.

Gough, D.A. (1988) 'Approaches to Child Abuse Prevention', in Browne, K., Davis, C. and Stratton, P. (eds) *Early Prediction and Prevention of Child Abuse.* Chichester: Wiley.

Gough, D.A. (1991) 'Preventive educational programmes for children', in Murray, K. and Gough, D.A. (eds) *Intervening in Child Sexual Abuse.* Edinburgh: Scottish Academic Press.

Gough, D.A. (1992) 'Survey of Scottish Child Protection Registers 1990–1991', in *Directors of Social Work in Scotland, 'Child Protection Policy, Practice and Procedure'.* Edinburgh: HMSO.

Gough, D.A. and Boddy, F.A. (1986) 'Family Violence', in Horobin, G. (ed) *The Family: Context or Client?* Research Highlights, No. 12. London: Jessica Kingsley Publishers.

Gough, D.A., Boddy, F.A., Dunning, N. and Stone, F.H. (1987) 'A Longitudinal Study of Child Abuse in Glasgow, Volume I, the Children who were Registered'. Report to Social Work Services Group, Scottish Office.

Gray, E. (1983) 'Final Report, Collaborative Research of Community and Minority Group Action to Prevent Child Abuse and Neglect'. Volumes 1–3, National Committee for Prevention of Child Abuse, Chicago.

Gray, J.D., Cutler, D.A., Dean, J.G. and Kempe, C.H. (1979) 'Prediction and prevention of child abuse and neglect'. *Journal of Social Issues 35(2)*, 127–139.

Hardiker, P., Exton, K. and Barker, M. (1991) *Policies and Practices in Preventive Child Care.* Aldershot: Avebury.

Holman, B. (1988) *Putting Families First.* Basingstoke: Macmillan.

Kitzinger, J. (1990) 'Sexual abuse and the violation of children', in James, A. and Prout, A. (eds) *The Social Construction of Childhood.* Oxford University Press.

Kraiser, S.K., Fryer, G.E. and Miller, M. (1988) 'Programming for preventing sexual abuse and abduction: What does it mean when it works?' *Child Welfare LXVII(1)*, 69–78.

Larson, C.P. (1980) 'Efficacy of prenatal and post-partum home visits on child health and development'. *Paediatrics 66(2)*, 191–197.

Lealman, G.T., Haigh, D., Phillips, J.M., Stone, J. and Ord-Smith, C. (1983) 'Prediction and prevention of child abuse – an empty hope?' *The Lancet,* June 25th.

MacLeod, M. and Saraga, E. (1991) 'Clearing a path through the undergrowth: A feminist reading of recent literature on child sexual abuse', in Carter, P., Jeffs, T. and Smith, M.K. (eds) *Social Work and Social Welfare.* Milton Keynes: Open University Press.

Mayes, G.M., Gillies, J. and Warden, D. (1991) 'An evaluative study of a child safety training programme'. Report to Economic and Social Research Council.

Melton, G.B. (1992) 'The improbability of prevention of sexual abuse', in Willis, D.J., Holden, E.W. and Rosenberg, M. (eds) *Prevention of Child Maltreatment: Development and Ecological Perspectives.* New York: Wiley.

Miller, K., Fein, E., Howe, G.W., Gaudio, C.P. and Bishop, G.V. (1984) 'Time-limited, goal-focused parent aid service'. *Social Casework 65(8),* 472–477.

Miller, K., Fein, E., Howe, G.W., Gaudio, C.P. and Bishop, G. (1985) 'A parent aide program: record keeping, outcomes and costs'. *Child Welfare 54(4),* 407–419.

Morreale, S. (1986) 'The Ontario Centre for the prevention of child abuse' presented at Sixth International Congress on Child Abuse and Neglect, Sydney, 1986.

Murray, L. (1992) 'The impact of postnatal depression on infant development'. *Journal of Child Psychology and Psychiatry, 33,(3),* 543–561.

National Resource Centre on Family-Based Services (1986) *Annotated Directory of Selected Family-Based Service Programs.* Fourth edition. School of Social Work: University of Iowa.

Nelson, K.E., Landsman, M.J. and Dentelbaum, W. (1990) 'Three models of family-centred placement prevention services'. *Child Welfare LXIX(1),* 3–21.

Olds, D., Henderson, C.R., Chamberlain, R. and Tatelbaum, R. (1986a) 'Preventing child abuse and neglect: a randomised trial of nurse home visitation'. *Paediatrics 78(1),* 65–78.

Olds, D., Henderson, C.R., Tatelbaum, R. and Chamberlain, R. (1986b) 'Improving the delivery of prenatal care and outcomes of pregnancy: A randomized trial of nurse home intervention'. *Paediatrics 77(1),* 16–28.

Olds, D.L., Henderson, C.R., Tatelbaum, R. and Chamberlain, R. (1988) 'Improving the life-course development of socially disadvantaged mothers: a randomised trial of nurse home visitation'. *American Journal of Public Health 78(11),* 1436–1445.

Parton, N. (1985) *The Politics of Child Abuse.* Basingstoke: Macmillan.

Pecora, P.J., Fraser, M.W. and Haapala, D.A. (1991) 'Client outcomes and issues for program design', in Wells, K. and Biegal, D.E. (eds), *Family Preservation Sertvices: Research and Evaluation.* Newbury Park: Sage.

Phelan, J. (1983) *Family Centres: A Study.* London: The Children's Society.

Poche, C., Brouer, R. and Swearington, M. (1981) 'Teaching self-protection to young children'. *Journal of Applied Behaviour Analysis 14,* 169–176.

Quinton, D. and Rutter, M. (1988) *Parental Breakdown: The Making and Breaking of Intergenerational Links.* Aldershot: Gower.

Rutter, M. (1989) 'Intergenerational continuities and discontinuities in serious parenting difficulties', in Cichetti, D. and Carlson, V. (eds) *Child Maltreatment. Theory and Research on the Causes and Consequences of Child Abuse and Neglect.* Cambridge: Cambridge University Press.

Rutter, M. (1981) *Maternal Deprivation Reassessed.* Harmondsworth: Penguin.

Scaife, J. and Frith, J. (1988) 'A behaviour management and life stress course for a group of mothers incorporating training for health visitors'. *Child Care, Health and Development 14,* 25–50.

Schinke, S.P., Schilling, R.F., Barth, R.P., Gilchrist, L.D. and Maxwell J.S. (1986) 'Stress-management intervention to prevent family violence'. *Journal of Family Violence* *1(1)*, 13–26.

Siegel, E., Bauman, K.E., Schaefer, E.S., Saunders, M.M. and Ingram, D.D. (1980) 'Hospital and home support during infancy: impact on maternal attachment, child abuse and neglect, and health care utilisation'. *Paediatrics 66(2)*, 183–189.

Spaid, W.M. and Fraser, M. (1991) 'The correlates of success/failure in brief and intensive family treatment: implications for family preservation services'. *Children and Youth Services Review 13*, 77–99.

Stainton Rogers, W. and Stainton Rogers, R. (1989) 'Taking the child abuse debate apart', in Stainton Rogers, W., Hevey, D. and Ash, E. (eds) *Child Abuse and Neglect: Facing the Challenge*. London: Batsford.

Stevenson, J. and Bailey, V. (1988) 'A controlled trial of post natal mothers' groups as psychosocial primary prevention. II: Evaluation of outcome'. Unpublished paper, University of Surrey.

Straus, M. and Gelles, R.J. (1986) 'Societal change and family violence from 1975 to 1985 as revealed by two national surveys'. *Journal of Marriage and the Family 48*, 465–479.

Tipton, M. (1986) 'Cumberland county child abuse and neglect council prevention plan', presented to Sixth International Congress on Child Abuse and Neglect, Sydney.

Van der Eyken, W. (1982) *Home Start. A Four Year Evaluation.* Leicester: Home Start Consultancy.

Violence Against Children Study Group (1990) *Taking Child Abuse Seriously: Contemporary Issues in Child Protection Theory and Practice.* London: Unwin Hyman.

Walker, H. (1991) 'Family centres', in Carter, P., Jeffs, T. and Smith, M.K. (eds) *Social Work and Social Welfare.* Milton Keynes: Open University Press.

Walker, J. (1991) 'Social work: A force for good or a suitable case for treatment?', in Carter, P., Jeffs, T. and Smith, M.K. (eds) *Social Work and Social Welfare.* Milton Keynes: Open University Press.

Wasik, B.H., Bryant, D.M. and Lyons, C.M. (1990) *Home visiting: Procedures for Helping Families.* Newbury Park: Sage.

Wekerle, C. and Wolfe, D.A. 'Prevention strategies for child abuse and neglect: A review and critique'. Submitted, autumn 1991.

Wells, K. and Biegal, D.E. (eds) (1991) *Family Preservation Services: Research and Evaluation.* Newbury Park: Sage.

Whittaker, J.K., Kinney, J. Tracy, E.M. and Booth, C. (1990) *Reaching High Risk Families. Intensive Family Preservation in Human Services.* New York: Aldine de Gruyter.

Willis, D.J., Holden, E.W. and Rosenberg, M. (eds) (1992) *Prevention of Child Maltreatment. Development and Ecological Perspectives.* New York: Wiley.

Wolfe, D.A., Edwards, B., Manion, I. and Koverola, C. (1988) 'Early intervention for parents at risk of child abuse and neglect: A preliminary investigation'. *Journal of Consulting and Clinical Psychology 56(1)*, 40–47.

Wurtele, S.K., Last, L.C., Miller-Perrin, C.L. and Kondrick, P.A. (1989) 'Comparison of programs for teaching personal safety skills to preschoolers'. *Journal of Consulting and Clinical Psychology 57(4)*, 505–511.

Wurtele, S.K., Saslawsky, D.A., Miller, C.L., Marrs, S.R. and Britcher, J.C. (1986) 'Teaching personal safety skills for potential prevention of sexual abuse: a comparison of treatments'. *Journal of Consulting and Clinical Psychology 54*, 688–692.

Zigler, E.G., Weiss, H.B. and Kagan, S.L. (1986) *Programs to Strengthen Families: A Resource Guide.* Chicago: Yale University and Family Resource Coalition.

The Contributors

Lorraine Waterhouse   Lorraine Waterhouse is Senior Lecturer in the Department of Social Policy and Social Work, University of Edinburgh. She has been researching and writing about child abuse since 1983. She has previously worked as a social worker in the Department of Child and Family Psychiatry, Royal Hospital for Sick Children, Edinburgh.

Jacquie Roberts   Jacquie Roberts is Project Head of Polepark Family Counselling Centre, Tayside Social Work Department, Dundee and Co-Director of Child Protection Certificate Courses at Northern College, Dundee. Jacquie has worked in social work practice and research since 1971. She is a member of the Executive Council of the International Society for the Prevention of Child Abuse and Neglect.

Cathy Taylor   Cathy Taylor is Research Fellow at the University of Stirling Social Work Research Centre. Cathy worked for seven years as a social work practitioner for Tayside and Fife region. She has worked in social work research for three years.

Elaine Farmer   Elaine Farmer is Research Fellow in the Department of Social Policy and Social Planning at the University of Bristol. Her previous research includes work on discharge of care orders and interim care orders for the Child Care Law Review and a study on restoring children to their families, which has been published under the title *Trials and Tribulations: Returning Children from Local Authority Care to their Families* (HMSO 1991).

Harriet Dempster   Harriet Dempster is Assistant Chief Inspector (Child Care) in the Social Work Services Inspectorate of the Scottish Home and Health Department. She has worked extensively in local authority social work. Her last post was Principal Officer Child Protection in Tayside. Her experience also includes teaching and research.

Tom Pitcairn

Tom Pitcairn is Senior Lecturer in the Department of Psychology, Edinburgh University. He started life as a biologist, and worked in the Max-Planck-Institüt Forschungs stelle für Humanethologie in Germany. He is a founder member of the Edinburgh Centre for Research in Child Development, and the Institute Européen pour le Développment des Potentialités des tous les Enfants in Paris.

Janice McGhee

Janice McGhee is part-time lecturer in the Department of Social Policy and Social Work in the University of Edinburgh. She holds degrees in Psychology and Law and teaches aspects of both disciplines to social work students. She is also a qualified social worker and works part-time with Lothian Region's social work department, based in their Emergency Duty Team.

Jenny Secker

Jenny Secker is research officer with Fife social work department. Prior to taking up her post in Fife she completed a PhD at Edinburgh University, where she also worked as a social work tutor and part-time research associate.

Cathleen Sullivan

Cathleen P. Sullivan has a PhD in Immunology and a Master's degree in social work. She is interested in parent-child relationships and is currently working on aspects of infant feeding.

David Glasgow

David Glasgow is Lecturer in forensic clinical psychology at Liverpool University. He is director of the multidisciplinary Diploma and MSc in forensic behavioural science and has worked with sexual and violent offenders for over ten years in maximum and medium security, and also outpatient settings. He was a member of the Committee of Enquiry convened by the National Children's Home on children and young people who sexually abuse other children. He is involved in research on multi-agency investigation, assessment and gender differences.

Russell Dobash

Russell Dobash is Senior Lecturer in the School of Social and Administrative Studies, University of Wales College of Cardiff. He has been researching violence in the family for a number of years and is the co-author of *Violence Against Wives* (Free Press 1983), and the recently published *Women,*

Violence and Social Change (Routledge 1992) and *Women Viewing Violence* (British Film Institute 1992).

James Carnie   James Carnie is Research Fellow in the Department of Social Policy and Social Work, University of Edinburgh. He has previously worked in a number of university and government departments and has published in the fields of criminal justice and social welfare.

Christine Hallett   Christine Hallett is Reader in Social Policy at the University of Stirling, Scotland. She has published widely in the fields of child protection and the personal social services and has recently directed a research study on interagency work in child abuse, funded by the Department of Health, London. She served as Consultant to the Council of Europe Select Committee on Medico-Social Aspects of Child Abuse from 1990–1992. She is Chair of the Central Region Child Protection Committee.

James Christopherson   James Christopherson is Lecturer in Social Work in the School of Social Studies, University of Nottingham. He has been researching the differences in the perception and management of child abuse in different European countries since 1979. He was also a member of the CIBA group on Child Sexual Abuse within the Family and the Training Advisory Group on the Sexual Abuse of Children. He is a member of the Council and Professional Advisory Committee of Childline.

Joe Thomson   Joe Thomson is Regius Professor of Law at the University of Glasgow. He is author of *Family Law in Scotland* and Deputy Editor of the *Stair Memorial Encyclopaedia of Scots Law.*

Robin Clark   Robin Clark is Regional Director for the North East Region Health and Community Services Department in metropolitan Melbourne, Australia, managing the full spectrum of the state government's responsibilities in community services. Until May 1988 she was Director of Child Protection for the state of Victoria. She has researched decision-making in child protection and been a member of a recent Australian committee of inquiry into a fatal child abuse case.

Siobhan Lloyd

Siobhan Lloyd is co-ordinator of the Counselling Service at the University of Aberdeen. She is also lecturer in Women's Studies in the Department of Sociology. Her current research is on specialist police units for investigating crimes of violence against women and children. She is the co-author of *Surviving Child Sexual Abuse: A Handbook for Helping Women Challenge Their Past* (Falmer Press 1989).

David Gough

David Gough is Associate Professor, Department of Social Welfare, Japan Women's University, Tokyo. Until May 1992 he was Senior Research Fellow at the Public Health Research Unit, University of Glasgow, where he undertook a number of studies both on child protection and services for children with disabilities. Up until 1991 he was also Scottish chair of the Social Services Research Group. He is Book Review Editor of *Child Abuse Review*. His publications include *Scottish Child Abuse Statistics, 1990*, *Intervening in Child Sexual Abuse* (co-edited with Kathleen Murray, Scottish Academic Press 1991) and a review of child abuse intervention studies, soon to be published by HMSO.